This is a scholarly piece of work, presented in a simple, readable style that should make it easily accessible and beneficial to all, scholars and non-scholars alike. In this book, Asamoah-Gyadu returns to many familiar themes; he dialogues with other scholars in the field and also engages with the leaders of Charismatic/Pentecostal Christianity themselves. He consistently allows them to speak for themselves. Though an ordained minister of the Methodist Church, Ghana, Asamoah-Gyadu often points out how the mission-founded churches in Ghana have fallen behind their Charismatic/Pentecostal counterparts and the need for the former to learn from the latter. It is clear that this learning process has already started.

Asamoah-Gyadu constantly demonstrates the primal and, therefore, African underpinnings of much that is in African Pentecostalism today. He clearly has soft spot for this brand of Christianity, but that does not deter him from pointing out elements that lack adequate biblical grounding.

We thus end up with is a very comprehensive and balanced examination of the African Pentecostalism that has a great deal to teach African Christians but even more so Christians elsewhere. After all, as AF Walls has often indicated, African Christianity will be, if it is not already, a major component of the representative Christianity of the 21st century. This makes this book required reading for all those interested in the current state of African Christianity and the future of Global Christianity.

Rev BY Quarshie, PhD, Rector, Akrofi-Christaller Institute of Theology, Mission and Culture, Akropong-Akuapem, Ghana

J Kwabena Asamoah-Gyadu is one of the foremost interpreters of African Pentecostalism today. He has the critical expertise to engage this vigorous movement at its religious center even as he brings to such important work a command of the secondary literature across the various scholarly disciplines that few theologically trained scholars of the movement possess. Readers of this book may sigh at what is happening on the African Pentecostal ground but no one interested in the present and future of African Christianity can ignore this analysis of the signs of Pentecostalism in this context.

Amos Yong, Professor of Theology and Mission, Fuller Theological Seminary

The book of Revelation paints an apocalyptic picture of prophecy of every nation, race, people and tongue standing before the throne and the Lamb praising God (Revelation 7:9-12). This in its own way portrays the faith's self-definition by Incarnation and Mission and the church as the Una Sancta. J Kwabena Asamoah-Gyadu's book reminds us that the two marks of self-identification are fundamentally about renewal, revival and revitalization. Thus the vibrant non-Western African initiatives in Christianity, represents Africans taking the ball and project of the Christian gospel to run with it in Africa. The title *Sighs and Signs of the Spirit* reminds us that the rational and intellectual characteristic of theological statements marked by fact and objectivity may not be the last word. For beyond intellectual pursuit, knowing may be measured by lived experience and the dynamics of love and response to God. The study then underscores Africa's emphasis on experience of the Holy Spirit as consistent with their religious and spiritual epistemology and ontology. The African Initiated Churches represents an option for pneumatic revivalist forms of the faith that stress the experience of the Holy Spirit in what Asamoah-Gyadu describes as "exercises of aggressive and glossolalic prayer, prophecy, healing, deliverance, visions and revelations" (p.3). This is a well-researched, intellectually honest, sensitive and sympathetic study written in a compellingly humble spirit. I am therefore more than enthusiastically happy to commend the volume to all interested in the place of Africa in the transformation of Christianity as a non-Western religion.

Emeritus Professor Canon John S. Pobee FGA
Anglican Diocese of Accra, Ghana

REGNUM STUDIES IN MISSION

Sighs and Signs of the Spirit

Ghanaian Perspectives on Pentecostalism and Renewal in Africa

Series Preface

Regnum Studies in Mission are born from the lived experience of Christians and Christian communities in mission, especially but not solely in the fast growing churches among the poor of the world. These churches have more to tell than stories of growth. They are making significant impacts on their cultures in the cause of Christ. They are producing 'cultural products' which express the reality of Christian faith, hope and love in their societies.

Regnum Studies in Mission are the fruit often of rigorous research to the highest international standards and always of authentic Christian engagement in the transformation of people and societies. And these are for the world. The formation of Christian theology, missiology and practice in the twenty-first century will depend to a great extent on the active participation of growing churches contributing biblical and culturally appropriate expressions of Christian practice to inform World Christianity.

Series Editors

A full listing of titles in this series appears at the end of this book

REGNUM STUDIES IN MISSION

Sighs an Signs of the Spirit

Ghanaian Perspectives on Pentecostalism and Renewal in Africa

J. Kwabena Asamoah-Gyadu

First published 2015 by Regnum Books International

Regnum is an imprint of the Oxford Centre for Mission Studies
St. Philip and St. James Church
Woodstock Road
Oxford, OX2 6HR, UK
www.ocms.ac.uk/regnum

09 08 07 06 05 04 03 8 7 6 5 4 3 2 1

British Library Cataloguing in Publication Data
A catalogue record for this book is available from the British Library

ISBN: 978-1-506477-24-4

Typeset by Words by Design
Cover design by Words by Design

The publication of this title is made possible through the generous financial assistance of Dr. Ato Essuman, Managing Director of Profile Education Consult Ghana; Former Lay President of Methodist Church Ghana and former member of the Council of State of Ghana's Fourth Republic.

Distributed by 1517 Media in the US and Canada

Dedicated to

Kwame Bediako

Teacher, Mentor and Friend

Contents

Preface

Pentecostalism is a very versatile and eclectic stream of Christianity. Together with its more recent charismatic versions, it constitutes a new and growing phase of Christianity in Africa. Although there are downsides to its constantly evolving quality, that it represents a movement of change accounts in part for the attraction that it holds for people in modern African societies. In a sense, this versatility is also an important characteristic of the Holy Spirit, who as the 'Breath' or 'Wind' of God has the ability to move the church in different directions. All depends on what the Spirit wants to accomplish and whom he wants to use. The changes inspired and directed by the Spirit and the flaws associated with human endeavours are both reflected in the developments that have occurred within Pentecostalism or pneumatic Christianity in Africa.

The data has mostly come from personal observations and encounters through participation as a resource person at various meetings. My reflections as both an outsider and an insider are based on listening to media presentations, reading books written by leaders of new Pentecostal churches and actively engaging with the growing numbers of contemporary Pentecostal pastors and leaders who write their dissertations under my supervision. In putting my findings together in essay form, I have sought to combine descriptive and theological approaches and to give as many examples as I can. My aim has been to make the material accessible to all those who want to know about contemporary Pentecostalism in Africa, whether or not they are academics. Indeed, much of the material has been presented in public seminars, academic conferences or lectures to seminary students.

The title Sighs and Signs of the Spirit reflects the fact that Pentecostalism always appears to be a movement in transition, with pains and glories in equal measure. On the one hand, it has helped to change the face of Christianity in Africa; on the other hand, it has generated new forms of spirituality and teachings that fall short of biblical and theological standards. One of these, for instance, is the prosperity gospel, which has a strong message of empowerment but in some ways fails to articulate an adequate response to pain and suffering. I hope that my readers will enjoy reading this book for what it is worth. During the writing of this book a few things changed and I have tried to incorporate those changes into the material as much as I could. One of them was that Bishop Charles

Agyinasare removed the hyphen from his name and joined together 'Agyin' and 'Asare' into a single name. The name of his church also changed from Word Miracle Church International to Perez Church International. I have retained 'Agyin-Asare' in the notes and bibliography but the new format has been used in the text. This book is a modest attempt to reflect on developments within Pentecostalism in Africa generally and within contemporary Pentecostalism of the Ghanaian type in particular. These are movements that are transforming the face of Christianity in Africa and our reflections on them are not likely to stop with this publication.

Acknowledgements

The publishers of this volume, led by Professor Mary Gillian Bediako, deserve my gratitude for helping me make these modest essays available to a wider reading public. Along the way, several others have helped to bring my thoughts to fruition. In particular I wish to acknowledge and thank Ingrid Lawrie of Leeds for her extensive editorial contribution to this work. Ingrid continues to provide me with professional and excellent editorial support, and I thank her for being so gracious. All our contacts had been by email until June 2011, when we met during a visit to Birmingham. It was such a delight to meet her in person and to thank her personally. I know I will have occasion to thank her again in the future. Final editing services were provided by Rona Johnston-Gordon of the Overseas Ministries Study Centre (OMSC) in New Haven. I spent a half-year sabbatical at OMSC in 2012 and I thank Rona and the then Director Jonathan Bonk, and his then assistant (now Director), Nelson Jennings, and all the staff for their support.

My brother and friend Rev. Dr. Casely B. Essamuah inspired me to work on this book. When my laptop gave up the ghost at the beginning of my writing, he made sure I had access to a brand new one for the project. I thank him sincerely for his support and sustained inspiration throughout my academic and pastoral career. I am also happy to thank Mavis Osei-Boakye and Type Company Ltd.for their continued support with my publications.

Parts of this work were put together in two other locations: first, Regent University Library, Virginia Beach, Virginia, and second, Laurel, Maryland, where our friend Gladys Akos Armah lives. At Virginia Beach, I lodged with Vinson and Carol Lee Synan. Scholars of Pentecostal Studies will know the name Vinson Synan as a veteran in the field of global Pentecostalism. The Synans received me into their home during a fortnight's stay in Virginia Beach, to write in the Regent University library and I am grateful for their hospitality. Professor Amos Yong arranged not only for me to visit Regent, but also for me to have a private carrel and mentioned my need for accommodation to the Synans. I am grateful for all he did for me during my stay at Regent. My friend and colleague Professor Clifton Clarke, also of Regent, provided much support during my time there, and I thank him and Marcia for their kindness.

Gratitude is extended to Martin Lindhardt and Afe Adogame for accepting to write forewords to this publication. I cannot thank enough my wife, Theodora, and our children, Theophil, Griselda and Emmanuel, for what they have come to mean to me. They have endured my frequent travels admirably and I appreciate them, together with my siblings, for their continued support. I thank the Lord for bringing them into my life. If this book helps anyone to better understand contemporary Pentecostalism in Africa, it will have been with the support and prayers of all those I have named here and many others too numerous to mention. Kwame Bediako motivated me to give more attention to a field that holds both experiential and academic interests for me. For all he did to help bring me up in my career, I dedicate this book to his memory.

J. Kwabena Asamoah-Gyadu, July 2014

Foreword

It is with great pleasure that I write this foreword to J. Kwabena Asamoah-Gyadu's latest book on Pentecostal renewal in Africa. Without doubt, the rapid growth and proliferation of Pentecostal-charismatic denominations and movements represent the most significant change in Africa's Christian landscape — and perhaps in Africa's religious landscape in general — within the last four decades. In the present book, Kwabena Asamoah-Gyadu offers his reader a comprehensive and highly perceptive account of the appeal and theological influence of this kind of Christianity, combining scholarly excellence with a deep insider understanding of resonances within African religious sensibilities. As in many of his previous writings, Kwabena Asamoah-Gyadu sheds light on the indigenous nature and particular histories of African Pentecostalism, including on the founding of African Independent Churches that preceded missionary Pentecostalism on the continent. Though Pentecostalism is now clearly a global religion and, many would argue, a prime example of cultural globalization, an understanding of why and how it has taken root in Africa requires a fine-grained analysis of African agency and initiative, and not least of the complex processes of enculturation through which it has been rendered meaningful to Africans. The present book offers exactly that.

Clearly, this is a book written by a theologian with an unashamed theological sympathy for the Pentecostal movement and its vigorous contributions to recent transformations of African Christianity. More 'secular' scholars (anthropologists, sociologist, historians, etc.) and students will probably be reluctant to accept that the hand of God is ultimately behind the Pentecostal renewal in Africa. Nevertheless, those scholars and students who mainly adhere to instrumentalist explanations of why so many Africans embrace this kind of Christianity, and who therefore tend to focus on historical and structural circumstances of conversion, and not least on its this-worldly effects, will do very well to read this book. Kwabena Asamoah-Gyadu does certainly not reject the kinds of analysis that emphasize this-worldly effects of conversion and he does a remarkable job in highlighting historical processes. But he also supplements historical and sociological analysis by consistently and forcefully reminding his reader that Pentecostalism is first and foremost a religious and spirit-centered movement that appeals to Africans because it offers a particular kind of religiosity, most notably the experience of the power of the Holy

Spirit. Acknowledging that people in Africa (and elsewhere in the world) embrace Pentecostal Christianity because they yearn for a particular kind of experience of the Holy Spirit may not always be easy for non-theologian scholars. On the other hand, ignoring that Africans embrace Pentecostal Christianity for that reason would be nothing short of a mistake. The present book is therefore to be welcomed as a significant and multifaceted contribution to a crowded scholarly field.

Prof. Martin Lindhardt
Cultural Sociologist
University of Southern Denmark

Foreword

The debut, visibility and mobility of the Pentecostal movement and the charismatization of mainline Christianity have combined to reshape the African religious landscape so profoundly that its footprints can hardly be sidestepped. Its stark emphasis on personal pneumatic experience, expression and committed evangelical re-engagement of depth spirituality has implications that transcend the religious sphere to how humans deploy religious power for economic, social and political gymnastics vis-a-vis the sacraments of life. Generally, in-depth Pentecostal studies in the global south are relatively in the liminal infancy phase with a historiography that is vitiated by the predominant theorization by social scientists that may have out-paced the quality of data. This book seem to checkmate the fairly one-sided anthropological mirroring of Ghana's new Christianities by interrogating the core spiritual DNA of these religious phenomenon instead of simply positing how external dynamics of globalisation, neoliberal politico-economies drive their raison d'etre, modus operandi and mobility.

Sighs and Signs of the Spirit provides thick descriptions, teasing out the fluidity of the spiritual *weltanschauung* through the historical trajectory of revitalization, revival and renewal of Ghanaian Christianity that now crystalizes in the Pentecostal ferment. In lacing a theological umbilical cord between the different phases, my dear colleague-friend Kwabena Asamoah-Gyadu demonstrates boldly how these streams of pneumatic Christianity "inspired by the Spirit of God", have together transformed the face and texture of Christianity in Ghana.

A cursory exploration of the anatomy of revivalism reveals how revivals are an endemic aspect of Christianity in Africa. Experiences and exercises of all pneumatic phenomena are cherished in African Christian revitalisation or renewal movements as being of the Holy Spirit. At several points in time, a movement would flare up as certain elements in the gospel, either its charismatic/pneumatic resource or its ethical imperative, would be emphasized enough to compel a new expression of its spirituality and structure. A revival is not the mere appearance of a new version of Christianity but one that elicits massive attention and acceptance; it brings a new life to an old religion. Revival, renewal and revitalization appeared amidst African efforts to cope with colonialism, white settlers and missionaries. The challenges of modernity and globalization has also triggered widespread revivalism in the quest for supernatural responses.

Amidst a multiplicity of explanations, the book echoes a religious explanation which emphasizes that God has constantly renewed His people through the out-pouring of the Holy Spirit. The cumulative effect of these revivals and renewals intensified the process of Christianization, catalysed vertical growth and increasingly stamped a charismatic character on African Christianity.

In this book, Kwabena Asamoah-Gyadu has combined his ethnographic acumen, participant observation, critical reflexivity of an outsider/insider researcher and theological pondering in a creative manner. The author makes bold at the instance of this book to dump his *social science face-cap* in favour of his *theological hat* in asserting that "the single most important reason for the rise of revitalisation movements in Africa is the experience of the Holy Spirit…Christian religious innovation in Africa has mostly had a pneumatic orientation, in which the reality of God is encountered primarily through the power of the Holy Spirit". He even prognosticates, albeit controversially, that "there is every indication that the future of Christianity in Africa will be determined by how seriously the churches remain open to the work of the Holy Spirit".

No doubt, the clarion call by the doyens of African Christianity such as Andrew Walls, Kwame Bediako, Ogbu Kalu is increasingly being heeded. Kwabena Asamoah-Gyadu falls under the coterie of scholars who has hearkened to the call to tell the African story without fear or favour; whose term of reference is to identify the major themes or story lines in African Christianity. It is also expedient to start the storyline from African primal religions and cultures. The doyen, Andrew F. Walls, has encouraged this endeavour through his writings, teaching, mentoring, deep insights, and friendship. Kwame Bediako, to whom this book is dedicated, also urged for a shift from a paradigm that conceives Christianity and African primal religion as the correlation of two entities thought to be independent. Thus, the pneumatic orientation privileged in this book resonates not just with the biblical material, but also with traditional religious piety.

With this book, *Sighs and Signs of the Spirit,* this author cuts right and deep with a descriptive and theological knife to illuminating Ghanaian perspectives on Pentecostalism and renewal in Africa. The book provides an enlightening description and analysis that makes for compelling reading. To borrow Ogbu Kalu apt remark elsewhere, "this book opens the possibility that African scholars will co-operate to tell the story of where the rain of the gospel met our ancestors, its thick showers on us, and the torrents that will meet our future generations as the gospel deluges Africa".

Afe Adogame, PhD
The University of Edinburgh, UK

Chapter 1
'We Are Here to Heal': Christian Revitalisation and Renewal in Africa

Christianity in Africa has had a history of revitalisations and renewals. In this collection of essays, I seek to argue that the single most important reason for the rise of revitalisation movements in Africa is the experience of the Holy Spirit. Other than in the Ethiopianist or Nationalist churches of the late nineteenth century, Christian religious innovation in Africa has mostly had a pneumatic orientation, in which the reality of God is encountered primarily through the power of the Holy Spirit. In a simple but central methodological statement for the study of revitalisation or pneumatic movements, Harvey Cox observes that 'knowing the gods and demons of a people and listening to their prayers and curses tells us more about them than any graphs and statistics one could assemble.'[1] This observation, which is made in a study of Pentecostalism as a global religion, is relevant for our purposes because African Christian revitalisation movements have always had a pneumatic character, even if they do not always or consciously describe themselves as Pentecostal. Thus N. Ngada, a leader of a South African renewal movement, has been quoted as saying:

> There is one enormous omission throughout the whole history that has been written by outsiders. The work of the Holy Spirit throughout our history has simply been left out. The events of our history have been recorded as if everything could be accounted for simply by sociology and anthropology. We would like to write our own history from the point of view of the Holy Spirit.[2]

This pneumatic orientation resonates not just with the biblical material, but also, and very much, with traditional religious piety. In the African primal imagination, through the presence of spirits and spirit possession, communications and interventions are sought from the supernatural realm of health and salvation. In 1962, in one of the earliest studies of

---

[1] Harvey Cox, 'Foreword', in Allan H. Anderson and Walter J. Hollenweger (eds.), *Pentecostals after a Century: Global Perspectives on a Movement in Transition* (Sheffield: Sheffield Academic Press, 1999), 12.

[2] Ruth Marshall, *Political Spiritualities: The Pentecostal Revolution in Nigeria* (Chicago and London: University of Chicago Press, 2009), 7.

revitalisation movements in sub-Saharan Africa, Christian Baëta of Ghana pointed to the way in which churches adopted the adjective 'spiritual' to define their brand. The word 'spiritual', as he explained, was 'intended to signify that, in their worship, the groups concerned engaged in various activities which (by their own assertion) were either meant to invoke the Holy Spirit of God, or were to be interpreted as signs of his descent upon worshippers'. These activities and 'signs' Baëta described as '[rhythmic] swaying of the body, usually with stamping, to repetitious music (both vocal and instrumental, particularly with percussion), hand-clappings, ejaculations, poignant cries and prayers, dancing, leaping, and various motor reactions expressive of intense religious emotion; prophesying, "speaking with tongues", falling into trances, relating dreams and visions, and "witnessing", i.e. recounting publicly one's own experience of miraculous redemption.[3] In other words, experiences and exercises of aggressive and glossolalic prayer, prophecy, healing, deliverance, visions and revelations – all pneumatic phenomena – are cherished in African Christian revitalisation or renewal movements as being of the Holy Spirit. Pneumatic movements emerged in Africa precisely because these revivalist phenomena were seen as neglected or marginalised in the historic mission churches with their orderly, staid and overly formal worship services.

Results of Renewal and Revitalisation

Africa's first renewal movements were the Spiritual churches or Sunsum sorè in Ghana, the Aladura (people of prayer) of Nigeria and Zionist churches in South Africa. They are often placed together under the general rubric of African Independent/Initiated/Instituted Churches (AICs). The AICs were usually formed around the personal religious experience of a charismatic figure who then started to exercise certain graces of the Spirit, particularly prophecy and healing. When these Christian religious innovations began in Africa at the beginning of the twentieth century, they were resisted by the historic mission denominations as aberrations to the faith. The older churches simply dismissed the pneumatic phenomena being displayed as alien to 'orthodox' Christian practice.

These newer churches take a militant attitude towards reformation that includes spiritual warfare, an area of ministry in which their historic mission church forbears proved deficient. A classic example of this radical stance is found in the origins in Ghana of the Musama Disco Christo Church (MDCC), also called the Church of the Army of the Cross of Christ. The use of militaristic idioms in the names of such churches has been sustained within contemporary forms of Pentecostalism in Africa. The

---

[3] Christian G. Baëta, *Prophetism in Ghana: A Study of Some Spiritual Churches* (London: SCM, 1962), 1.

words of Pastor M.O. Ojewale, cited in Ruth Marshall's study of Nigerian Pentecostalism, allow us to access this mindset: 'The warfare we are presently engaged in is the battle of translating the victory of Jesus over the devil into the everyday, natural realities of our personal lives and also of our political, religious, economic, and social systems.'[4]

In the early 1920s, Methodist catechist William Egyanka Appiah began to manifest powers such as speaking in tongues and healing, but his superintendent minister simply described these activities as belonging to the occult and instigated Appiah's dismissal. Interpreting the superintendent's actions as a form of assault on the cause of Christ, Appiah and his followers, who came under severe persecution for promoting what in Methodist eyes was 'occult religion', went on to found the MDCC. The MDCC has been in existence since 1923, and until its recent leadership succession problems the church was one of the most popular Spiritual Churches in Ghana.

The various forms of Christian revitalisation movement that have developed in Africa since the beginning of the twentieth century account in large measure for the emergence of Africa as a heartland of Christianity today. What movements have emerged within the last century? How are we able to define models of revitalisation within African Christianity? How has the rise of revitalisation movements contributed to new African understandings of church? What can we say about the central themes of Christian revival and renewal in Africa? This volume responds to these and related questions. In light of the socio-religious location of my personal experience and knowledge, my examples come mainly from Ghana, but more broadly this work mirrors developments in other parts of sub-Saharan Africa. Writing on Christianity and African initiatives, Andrew Walls has noted that the sheer size of Africa's professedly Christian community is one reason for taking Africa seriously.[5] This significance, I contend, has come through Africa's revitalisation movements and the pneumatic Christianity for which they are known.

Types of Christian Revitalisation Movements

At least four main Christian revitalisation movements have emerged in Africa since the first World Missionary Conference, held in Edinburgh in 1910. Allowing for internal variations, and bearing in mind that there are also movements that are syncretistic and eclectic or even promote religious messianism, we can identify the best known movements according to the following schema:

---

[4] Quoted in Marshall, *Political Spiritualities*, 1.

[5] Andrew F. Walls, *The Missionary Movement in Christian History: Studies in the Transmission of Faith* (Maryknoll, NY: Orbis Books, 1996), 83.

(1) Independent itinerant charismatic prophets led revivals with massive conversions of people from traditional African religions to Christianity from about 1910. They include William Wadé Harris of Liberia, Garrick Sokari Braide of the Niger Delta, Simon Kimbangu of the Congo and Isaiah Shembe of South Africa. Ogbu Kalu has written of their historical influence:'These prophets tilled the soil on which modern Pentecostalism thrives. They were closer to the grain of African culture in their responses to the gospel and so felt the resonance between the charismatic indigenous worldviews and the equally charismatic biblical worldview.'[6]

(2) African Initiated Churches emerged as a direct result of the work of the indigenous prophets listed in (1) above. The churches concerned emphasised the charismatic triad of prayer, prophecy and healing. Healing is a fundamental quest in African religious practice, and so it is not surprising that it has become a central concern of Christian revitalisation on the continent.

(3) Renewal movements within historic mission denominations were a product of the desire to emulate the hugely popular ministries of the AICs. Through these local charismatic movements the renewal and revitalisation that was drawing people into the AICs were introduced into historic mission Christianity. The haemorrhage was not halted, but the flow from the older churches to the newer ones was stemmed. In Ghana, for example, the Bible Study and Prayer Group of the Presbyterian Church, the Methodist Prayer and Renewal Program and the Catholic Charismatic Renewal movement are all very popular for the dynamism they bring into their historic mission denominations.

(4) Neo-Pentecostal or contemporary Pentecostal movements and ministries have been burgeoning in Africa since the late 1970s. These are indigenous movements, but the influence of American prosperity-style televangelism on their ecclesiology is undeniable. There are strong parallels between African neo-Pentecostalism and the churches in North America designated by Donald E. Miller as 'new paradigm churches'.[7] My own work, Contemporary Pentecostal Christianity: Interpretations from an African Context, deals with the nature and teachings of African neo-Pentecostal movements.[8] With their very modern outlook, relaxed dress codes, internationalism, innovative use of modern media and contemporary forms of worship, the neo-Pentecostals have proven very attractive to

---

[6] Ogbu Kalu, *African Pentecostalism: An Introduction* (Oxford: Oxford University Press, 2008), x.

[7] Donald E. Miller, *Reinventing American Protestantism: Christianity in the New Millennium* (Berkeley: University of California Press, 1997).

[8] J. Kwabena Asamoah-Gyadu, *Contemporary Pentecostal Christianity: Interpretations from an African Context* (Oxford: Regnum International; Akropong-Akuapem: Regnum Africa: 2013).

Africa's upwardly mobile youth and have transformed the face of Christianity on the continent.

In these four revitalisation movements, we find what African Christians consider important to their faith. These characteristics include an emphasis on the experience of the Spirit, empowerment, dynamism in worship and a spirituality that is felt within everyday endeavours and issues forth in health, wholeness and prosperity. While in Ghana the older AICs are known as Spiritual churches, in Nigeria they are mainly called Aladura, meaning people of prayer. On account of the central role played by charismatic personalities and their ministries of healing within the AICs, Harold Turner has termed the AICs prophet-healing movements.[9]

We can discern that the charismatic triad of 'prayer', 'prophecy' and 'healing' is present in all the forms of African revitalisation movements listed here. This character underscores an observation by Andrew Walls that although they have differences in outlook – an inevitable result of their emergence from within different historical circumstances – the various streams of African revitalisation share the same religious characteristics. Writing with reference to the similarities between the prophet-healing churches and the neo-Pentecostals, Walls observed:

> Like the prophet-healing churches, they [the neo-Pentecostals] proclaim the divine power of deliverance from disease and demonic affliction, but the style of proclamation is more like that of American Adventist and Pentecostal preaching … All the new movements share with the prophet-healing churches a quest for the demonstrable presence of the Holy Spirit and a direct address to the problems and frustrations of modern African urban life.[10]

The theological emphases, styles of worship and ecclesiology of these movements reveal certain underlying themes that help to define revitalisation or, as some would prefer, renewal, within the African Christian context. The most important of these common themes we have identified as experience of the Holy Spirit. The key theological emphases of the AICs, as summarised by Turner, are equally present in the revitalisation or renewal movements that emerged in Africa during the twentieth century and into the twenty-first. Harold Turner and Christian G. Baëta point out that the prophet-healing movements or Spiritual churches stress two aspects of the totality of Christian belief: first, a 'pneumatological' emphasis in which the Godhead is envisaged as present and powerful through the Holy Spirit, who reveals the will of God and the destiny of the individual, guides through dangers, and fills men with new powers of prophecy, utterance, prayer and healing; second, a

[9] Harold W. Turner, *Religious Innovation in Africa: Collected Essays on New Religious Movements* (Boston, MA: G.K. Hall, 1979).

[10] Walls, *Missionary Movement*, 93.

'soteriological' emphasis in which the movements consisted of 'those who have rejected both the spirits and deities of the traditional pantheon, and the medicine-man with his magical powers and techniques, [and] have turned to the Christian God for their salvation when in trouble, and for their protection from the host of evil forces that surrounds them.[11] Salvation has been interpreted in an extremely practical this-worldly fashion.'[12]

These characteristics suggest that the streams of Christianity that have appealed to Africans most are those that have placed considerable emphasis on the power of Jesus Christ as experienced through the Holy Spirit. In the discourse of Jesus Christ on the Holy Spirit, particularly in John 14 and 16, the Holy Spirit is presented as the continuing Presence of Jesus Christ with the disciples and, by extension, all believers. Belief in the continuing experience of the Holy Spirit is the reason for the oral nature of renewal theology and its effective enculturation and innovative gender ideology. The Spirit of God described by Jesus Christ as 'the promise of the Father' is an inclusive Spirit, as we see in the way in which he brought the nations together at Pentecost. Almost eighty years before any mainline Protestant denomination ordained women, the independent churches of Africa had already recognised the inclusive power of the Holy Spirit and accepted his call on women who were founders of African churches.

How is the Spirit manifest in such movements? The founder of an African Christian revitalisation movement is first and foremost a 'receiver' of revelation from the realms of the Spirit. Those who choose the Christian alternative come to him or her to seek God's intervention in their problems instead of visiting traditional religious shrines, which in the Christian mindset are demonised as under the control of Satan.[13] The power of the Holy Spirit is deployed by the Spiritual churches in situations of crisis and ill health in particular. It is here that African revitalisation movements – both Spiritual churches and neo-Pentecostals – connect most closely with African religio-cultural worldviews. Within African cultures, concepts of illness and health are usually more social and cultural than biological. Etiology and diagnosis in the context of traditional African thought, as Masamba ma Mpolo rightly points out, pose the following basic question: '"Who is the cause of my illness?" In this context of spiritual causality, organically manifested symptoms are always the result of some external aggression.'[14] The world of the traditional African is an 'intentional' one in

[11] Baëta, *Prophetism in Ghana.*

[12] Turner, *Religious Innovation in Africa,* 98.

[13] For a useful study on this, see Birgit Meyer, *Translating the Devil: Religion and Modernity among the Ewe of Ghana* (Edinburgh: Edinburgh University Press, 1999).

[14] Masamba ma Mpolo, 'Perspectives on African Pastoral Counseling', in Masamba ma Mpolo and Wilhelmina Kalu (eds.), *The Risks of Growth: Counselling and Pastoral Theology in the African Context* (Geneva: WCC, 1985), 9.

which nothing happens by chance, and 'the unseen powers are held to be active also in the natural order.'[15] Thus the working of the Spirit within pneumatic movements is very much evident in the interventionist nature of their theology. The Spirit intervenes when lives are turned around in Born-again experiences; the Spirit intervenes with 'groans too deep for words' in prayer (Romans 8:26) and also in healing, deliverance and other such ministries meant to restore lives to proper functioning order.

Holy Spirit in Renewal and Revitalisation

Historically, wherever Christian revitalisation has occurred, it has defined itself in terms of a recovery of the activity of the Holy Spirit for the church and has positioned itself as a critique of the ecclesiastical status quo. Thus a number of Pentecostal movements talk about their existence in terms of the Spirit pouring out the 'latter-rain' upon the church. The inspiration for this interpretation comes from Joel 2:23, where in response to prayers of repentance following drought and devastation in the land, God promises through the prophet: 'Be glad O people of Zion, rejoice in the Lord your God, for he has given you the autumn rains in righteousness. He sends abundant showers, both autumn and spring rains as before.' Like pouring rain, rushing waters or blowing wind (Ezekiel 37), the Holy Spirit is associated with the 'power of God in action', or 'anointing' as the contemporary or neo-Pentecostals like to call it. A revitalised or renewed Christian community is therefore an empowered community. The Holy Spirit is supposed to bring the word of God to life and return power to the church just as happened in the post-Pentecost apostolic era.

These stirrings of the Spirit lead to certain developments including rebirth, inspiration, renewal, revival, transformation, enthusiasm, ecstasy, health and wholeness, and restoration. Within the African Christian context in particular, it is normal to view revitalisation or renewal in terms of supernaturally inspired attempts to rescue religion from a moribund fate at the hands of traditional representatives of its belief systems and practices. To quote Ojewale again:

> It is a battle of reclamation: to reclaim from the devil what he illegally holds in his control … It is warfare. But we are on the winning side. This is the time to muster the army – the Lord's army … We are disadvantaged if we lean on carnal weapons. Prayer – militant, strategic and aggressive prayer – must be our weapon of warfare at this time. It is a spiritual warfare that needs spiritual weapons.[16]

[15] Kwesi A. Dickson, *Theology in Africa* (Maryknoll, NY: Orbis, 1984), 49.
[16] Quoted in Marshall, *Political Spiritualities*, 1.

In Christian revitalisation, as evidenced in the ministries of such African movements, revivalism replaces formalism; exuberant worship replaces dry liturgy, spontaneity replaces routinised services and written prayers or collects; faith replaces doubt; material prosperity on this earth becomes a possibility, and holiness replaces carnality and moral permissiveness. When a church is renewed, charismatic experiences are normalised in its worship, and the dichotomy between body and soul is bridged in rituals of salvation and healing. Additionally, there is an ardent desire to experience the immediacy of the Presence of God in personal and communal Christian lives. That sort of religious experience breaks the monopoly of patriarchal clergy over religious affairs because individuals, both men and women, receive dreams and visions through which they are also called to minister through their charisms.

All this suggests that in both the older Spiritual churches and contemporary Pentecostal forms, revitalisation movements in Africa define their ministries in terms of zeal, activity, power, experience and spiritual warfare, all of which are explained in terms of the work of the Holy Spirit. This experience of the Holy Spirit can be deemed missing, neglected, marginalised or downplayed in the life of the historic Christian traditions. This lacuna is not lost on the older compatriots of African revival movements. In the mid-1960s, for example, the Presbyterian Church of Ghana established a committee to look into why its members were drifting towards the burgeoning Spiritual churches. Four out of the eight reasons provided by the committee as possible explanations for the attractiveness of the Spiritual churches for Presbyterians in Ghana are most instructive for understanding models of the church for revitalisation in Africa:

1. A large number of Christians joined the Spiritual churches because they were disappointed with their former churches. They complain that the worship there is dull, that there is no 'spiritual power', that church agents are hypocrites, and that there is not sufficient prayer in the old churches. They therefore seek a younger, more zealous and more 'spiritual' fellowship.
2. Pagans find their way more easily into these churches [because] worship is less intellectual.
3. Their worship is appealing, and people take an active part in it and obviously enjoy it.
4. Divine healing plays a prominent role in all these churches and obviously satisfies a great desire for giving due attention to the spiritual side of sickness and healing.

The references to 'dull worship', 'lack of spiritual power', 'intellectual worship', and 'lack of divine healing' are important indicators of what Africans expect in renewed and revitalised Christianity. Unlike the historic mission denominations, in which such ideas were dismissed as nonsensical and even as belonging to the occult, revitalisation movements take seriously both the message of the Bible in terms of the activity of the Spirit and also primal worldviews of causality. These movements are therefore able to create ritual contexts within which appropriate responses to the anxieties and fears that these understandings generate can be articulated. Revitalisation movements in Africa, as elsewhere, are therefore meant to be movements of restoration of life to the church, and this through the Presence of the Spirit. For this reason, African Christian revitalisation movements generally tend to have a pneumatic orientation.

Historically, revitalisation movements were formed and grew largely in response to the failure of western-mission–founded churches to accept or integrate 'charismatic experiences', especially healing, into their faith and practice. As Emmanuel Lartey notes from the perspective of a pastoral theologian:

> Foremost in the faith and practice of these churches is divine healing. In many respects, their practice of divine healing is phenomenologically similar to the activities of the traditional priest healers. This renders them culturally and religiously very amenable to the masses of people who find in them a congeniality and familiarity absent from the staid, silent, 'orderly' form of worship and liturgy in the western mission-founded churches with their non-interventionist theology.[17]

This is often evident in the charismatic triad of prayer, prophecy and healing, but even these are based on particular understandings of the work of Jesus Christ. It has been said of Prophet Garrick Braide, who ministered in the Niger Delta around 1915, that 'he mobilized masses of the citizenry in a bid to make Christianity more relevant to contemporary needs'.[18]

Model of Revitalised Church

On the charismatic triad named above, Lamin Sanneh draws attention to the importance of prayer in African revitalisation movements and points out how the emphasis on prayer is connected with indigenous religious worldviews:

> Prayer was understood in two specific ways. First, it was the means whereby the individual received certain benefits, including the fulfilment of wishes and desires; secondly, it was the obtaining of guidance. In this way personal need and

---

[17] Emmanuel Y. Lartey, 'Healing: Tradition and Pentecostalism in Africa Today', *International Review of Mission*, 75, no. 297 (January 1986), 75.

[18] Lamin O. Sanneh, 'Translatability in Islam and Christianity in Africa: A Thematic Approach', in Thomas D. Blakely, Walter E.A. van Beek and Dennis L. Thomson (eds), *Religion in Africa: Expression and Experience* (London: James Currey; Portsmouth, NH: Heinemann, 1994), 41.

control, which used to form a prominent part of traditional religious life and practice, acquired a new lease of life in a Christian setting.[19]

Writing on contemporary forms of revitalisation, André Corten and Ruth Marshall-Fratani in their introduction to Between Babel and Pentecost refer to how the newcomers have shifted the emphasis from simply 'speaking in tongues' and 'retreat from the world', which characterized the theology of the classical Pentecostal denominations. In contemporary Pentecostalism in Africa, they note, the emphasis is now on miracles of prosperity and of divine healing, which are 'understood in the broadest sense of alleviating the causes of suffering, be they physical, financial, spiritual or social'.[20] In this new type of African revitalisation movement, 'salvation is now resolutely this- worldly and the evidence of new life has become as much material as spiritual'.[21] The point here, as Andrew Walls suggests, is that there is clear continuity between the two sets of revitalisation movements in Africa – the classical AICs represented by the Aladura or Spiritual churches and the contemporary Pentecostals or charismatic ministries – which underscores my submission above on what Africans consider important as far as renewed Christianity is concerned.

The issue of translation of the Scriptures has also been identified as pivotal for the rise of reform, renewal and revivalism in Africa. The vernacular principle was thought to be 'the pulse' of the revival movements that swept across sub-Saharan Africa in the early decades of the twentieth century.[22] This work does not question that claim, for access to the Scriptures in mother tongues betrayed the gaps between what came to be understood as biblical Christianity and the liturgical forms of worship that mission agencies made available. Through vernacular Bibles, God, who revealed himself in Jesus Christ, came to be understood as the one who, by the power of the Holy Spirit, is our healer. A popular chorus sung widely in African Pentecostal churches should be understood against the backdrop of that understanding of God as one who intervenes in human situations:

He is a miracle-working God
He is a miracle-working God
He is the Alpha and Omega
He is a miracle-working God

---

[19] Lamin O. Sanneh, *West African Christianity: The Religious Impact* (Maryknoll, NY: Orbis Books, 1983), 191.

[20] André Corten and Ruth Marshall-Fratani (eds.), *Between Babel and Pentecost: Transnationalism in America and Latin America* (Bloomington and Indianapolis: Indiana University Press, 2001), 5.

[21] Corten and Marshall-Fratani, *Babel and Pentecost*, 7.

[22] Sanneh, 'Translatability', 42.

The efforts of Prophet Harris, in particular, led to the formation of the Church of the Twelve Apostles by two of his most prominent converts: John Nackabah and Grace Tani, both of whom were former custodians of powerful traditional shrines. The names 'John' and 'Grace' were adopted, we can presume, after conversion to Christianity. A third member of the group, John Hackman, was converted through the ministry of Nackabah. In his work on these churches as they formed in Ghana, Baëta refers to all three as having had gifts of prophecy and spiritual healing.[23] He provides an apt summary of what the Church of the Twelve Apostles stood for in terms of what these new movements brought to bear on African Christianity as revitalisation movements: 'emphasis is laid, to the exclusion of all other matters, upon the activity of the Holy Spirit in enabling certain men and women to predict future events, warn of impending misfortunes, detect evil-doers and, above all, to cure illnesses. Asked to put in a nutshell what their Church stood for, Mr. Nathan [an important leader] had no hesitation in exclaiming: "We are here to heal."'[24]

Healing has been central to the work of African revitalisation movements. It takes place within the context of prayer, rituals and prophecy, especially if the source of affliction is determined to be supernatural. The ministry of Jesus Christ as healer is an indication that the source of health is divine, and in the African context, healing is related to prophecy because, like divination in the traditional setting, prophecy reveals destinies and the sources of predicaments. Healing in this context encapsulates something more than just the cure of ailments. It includes all those divine interventions made possible by such spiritual disciplines as waiting, fasting and prayer, through which health and fortunes are restored and deliverance received from one's enemies. In healing, divine resources are deployed to provide release for the sick, demon-possessed, demon-oppressed, broken, disturbed and troubled persons, in order that victims may be restored to proper functioning order (which means health and wholeness) that 'they may enjoy God's fullness of life understood to be available in Christ'.[25]

Significance of Revitalisation and Renewal in Africa

Christian revitalisation in Africa, one could say, is constituted by indigenous attempts to answer a basic Christological question. The late Kwame Bediako drew my attention to how J.V. Taylor, himself a former missionary to East Africa, articulated this very question:

---

[23] Baëta, *Prophetism in Ghana*, 9.

[24] Baëta, *Prophetism in Ghana*, 15.

[25] J. Kwabena Asamoah-Gyadu, *African Charismatics: Current Developments within Independent Indigenous Pentecostalism in Ghana* (Leiden: E.J. Brill, 2005), 165.

> Christ has been presented as the answer to the questions a white man would ask, the solution to the needs that Western man would feel, the Saviour of the world of the European world-view, the object of the adoration and prayer of historic Christendom. But if Christ were to appear as the answer to the question that Africans are asking, what would he look like?[26]

The idea of 'religious movements' implies an organised attempt to introduce change in religion. Such change, James Beckford has written, 'is normally accompanied by strain and conflict between religious movements and their competitors or opponents'.[27] In this context, the competitors or opponents of African Christian revitalisation movements have been the historically older and more administratively and doctrinally firmly established mission denominations. Their vision of Christ was of the one who saved people to take them to heaven. The revitalisation movements took a different approach. When a member of the Church of the Twelve Apostles said 'we are here to heal', those words were an indirect indictment of that church's older compatriots for being closed to those experiential aspects of the Christian faith that allowed for charismatic experiences, such as healing, to take place within the context of Christian worship.

Religious movements, like social movements, usually attempt to cause change; for religious movements, that change is brought to a system of beliefs, values, symbols and practices concerned with providing supernaturally based general compensators.[28] For the movements under study here, the provision of ritual contexts (prayer places, dynamic Spirit-inspired fellowships, healing camps, for example) for the purpose of providing supernatural interventions for people seeking help in times of need, was key to their religious and theological identity. Because the worldview of supernatural causality within which they functioned resonated with traditional religious ideas, it served to underscore the significant place occupied by these movements within the African Christian religious landscape.

Conclusion

'When Edinburgh 1910 was constituted, no one foresaw the emergence of a vibrant Christian presence in Africa, let alone the emergence of a distinctly

[26] John V. Taylor, *The Primal Vision: Christian Presence amid African Religion* (London: SCM, 1963), 16.

[27] James A. Beckford (ed.), *New Religious Movements and Rapid Social Change* (London: Sage, 1986), x.

[28] Rodney Stark and William Sims Bainbridge, *The Future of Religion: Secularization, Revival, and Cult Formation* (Berkeley, Los Angeles and London: University of California Press, 1985), 23.

African experience of Jesus Christ', wrote Kwame Bediako.[29] Yet around 1910, as European missionary leaders gathered in Edinburgh to map out the future of mission in Africa and the rest of the world, Prophet Wadé Harris trekked from Grebo Island through the Ivory Coast to the Gold Coast, baptising, healing, teaching new choruses and charismatising the religious landscape. The charismatic fire that he lit, Kalu has said, proved more important for the future of Christianity in Africa than the grand Edinburgh conference that shut out African voices.[30] When the Conference reconvened in Le Zoute, Belgium, in 1926, it considered a recommendation for the setting up of mission boards, committees and agencies to provide resources to African missionaries in terms of recognised courses at home and in the field, so they could take an effective approach to mission. By then, Africans had already taken their spiritual destiny into their own hands. Through the translated Scriptures and openness to pneumatic activities, African Christians had acquired the means to make their own responses to the Christian message in terms of their own needs and categories of meaning. Through these revitalisation movements, Lamin Sanneh has noted,

> A process of internal change was thus initiated in which African Christians sought a distinctive way of life through mediation of the spirit, a process that enhanced the importance of traditional religions for the deepening of Christian spirituality. The charismatic churches, therefore, combined the two fundamental elements of Christianity and African culture in a way that advertises their Christian intentions without undervaluing their African credentials. Biblical material was submitted to the regenerative capacity of African perception, and the result would be Africa's unique contribution to the story of Christianity.[31]

The older independent churches about whom Sanneh writes here may no longer be paradigmatic of Christian religious innovation in Africa. In terms of numbers, infrastructure and influence, their place has been taken by the contemporary Pentecostal churches and their better educated and media savvy charismatic leaders. Their ability to present an alternative to historic mission Christianity that seeks the integration of charismatic experiences, especially healing and prophecy, into Christian life and worship in Africa at the beginning of the twentieth century, has served as a source of inspiration, if not as a model, for indigenous renewal movements on the continent. Contemporary Pentecostals, to whom we turn in the next chapter, have drawn in turn from the pneumatic orientation of older forms of renewal .

[29] Kwame Bediako, *Jesus in Africa: The Christian Gospel in African History and Experience* (Akropong-Akuapem, Ghana: Regnum Africa, 2000), 4.
[30] Kalu, *African Pentecostalism*, x.
[31] Sanneh, *West African Christianity*, 180.

Chapter 2
'Taking Territories and Raising Champions': The Force of Contemporary Pentecostalism

'Taking Territories; Raising Champions' is how the Kingsway International Christian Centre in London led by Pastor Matthew Ashimolowo captures its mission. The slogan says something about the force of contemporary Pentecostalism in world Christianity today. In chapter 1, I sought to define contemporary Pentecostalism, showing how it stands in continuity with the older independent church movement and drawing attention to the significance of what I refer to collectively as 'pneumatic movements' to the current renewal that Christianity in Africa is experiencing. In this chapter I discuss some of the specific ways in which this new form of Pentecostalism is making its presence felt within public space. The importance of this charismatic Pentecostalism with its contemporary approach to Christian expression is evident in many ways that cannot escape even the most casual of observers: magnificent church buildings, with some christened 'cathedrals'; mega-size congregations; the youthful nature of the membership; an overwhelming presence in the mass media and popular media; charismatic and high-profile leaders; a growing number of academic studies of the phenomenon; influence on the worship style of the historic mission churches; and a theology of dominion, empowerment and fruitfulness. The gospel of contemporary Pentecostalism is very much a message of upward mobility and redemptive uplift.

In this new type of Pentecostalism, André Corten and Ruth Marshall-Fratani note that 'believers no longer retreat among themselves in order to maintain the purity of their beliefs and their moral rigor ... salvation is now resolutely this-worldly, and the evidence of new life has become as much material as spiritual'. The notion of transformation, they note, 'has been broadened to include the possibility of material change in everyday life', to preserve an image of salvation that 'increasingly means upward mobility and personal success.'[1] Leaders of contemporary Pentecostal churches and ministries such as Matthew Ashimolowo in London and Sunday Adelaja in Ukraine, and their Africa-based compatriots – Enoch A. Adeboye

---

[1] André Corten and Ruth Marshall-Fratani (eds.), *Between Babel and Pentecost: Transnational Pentecostalism in Africa and Latin America* (Bloomington and Indianapolis: Indiana University Press, 2001), 7.

(Nigeria), David O. Oyadepo (Nigeria), Ezekiel Guti (Zimbabwe), Chris Oyakhilome (Nigeria/South Africa), Nicholas Duncan-Williams (Ghana), Mensa Otabil (Ghana), Charles Agyinasare (Ghana), Eastwood Anaba (Ghana), Sam Korankye Ankrah (Ghana), Dag Heward-Mills (Ghana), Nevers Mumba (Zambia) and many others – have, within a generation, transformed and 'pentecostalised' the global Christian landscape.

In the writings of Andrew Walls, Kwame Bediako, Ogbu Kalu and others interested in world Christianity, much is made of the fact that Christianity has become a primarily non-western religion. I understand this shift not necessarily in terms of change in ownership but rather in terms of growth and theological influence. From an African perspective, contemporary Pentecostalism has hastened that process, which was started by the older African independent churches at the beginning of the twentieth century. They have taken territories in terms of numbers. They have also spread and raised new champions of mission who have transnational influences across the world and are challenging the old paradigms that marginalised the experiential presence of the Holy Spirit and reduced the message of salvation to an eschatological aspiration. This growing importance of Pentecostalism in the southern continents invites us to reinterpret even older theological forms of liberation and inculturation in the light of Spirit-inspired renewal and dominion theologies that have proven extremely popular in several non-western contexts.

In Ghana, for example, Mensa Otabil of the International Central Gospel Church has emerged as an important advocate of popular liberation theology hermeneutics and black empowerment discourse. His annual Destiny Summit features individuals such as Matthew Ashimolowo, Mike Murdock and Randy Morrison as regular speakers. That Randy Morrison – a Jamaican American – of Speak the Word Church in Minnesota, USA, carries the official designation 'Life Coach' in his church, is an indication of the new dimension that contemporary Pentecostalism brings to pastoral ministry. It also explains why their brand of Christianity appeals to a media-savvy technology-sensitive generation. In the new Christian context of religious revitalisation in Africa, the Bible is applied in very practical or existential ways to meet the needs of urbanisation. It is used to address issues of upward mobility and success, wealth creation, the importance of higher education, investment and a Christian life that must be evident in progressive family life. Looked at this way, even the much criticised message of prosperity that is associated with contemporary Pentecostalism emerges in other forms, as a means of encouraging people to take their destiny into their own hands and move forward in life. This message can have a distinct impact on the aspirations of young people, in particular when political leadership has proven deficient in many ways and has let people down badly.

Beyond the Rivers of Ethiopia

Pastor Eastwood Anaba of the Fountain Gate Chapel in Ghana talks about the development of contemporary charismatic Christianity in terms of a religious change that is reminiscent of the political revolutions that occurred in Africa at the time the new Pentecostal movements were emerging. I have examined his ideas in two of my books, African Charismatics and Contemporary Pentecostal Christianity. For Eastwood Anaba, the new churches were born to chart new paths in Christian mission:

> Whilst there is nothing new under the sun, these [new Pentecostals] are born for modification, alteration, revolution, modulation and variation. These latter ones are born to resurrect great things long abandoned and forgotten. This is a revival and restoration … You may not have an example to follow but you can create your own path.[2]

Mensa Otabil of Ghana is a personal embodiment of this sort of new Christianity and its message of positives and possibilities in this life. He is only one of the most popular among a number of contemporary Pentecostal pastors who have adopted this new strategy of preaching that uses the Bible to offer practical information for personal development and self-improvement. This approach partly explains their wide appeal to upwardly mobile youth, who may be looking for new sources of inspiration in religion. Thus, one way in which the new churches have come to dominate public space is through the writing of books. Those familiar with the religious thought of Pastor Mensa Otabil of the International Central Gospel Church will know that his work Beyond the Rivers of Ethiopia was written to affirm the important place that the Black race occupies in God's economy:

> I believe what we are seeing is the beginning of more fundamental and foundational changes. There is a shaking in the land! God is going to visit the black peoples of this world to bring them out of the state they are in, into their portion … There is the sense of urgency and a feeling of an appointment with destiny among black people. It is a feeling that makes you know that your time has come and God is bringing to fruition the days of intense intercessions, for his justice to prevail.[3]

In Beyond the Rivers of Ethiopia, Otabil challenges the general Black perception of our race as inferior to whites and points to several people of

---

[2] Eastwood Anaba, *God's End-Time Militia: Winning the War Within and Without*, rev. ed. (Accra: Design Solutions, 1997), ix.

[3] Mensa Otabil, *Beyond the Rivers of Ethiopia: A Biblical Revelation on God's Purpose for the Black Race* (Accra: Altar Media, 2004), 8, 64.

dark complexion whom God used to achieve his purposes. In his attempt to inspire Africans to exploit their potentialities and abilities to the full, Otabil even challenges the simplistic approach to prosperity that preaches a 'name it and claim it' theology of success and material well-being. His emphasis is that claims on God to provide money must give way to the application of the principles of wealth creation through the wisdom that God grants those who ask him.[4] He has clearly chosen a different path from those new prophetic, healing and deliverance ministries that specialise in seeing demons lurking everywhere and interpret every problem of life in terms of the work of evil spirits and curses. Prophecy, healing and deliverance are certainly biblical, but the African Pentecostal obsession with them is destroying the image of the movement.

In some of my earlier writings, I have argued that Eastwood Anaba's use of the word 'revolution' to describe the new Pentecostals is very instructive. The militaristic idiom we saw in chapter 1 was present in the discourse of the older independent churches, but has now re-emerged with a completely different connotation. Contemporary Pentecostalism, in Anaba's understanding, constitutes God's End-Time Militia brought into being by the Holy Spirit as movements of revival and restoration. In his many books, Anaba has sustained the argument that contemporary Pentecostals are called by God to chart a new path for Christianity by democratising ministry, a process made possible by their individual and corporate experiences of the Spirit. Taking an experiential, rather than an administrative, approach to the Protestant principle of the priesthood of all believers, Anaba contends that the work of ministry must never be abandoned to professional clergy, but each person must function in the gifts and graces of the Spirit to the glory of God.[5]

Renewal Theology in Context

The sighs and signs of the Spirit have, through revitalisation movements, generated new forms of Christian expressions and theological renewal. Not everything with these African renewal movements is not necessarily perfect, but the wind of the Spirit is indeed in action, as Jesus sought to tell Nicodemus in John 3. In African renewal theology, graces or gifts of the Spirit are central to ecclesiology. This understanding of the use of spiritual gifts recalls Paul's admonition to the Corinthians on how these gifts are to be deployed within the context of the believing community:

---

[4] For full discussion on Otabil and his message see Paul Gifford, *Ghana's New Christianity: Pentecostalism in a Globalizing African Economy* (London: Hurst and Co., 2004), chs 5-7.

[5] Anaba, *End-Time Militia*, 1.

> Now to each one the manifestation of the Spirit is given for the common good. To one there is given through the Spirit the message of wisdom, to another the message of knowledge by means of the same Spirit, to another faith by the same Spirit, to another gifts of healing by that one Spirit, to another miraculous powers, to another prophecy, to another distinguishing between Spirits, to another speaking in different kinds of tongues, and to still another the interpretation of tongues. (1 Cor. 12:7-10)

We will return below to the implications of this text for contemporary Pentecostal ecclesiology, but we should note here the fundamental position in Paul's thought that is stated in verse 11: 'All these are the work of the one and the same Spirit, and he gives them each one, just as he determines.' The justification for Anaba's position is seen, firstly in the way the new Pentecostals have grown, with many individuals establishing their own ministries based on their particular spiritual gifts, and secondly, in the ways in which, within particular charismatic churches, people bring their gifts and graces together to ensure charismatic functionality in worship life.

Spirit, Dominion and Globalisation

This chapter treats how contemporary Pentecostalism expresses itself in terms of taking new territories and raising new champions in mission. We have already encountered these ideas in the new focus on the mission of the church in Otabil's message of Black/African empowerment. The ministries that Pentecostalism has developed are understood as a fulfilment of biblical promise and an application of the territorial dominance associated with the power of the Holy Spirit. Birgit Meyer explains that this self-understanding is also part of a process of Pentecostal insertion into globalisation:

> In principle, anything can be imbued with the Holy Spirit and thus be part of a Born-again believer's life. This is what accounts for the close connection between the spread of capitalism, consumption, and the appeal of Pentecostalism: Pentecostalism 'embeds' neoliberal economic policies. Likewise the realm of politics can easily be subjected – and it seems increasingly so – to extensive prayers. And even a football match is an appropriate target for the Holy Spirit.[6]

In contemporary Pentecostalism, for those familiar with the messages of Otabil, Ashimolowo and others, the Scriptures are applied in ways that encourage members to invest in financial markets, seize opportunities in education, business, politics and entertainment and, wherever possible, enlarge their spheres of influence in the world. The establishment of

---

[6] Birgit Meyer, 'Pentecostalism and Globalization', in Allan Anderson et al. (eds.), *Studying Global Pentecostalism: Theories and Methods* (Berkeley: University of California Press, 2010), 118.

institutions of higher learning, such as the Central University College of Mensa Otabil's ICGC and Covenant University of David Oyedepo's Living Faith Church Worldwide or Winner's Chapel, is a response to their calls to take territories and influence public life. Contemporary Pentecostal messages challenge the youth to make a difference in every conceivable area of life: education, information, sports, entertainment, economics, business, banking, land acquisition, politics, landed property, money, international travel, transport, universities, mining, technology, science, law, agriculture, marketing, leadership, etc.

Here we see what I have termed the 'theology of dominion', because even in the purchase of lands for building, for example, sustained prayer and fasting may be undertaken in order to ward off negative supernatural interests. In this type of Christianity the line between what is physical and what is spiritual may be very thin indeed. The payment of tithes may be a physical activity, but it is understood as the single most important act for opening doors to success or prosperity in life. The lack of faithful payment of tithes and offerings conversely accounts for the failures and curses that have accompanied the endeavours of people in this world. Thus Bishop Dag Heward-Mills of the Lighthouse Chapel International in Ghana writes in a very straightforward manner: 'Prosperity in its most basic form consists of someone sowing a seed and later harvesting the returns. Not paying your tithes separates you from this most basic principle of sowing and reaping. When you do not pay your tithes you harm your finances because you take away the foundations of prosperity.'[7]

In the chapter on giving and tithing in my work Contemporary Pentecostal Christianity, I share the story of once sitting beside a gentleman at a prophetic meeting in a charismatic church in Ghana.[8] At the end of proceedings each person was supposed to 'bless' the prophet by sowing some offering into his life. Respondents had to record a single need on the envelopes in which these offerings were to be placed. My neighbour wrote simply, 'for open doors'. In other words, the sower of the seed offering was looking for opportunities in life, whatever they might be. The sowing of offerings as 'seed' does not necessarily preclude working hard. In this type of religion the sacred and secular remain inseparable, and the faithful discharge of religious obligation is only a sign of faith in the God who is the source of one's blessings. Increasingly for many young people in Africa, the opportunities being sought relate to higher education, employment, business, marriage and at the top of the pile these days, international travel. One may question the simplistic connection often made

[7] Dag Heward-Mills, *Why Non-Tithing Christians Become Poor and How Tithing Christians Become Rich* (Wellington, South Africa: Lux Verbi.BM, 2009), 1.

[8] J. Kwabena Asamoah-Gyadu, *Contemporary Pentecostal Christianity: Interpretations from an African Context* (Oxford: Regnum International, 2012).

between seed-sowing and success, but the difference that the new churches have made in getting people to believe that nothing can stop them from achieving personal goals can only be commended. All the requests amount to seizing opportunity, taking territories and raising or becoming champions in an increasingly competitive world.

Spiritual Territories

Territorial conquests are not mere physical activities. Contemporary Pentecostals take spiritual territories by controlling the spiritual atmosphere. Let me cite Eastwood Anaba again, from one of his earliest writings, in which he indicated not only that believers must take territories and be champions, but also that there is a connection between physical and spiritual territories:

> The Scripture piles up evidence upon evidence that it is the will of God for believers in the Lord Jesus Christ to possess the land wherever they are. Everything you see on earth is supposed to be used to glorify God. However, because a good portion of these things are in the hands of unbelievers, the agenda of Satan is promoted. To spread the gospel there must be an ejection of the heathen from the possession of the land. Believers must move in quickly to take possession.[9]

This exercise in dominion is accomplished through religious activities that include massive revival meetings, summits and conferences, all-day prayer services and all-night prophetic vigils and mass evangelistic crusades. Thus Anaba further notes: 'When believers in any land become very aggressive in prayer and preaching, they attract the attention of the inhabitants … Our possession of the land must be two dimensional; in the Spirit realm and in the physical realm. Our faith and belief must supersede any other religion. Demons and powers of darkness must be subject to us.'[10]

'Taking territories', then, is not a reference only to physical land, important as that practical presence may be to the development of contemporary Pentecostalism.[11] 'Possession of the land' refers to something more than geographical space, as Anaba explains: 'One praying man on his

---

[9] Eastwood Anaba, *Breaking Illegal Possession: Dislodge the Enemy and Possess the Land!* (Accra: Design Solutions, 1996), 49.

[10] Anaba, *Breaking Illegal Possession*, 51.

[11] As far back as the mid 1990s, Anaba had pointed out that the new churches needed to move in quickly to buy land and erect their own chapel buildings, as they could be ejected by the owners of the school buildings in which many of them had been meeting at the time. In his own experience, recounted in several of his publications, the mission churches in whose school buildings his church started literally 'persecuted' the new church, including dismissing teachers of the mission school who had joined the new church, then called Broken Yoke Foundation.

knees can determine the prices of goods, the weather conditions and the health situations of a land though he does not belong to the ruling government … Again in the spirit realm, the joy, wisdom, discipline, and self-control of Christians should dominate the land.'[12] The experiences of the Spirit, Christian ethics, prayer and other such related acts of Christian life and ministry all constitute ways in which God's End-Time Militia has been brought into being, to break the hold of Satan and demonic powers over God's creation, seize opportunities and spread the influence of the Spirit over even the most mundane of things in this world. Indeed, this movement is bent on 'conquering Satan, principalities and powers', as one chorus has it, in order that it may insert itself into the world's globalisation process … and without doing so, I must add, no social movement will survive.

Crossover Services

We encounter a similar worldview and theology of dominion in another of Mensa Otabil's earliest books, Four Laws of Productivity, to which I shall return below.[13] David Oyedepo of Winners' Chapel specialises in titles that directly address issues of dominion, two of the most important being Possessing your Possessions and Walking in Dominion.[14] Periodic Empowerment and Destiny Summits, Convention of Saints, Holy Ghost Action Campaigns and end-of-year 'Crossover' services organised by the new churches have also proven very popular in the transformation of the religious landscape of Africa as a means of 'taking territories and raising champions'. Crossover services refer to the traditional New Year's Eve church service that for many years was associated with the Wesleyan tradition. In Africa, and in Ghana for example, that service is known as the Watchnight Service and is very well attended, with Methodist Churches in particular usually packed full with worshippers seeking to put behind them the sins and failures of the old year, in order to begin afresh with God. The services usually begin with singing, biblical exhortations and prayers, and then close to midnight come prayerful resolutions for the New Year. When the New Year is ushered in, there is much singing, dancing and hugging, and increasingly these days the 'sowing of first fruits', that are offerings for breakthrough during the year ahead.

The new Pentecostal churches have integrated the Watchnight Services into their system with different designations: Crossover, Jump Over,

[12] Anaba, *Breaking Illegal Possession*, 54.

[13] Mensa Otabil, *Four Laws of Productivity: God's Foundation for Living* (Tulsa, OK: Vicom Inc., 1991).

[14] David O. Oyedepo, *Possessing Your Possessions* (Ota, Nigeria: Dominion Publishing House, 2007); *Walking in Dominion* (Ota, Nigeria: Dominion Publishing House, 2006).

Passover, Shift Over, Change Over and at the end of 2013, for the first time, I saw a banner advertising Triumphant Entry. The masses have shifted their allegiance to the charismatic meetings because these services are heavily advertised and, more importantly, they include anointing for people to breakthrough by defeating their enemies, and prophetic declarations over people's lives. The services have therefore been embellished into nights of encounter with God and defeat of one's enemies, a discourse that appeals to the imagination of the ordinary African, with his or her belief that supernatural powers are constantly at work to frustrate efforts in life. Mensa Otabil has translated his Crossover services into a non-denominational meeting that he hosts at the Accra Sports Stadium. The stadium is usually filled to capacity as people seek to Crossover under the anointing that will help them succeed where they may have failed the previous year. The bottom line in the new churches' structuring of the Watchnight services is that power in the Spirit is available to cancel negative development and enhance opportunity as people embrace the New Year.

Restoring Experience to Christianity

We can return our focus now to the power of the Spirit in Christian revitalisation in Africa. As my definition of Pentecostalism indicated, the movement draws particular attention to the importance of the experience of the Holy Spirit to the Christian faith. 'I believe in the Holy Spirit' and 'I have experienced the Holy Spirit' are not necessarily the same thing, but they are connected. In Acts 6, the Apostles asked the leadership of the Christian community to 'choose seven men' from among their ranks who are known to be full of the Holy Spirit, indicating that such persons could be distinguished from those who were not so filled. At the official doctrinal level in a typical Pentecostal church or community, manifestations of the Spirit constitute part of normal expressions of faith. The process, though, begins with the experience of the individual believer, as this movement offers a direct and intense encounter with God that will make possible profound changes in the lives of those experiencing it. Through this direct and experiential encounter with the Holy Spirit, God is felt to make himself accessible to those who seek him. These personal transforming and charismatic experiences have had implications, both for the emergence of new pastors and pastoral ministries, and for the formation of new Christian communities without any allegiance to mission organisations with denominational encumbrances:

> The new person, who is incorporated into the Pentecostal community through conversion, receives, and is acknowledged by the church to have received, a gift which will enable him or her to begin to participate in the carrying out of the

> evangelizing mission of the church. In this way, Pentecostalism carries into practice in a very radical way the idea of the 'universal priesthood of the believers'.[15]

Contemporary Pentecostalism has changed the face of Christianity in both ecclesiological and practical terms. The days in which young people seeking to express Christian ministry had to go through denominationally structured formal theological education and fit into monolithic clerical vocations are a thing of the past. The flexibility introduced into Christian ministry by the new churches means that once personal transformations and gifts of ministry are authenticated, people may be invited to serve. The edges of Christian ministries have expanded, and that development is evidence of the new Pentecostals' sensitivity to the challenges of the times and of their responses to those challenges. The encouragement of ordinary lay people to function within their gifts in ministry seriously challenges the definition of ministry which understands that role simply in terms of liturgical ordination within given denominations. Eastwood Anaba explains what this means for the new approaches to Christian pastoral ministry:

> People come to church with marriages on the verge of falling apart, others with terminal diseases, others with spiritual dryness and desolation, others with financial crisis. They don't come for a picnic. Everyone in the church is a minister to such people. We all help to create a suitable atmosphere for the flow of the rivers of oil to meet the needs of these people. The preacher must come prepared, the choir must come tuned to the preacher and the Holy Ghost. Ushers must stand as flaming messengers of God ... Somebody is depending on whatever you are doing for his blessing and if you don't do it well, quit doing it.[16]

This 'democratisation of charisma' occurs through the outpouring and experiences of the Holy Spirit. It helps people to function in their gifts and graces, making the church 'charismatically functional'. The idea is that the experience of the Holy Spirit grants 'ministries' to beneficiaries. The democratisation of ministry, according to James Dunn, puts a large question mark against the traditional understanding of 'ministry' that takes the word to mean 'the ordained ministry'. Contrary to this understanding, 'ministry' in contemporary Pentecostalism coheres with Pauline thought in 1 Corinthians 12 and Romans 12, where Paul envisages the local church as a 'charismatic community where each member, by definition, has a function within the body, a role within the community of faith'.[17]

---

[15] Juan Sepúlveda, 'Reflections on the Pentecostal Contribution to the Mission of the Church in Latin America', *Journal of Pentecostal Theology*, 1 (1992), 100, 103.

[16] Anaba, *End-Time Militia*, 12.

[17] James D. G. Dunn, 'Ministry and the Ministry: The Charismatic Renewal's Challenge to Traditional Ecclesiology', in Cecil M. Robeck, Jr.(ed), *Charismatic Experiences in Christian Worship* (Peabody, MA: Hendrickson, 1985), 82.

The experience of the Spirit, then, democratises charisma and access to the sacred, and thereby redefines ecclesiology. This is how Anaba interprets the cardinal text of the Pentecostal movement: 'And it shall come to pass afterward, that I will pour out my Spirit upon all flesh; your sons and daughters shall prophesy, your old men shall dream dreams, your young men shall see visions' (Joel 2:28). The expression 'all flesh' in this passage, according to Anaba, defies skin colour, educational status, natural abilities and social standing: '"Professional believers", baptized, confirmed and complacent are being sidelined … We are God's end-time militia being released in these end-times to replace, or augment the services of professional, regular and institutionalized Christendom. This militia is made up of Born-again believers who are not bound by rituals and religious limitations.'[18] Contemporary Pentecostalism in its pristine form therefore reminds us that the work of ministry is about functioning in our spiritual gifts or ministries to the glory of God and blessing of his people.

Transforming the Face of Mission

Our new task in the twenty-first century, Allan Anderson suggests, 'is to reflect on the role of Pentecostalism in the majority world in the transformation of Christianity.'[19] But how have the new Pentecostals transformed Christianity in the global south? We have already referred to the messages of empowerment directed at those from the underside of history. In 1979 Archbishop Nicholas Duncan-Williams, with much inspiration from the late Archbishop Benson Idahosa of Nigeria, pioneered the formation of contemporary Pentecostal churches in Ghana. In his revised autobiographical book Destined to Make an Impact, he reflects on his pioneering work after his calling:

> The church, which I later called Christian Action Faith Ministries, began to grow … The ministry attracted many young people from schools, colleges as well as adults from the mainline churches because of the visible miracles, healings, and great teachings on faith and prosperity. Today, many of these young people have also pioneered churches and have become general overseers, with some already ordained as bishops. The work God started with me, by His grace, has had a far-reaching influence, both nationally and internationally.[20]

---

[18] Anaba, *End-Time Militia*, 3, 5.

[19] Allan Anderson, 'Varieties, Taxonomies, and Definitions', in Allan Anderson et al. (eds.), *Studying Global Pentecostalism: Theories and Methods* (Berkeley: University of California Press, 2010), 13.

[20] Nicholas Duncan-Williams, *Destined to Make an Impact* (Lanham, MD: Pneuma Life Publishing, 2004), 120.

As part of this new type of religious revolution, as I have termed it, Mensa Otabil's ICGC says it is 'Raising Leaders, Shaping Vision, and Influencing Society through Christ.' Sam Korankye-Ankrah's Royalhouse Chapel International advertises itself as a church that is 'Touching our Generation with the Power of God.' Charles Agyinasare's Perez Church International (formerly Word Miracle Church International) is 'A Place Where Jesus Makes Everybody Somebody.' These are not idle claims and empty catchphrases, for there are profound testimonies of lives that have been turned around and of different kinds of elevations in life that have come to people through the new ministries under discussion here. As a result of the powerful and dynamic presence of Pentecostal churches, Latin America, a context previously synonymous with Catholicism, is turning into Protestant territory.[21]

Internationalism, Globalisation and Power

There are several other ways in which contemporary Pentecostals have taken the initiative and transformed the face of Christianity in Africa and beyond. In Ghana's New Christianity, Paul Gifford identifies 'success' as an emphasis that is found everywhere in Ghanaian charismatic culture, and identifies the choice of names as one area in which this is evident.[22] Given the transnational nature of contemporary Pentecostal ministries, it is not for nothing that each of these churches invariably includes in its name expressions such as 'worldwide', 'international', 'global' and, more recently, 'transcontinental'. The globe, usually combined with the symbol of the dove, remains a favoured element in the design of church logos. This movement has an international understanding of its missionary mandate, which explains why the globe (representing the world) next to the dove (representing the Holy Spirit) and the eagle (representing height, strength, survival, opportunities, reach in terms of sight, and renewal) is an important symbol in charismatic Christianity.[23]

The process of transformation includes a deliberate attempt to take Christianity back to the former heartlands of the faith in the west. A new breed of pastors heads contemporary Pentecostal churches today, including Charles Agyinasare, Dag Heward-Mills and Ampia Kwofie of Ghana; they preach frequently and hold mass evangelistic crusades in foreign lands that attract the large crowds usually associated with high-profile North

---

[21] David Stoll, *Is Latin America Turning Protestant? The Politics of Evangelical Growth* (Berkeley: University of California Press, 1990); David Martin, *Tongues of Fire: The Explosion of Protestantism in Latin America* (Oxford: Basil Blackwell, 1990).

[22] Paul Gifford, *Ghana's New Christianity: Pentecostalism in a Globalizing African Economy* (London: Hurst and Co., 2004), 44.

[23] See chapter 3 for further details of these developments.

American international evangelists. Bishop Agyinasare, for example, has a healing-miracle ministry that has taken him to more than seventy countries. At his meetings, cripples walk, the deaf hear, the eyes of the blind are opened, and souls are won for Christ. Those who have gone from Africa to establish churches abroad are also helping to keep Christianity as a non-western religion and in the same breath are keeping the hope of its message alive in otherwise largely secular areas, for example, Europe. It is not surprising that the African immigrant churches in European countries like Germany, on looking at what is happening to Christianity in those countries, insist on being called 'New Mission Churches' and not Migrant Churches. This name, they claim, avoids emphasis on their 'foreignness' and instead stresses the reason that they are in Europe, that is, to execute a missionary calling from the south to the north.[24]

Charisma, Media and Globalisation

The transformation of Christianity through contemporary Pentecostalism has involved extensive deployment of modern media technologies for Christian ministry. The new churches now dominate televangelism and radio ministries. Additionally, it would be difficult to find any senior pastor of charismatic persuasion who has not compiled a book from his sermons. The usage of modern media technologies by contemporary Pentecostals is largely responsible for the omnipresence of this stream of Christianity in African public life today. The centre of Christian influence and power has therefore shifted from the historic mission denominations to these new representatives of the faith. Its media presence has been very important for crafting the public face of contemporary Pentecostal Christianity. Posters and handbills, street banners and other such popular forms of communication enhance the presence of these churches in Africa. My 2007 study of Pentecostal uses of the internet demonstrated that whereas the historic mission churches used the internet in a limited way, as a means to talk about the historical importance and legacy of their churches, contemporary Pentecostals used the same medium with highly evangelistic intent. At the website of Mensa Otabil's ICGC for example, one could learn how to be Born-again and, depending on the user's location, how to find a place of worship. In 2007, most historic mission church websites were non-existent, out-of-date or simply filled with history, lengthy lists of bishops, pictures of cathedrals and similar material. Yet it is possible to listen to every single sermon preached by Heward-Mills of Lighthouse Chapel in Ghana, or by Sunday Adelaja of the Church of the Embassy of the Blessed Kingdom of God for All Nations in Ukraine on their websites; an indication

[24] Claudia Währisch-Oblau, *The Missionary Self-Perception of Pentecostal-Charismatic Church Leaders from the Global South in Europe* (Leiden: E.J. Brill, 2009), 35.

of how slow the older churches have been to realise that the media can serve as a powerful instrument of mission and renewal.

In the world of globalisation, the media is a source of empowerment, a role that comes from its primary function of communication. The more people read charismatic pastors' books or listen to their sermons, the more their lives are shaped by the information received. In Communication Power, Manuel Castells argues that power is based on the control of communication and information, and communication power is at the heart of the structure and dynamics of society.[25] By seizing the opportunities offered by the media, the contemporary Pentecostal movement has been able to take control and exercise the power of religion in public space. They have taken territories, raised champions – for that is how I understand power in this context – and are set to dominate the religious life of Africa for the foreseeable future. The media, which they use extensively, provides communication power and, as Castells has written, 'the most fundamental form of power lies in the ability to shape the human mind'.[26]

Pentecostalism, Politics and Public Life

The churches I have discussed in this chapter may not possess the intellectual heritage associated with historic mission denominations. Traditionally their 'weapons' have not been memoranda and pastoral letters. In the early 1980s, when Ghana's economy collapsed and the plight of people was worsened by drought and hunger, the Pentecostals referred to biblical passages to interpret what was going on and responded to the developments with prayer and prophetic declarations. They instituted prayer meetings to ask for God's intervention. The Pentecostal churches called for periods of fasting, and prayer meetings were initiated around passages such as: 'If my people who are called by my name humble themselves, pray, seek my face, and turn from their wicked ways, then I will hear from heaven, and will forgive their sin and heal their land' (2 Chr. 7:14). I am not suggesting that the historic mission churches do not pray for situations to change, but certainly, in dealing with the supernatural influences believed to be at work within public space, the Pentecostals have been at the forefront, creating ritual contexts that appeal both to the biblical material and to African religious sensibilities.

Emeka Nwankpa, a Nigerian charismatic author, has even articulated the problems of Africa in terms of the influences of 'territorial spirits' and spiritual bondage as a result of idolatry and sin. In this type of Christianity, the ancestors and spirits of traditional religion have survived as territorial demons that must be exorcised in order to 'redeem the land'. In Redeeming

[25] Manuel Castells, *Communication Power* (Oxford: Oxford University Press, 2009), 3.
[26] Castells, *Communication Power*, 3.

the Land, Nwankpa presents the International Monetary Fund and World Bank, popularly regarded as contributing to the economic problems of Africa, as 'oppressive agents of the devil that need to be resisted by prayer and the force of the Spirit'.[27] This resistance amounted to the invocation of the power of the Holy Spirit to tackle the agents of supernatural evil that had brought certain African countries to their knees. If the land needed healing, then that healing would come through prayerful interventions.

Conclusion

Pentecostalism, as Peter forcefully underscored in his Pentecost Day sermon, is the direct fulfilment of divine promise. This promise moved the activity of the Spirit of God far beyond the Jewish understanding, to another level in which nonentities such as menservants and maidservants also became entities. The Holy Spirit takes 'nobodies' and turns them into 'somebodies'; when the Spirit of God overshadowed Mary, making her the carrier of the Eternal Word in physical form, she could sing, 'My soul glorifies the Lord and my spirit rejoices in God my Saviour, for he has been mindful of the humble state of his servant. From now on all generations will call me blessed, for the Mighty One has done great things for me – holy is his name' (Luke 1:46–49).

Through the new Pentecostals, God may well be taking new territories and raising new champions of mission out of what Paul describes to the Corinthians as the 'foolish', 'weak', 'lowly' and 'despised' things of this world. Pentecostalism has become so central in African Christianity that the expression 'mainline' can no longer be employed to describe the historic mission churches. Whether we are talking in terms of numbers, geographical spread, doctrinal orthodoxy or public influence, contemporary Pentecostals have taken territories and raised new champions of mission. The older denominations have not ceased to matter as a result. The new developments mean that God remains sovereign. He remains the God of renewal, who determines and chooses how to carry on his mission with whatever instruments are available to him at any particular time. Our response must be openness to what God is doing by his Spirit. For, if the history of Reformations is anything to go by, we must be aware that, if we cease to do God's bidding, he is mighty enough even to raise up stones to carry out the mission laid down for us in Jesus Christ our Lord and empowered by his Holy Spirit.

---

[27] Emeka Nwankpa, *Redeeming the Land* (Accra: ACP, 1994).

Chapter 3
Dove, Eagle and Globe: Symbolising Dominion Pneumatology

In the last chapter we considered the rise of contemporary Pentecostalism and the changing nature of ecclesiology in the African Christian context. We have noted that Pentecostalism is basically a movement of the Holy Spirit in which encounters with the Holy Spirit are usually privileged over rational and systematic reflections on the faith. Until recent decades, for example, many Pentecostals refused to take formal theological education seriously, accusing theologians of rationalising religious experiences, demystifying Christianity and turning it into 'mere' religion devoid of experience. This attitude has been changing, with many Pentecostals in Africa now embracing theological education. Pentecostal churches are even establishing theological institutions, leading to a concern that in much of sub-Saharan Africa every Pentecostal church is attempting to establish its own Bible School to train its people in-house. In this chapter, we continue with the changing nature of mission with the rise of Pentecostalism, looking at new ways of symbolising the Spirit and his work. Through new symbols, contemporary Pentecostals have pushed for a practical pneumatology, in keeping with the focus on power, transformation and expansion 'to the ends of the earth' (Acts 1:8).

The traditional symbol of Pentecostalism has been the dove. The recent focus on motivation, expansion of territory and empowerment means, however, that other symbols have been adopted by contemporary forms of the movement. Among these symbols are the globe, which represents the international mission, aspirations of contemporary Pentecostalism and its leadership. Of particular significance in the African context is the eagle, a symbol of emancipation, accomplishment, power and dominion that has been widely adopted based on the text in Isaiah 40:28-31. Here the prophet talks about the renewal of the strength of those who wait upon the Lord, and when we consider what the Spirit does in the lives of people and the church, then the motif of the eagle comes together perfectly. In other words, the globe and the eagle have become important symbols of the theology of dominion associated with contemporary Pentecostalism, and they fit into the prosperity and possibilities mindset of the movement.

This chapter considers the meaning of these symbols as found in contemporary Pentecostalism, and the ways in which their use can help our understanding of how the theology of this movement differs from its two main compatriots, the classical African initiated churches of the early twentieth century and the classical Pentecostals who came a little later. I will argue that in the practice of contemporary Pentecostalism, the myopic understanding of the work of the Spirit that restricted his activities to speaking in tongues and granting spiritual gifts has been broadened to include what might be considered secular areas of life.

Pentecost and Religious Symbolism

In relation to pneumatic movements, as with most religions, symbols possess a depth of meaning that may not be exhausted by what is seen. Symbols in this context convey levels of meaning and reality through that which is visible, with great significance for the invisible, i.e. belief in the supernatural and experience. Religious symbols possess the power to remind people of faith that reality can be complex and is not always communicated adequately in words. This engagement of the invisible by symbols explains why there is much within Pentecostal worship that is symbolic, including gestures of lifting hands, kneeling or simply walking up front during word- or song-ministration to drop an offering. I have witnessed cases in which people 'speak' to the offering before placing it at the feet of the preacher, for their offering – referred to as a 'point of contact' – is the symbol that carries their heartfelt needs to God. 'Speaking the word' and seeing the word come alive in real life situations have developed as significant elements of the spirituality of African Pentecostalism. Religious symbols enable people to communicate profound truths and realities in concrete and accessible ways.

The logo of most new Pentecostal churches is invariably formed by a combination of the globe and eagle, a representation of their belief in the movement of the Spirit with its transnational callings and influences. In Pentecostal Christianity, generally the dove symbolises the presence of the Holy Spirit, the harbinger of the new creation who descended on Jesus Christ at his baptism: the eagle has now been adopted to depict aspiration, empowerment and motivation, and the globe underscores the movement's worldwide aspirations because its mission mandate was to witness in Jerusalem, Judaea, Samaria and to the 'ends of the earth'. Modern Pentecostalism thus stands in direct continuity with the Jesus movement that followed Pentecost and sees the world as 'their parish'. Many of the early leaders of modern Pentecostalism from Africa, the late Archbishop Benson Idahosa of Nigeria in particular, referred to themselves as 'Apostles to the Nations'. This understanding also explains why each of the churches has the expression 'international', 'global' or 'worldwide' as part of its name. The mandate of Jesus for the disciples to take the Gospel to the whole world, making disciples of all nations, is surely key to explaining why, at the experience of the Holy Spirit, most Pentecostal movements engage in aggressive evangelisation beyond their local contexts. Each of these symbols has a significant role in Pentecostal thought because, first, it is present in the Bible, second, it is associated with the Holy Spirit, and third, it has features and characteristics that resonates with the self-definition of contemporary Pentecostalism as a movement of transnational significance.

The underlying theological principles of all three symbols as articulated within the pneumatic Christianity under study here are 'dominion', 'empowerment' and 'influence'. This interpretation must be understood in light of the African socio-religious context, within which the new Pentecostals stake their claim as brought into being by God to influence the course of events. That context explains the popular African/liberation theology hermeneutics found in the messages of Mensa Otabil, Matthew Ashimolowo and Andrew Wutawunashie. Other paradigms for Pentecostal hermeneutics of empowerment and liberation are the messages of Bishop T.D. Jakes and African/American Pentecostal leaders like him who, in the power of the Spirit, use the Bible to inspire confidence in people with faith in the God of the oppressed. I see in the new African Pentecostalism the development of a movement that may be considered the more popular and pastoral equivalent of Black theology within an African context of poverty, squalor and deprivation. James Cone is arguably one of the most popular African/American voices in that theology in the twentieth century. I quote here his words on the new hermeneutics in his context and experience:

> Black Theology's answer to the question of hermeneutics can be stated briefly: The hermeneutical principle of an exegesis of the Scriptures is the revelation of God in Christ as the Liberator of the oppressed from social oppression and to political struggle, wherein the poor recognize that their fight against poverty and injustice is not only consistent with the gospel but is the gospel of Jesus Christ. Jesus Christ the Liberator, the helper and the healer of the wounded, is the point of departure of valid exegesis of the Scripture from a Christian perspective.[1]

Thus the Spirit is understood within the new hermeneutics as the one in the Godhead who makes the difference in lives, including those of preachers with mega-size congregations and prosperous lifestyles. In terms of their entrepreneurial spirit and escapades, some preachers in the current wave of leadership have shown themselves to be examples of what they preach. Their success stories include the size of their churches, personal material acquisitions and private businesses that operate alongside the work

---

[1] James H. Cone, *God of the Oppressed* (Maryknoll, NY: Orbis Books, 1975),74-75.

of ministry. The Spirit of God in Christ is both powerful and influential, two attributes that can be read in the symbols employed by Pentecostal movements. As we have seen in the previous chapters, within the term 'Pentecostalism' I include all forms of pneumatic religious movements that have a definite Christian character. Such movements believe in God as Creator, Provider and Sustainer of all things, in Jesus Christ as his ultimate revelation and the sole mediator of salvation, and in the Holy Spirit as God's empowering presence. The Spirit of God is usually synonymous with the power of God, and therefore in the new hermeneutic of empowerment people accomplish great things when the Spirit comes upon them. This is an understanding of the work of the Spirit that has been sustained in contemporary Pentecostal theology.

Empowered with Skill

We have seen how Mensa Otabil of Ghana and Matthew Ashimolowo, for example, preach to encourage people to acquire skills and use their natural talents in order to progress in life. These messages make sense in African contexts of poverty and deprivation and within Black and African/American contexts of disempowerment stemming from the historical experience of slavery. One biblical example in the story of Spirit and empowerment is provided by Bezalel and Oholiab, who were said to have been filled by the Spirit of God and endowed with skill for work. The infilling of the Spirit of God enabled them to be craftsmen, working in metal, wood and precious stones and producing all kinds of artistic design. They were also able to teach others those skills and thus empower them, to use an important charismatic expression (Ex. 35:30–36:1). That the Spirit of God not only endows people with new tongues and ministry gifts of the Spirit, but also empowers them to acquire practical skills and knowledge, has become a vital element in the teaching and preaching ministries of the charismatic leadership in Africa's contemporary Pentecostal churches.

In fact, some leaders are now referred to as 'motivational speakers' or 'life coaches', rather than the traditional term 'pastors', signifying their new roles as people chosen by God to empower others to rise above limitations and debilitating conditions and reach the top of secular careers. Such messages have proven very attractive in Africa, where the desire to improve one's lot is now very high and where young people constantly seek local and international opportunities to succeed in life. In 2009, at the twenty-fifth anniversary celebration of Mensa Otabil's International Central Gospel Church in Ghana, I heard the testimony of a bank manager who said she had started with only a high school certificate, but inspired by the motivational messages of Mensa Otabil, she had returned to education and now had a Master's degree in business administration. There are many such testimonies that demonstrate the charismatic leaders' roles in empowering people to take the opportunities that come their way in life. Since 2000, as Ghanaian contemporary Pentecostals have started taking the academic study of theology seriously, Charles Owiredu, Michael Perry-Tettey and Charles Aye-Addo, all of the International Central Gospel Church, have taken doctoral degrees from Durham (UK), Edinburgh (UK) and Drew (New Jersey, USA) respectively. Joseph Quayisi-Amakye of the Royalhouse Chapel and Sylvia Owusu-Ansah of the Perez Church International (formerly Word Miracle Church International) have both been awarded doctoral degrees in theology at the Vrije Universiteit, Amsterdam. These individuals are only a few of the many Pentecostals who are now in doctoral education at the highest level, and yet the Pentecostal movement not too long ago considered academic theology an aberration from genuine spirituality.

Pentecostalism, Power and Dominion

The bottom line in the new hermeneutics of empowerment is what I refer to as 'dominion theology'. For example, contemporary Pentecostalism is generally depicted in modern mass media as a religion of power. Its functionaries are people with influence over both physical and spiritual entities as a result of the experience of the Spirit. In popular media such as Ghanaian and Nigerian video films, the Pentecostal pastor symbolises the presence of alternative, more auspicious and more potent forms of religious power, especially in confrontations between agents of Christianity and demonised traditional religions. In scenes in which a pastor must deal with the powers of evil, for example in the termination of witchcraft, or to cast out a demon, to subdue the possessed, to deliver the spiritually oppressed or exorcise a haunted home, the preferred image is of a Pentecostal pastor, rather than a Methodist or Presbyterian pastor (who is more likely to appear at liturgical occasions such as wedding and funeral ceremonies). For funerals, images of historic mission pastors are used, as if to re-enact within existential situations the words of Jesus, 'let the dead bury their dead'.

Historically, each of the Pentecostal groups discussed in the volume emerged as a 'movement of renewal' in its time. The older AICs emphasised the importance of 'healing' and the 'prophetic' in their brand of Pentecostalism, as a result of which Harold Turner designated them 'prophet-healing' churches.[2] From the beginning, the classical Pentecostals were keen to emphasise the Born-again experience and the doctrine of the Baptism of the Holy Spirit. Their core message, however, had a strong eschatological tone. This characteristic did not mean that the AICs did not encourage speaking in tongues, but that practice was not highlighted as a

---

[2] Harold W. Turner, *Religious Innovation in Africa: Collected Essays on New Religious Movements* (Boston, MA: G.K. Hall, 1979).

doctrinal issue and means of determining who was filled with the Holy Spirit. In addition to their emphasis on being Born-again and Spirit baptism, the classical Pentecostals, especially the indigenous forms such as the Church of Pentecost, also pushed a certain religious agenda of personal witnessing that was linked to preaching on the Second Coming of Christ.

One chorus of choice for the classical Pentecostal denominations has been: 'I have another world in view; my Saviour is gone to prepare me a place; I have another world in view.' This expectation of heaven called for renunciation of the 'world' of materialism and embracing a life of holiness. It affected the classical Pentecostal approach to public life, including engagement with/disengagement from politics as outlined by Amos Yong:

> [Pentecostalism] ... has been largely comprised of biblical literalists who have taken Jesus' sayings like 'My kingdom is not of this world' (Jn. 18:36, KJV) straightforwardly. Hence Pentecostal focus has remained, in a real sense, on the coming kingdom ... An apocalyptic mentality suggests that things are going to get worse before they get better, and they will get better after the return of Jesus Christ, since only he can right the wrongs of the world.[3]

Contemporary Pentecostals have all but dropped matters to do with the Second Coming of Christ from their theological discourse. Its absence is not an indication that they do not believe that Jesus Christ will return to judge the world; they do believe in Christ's return. It is simply that, like initial evidence or subsequence in the ministry of the AICs, the Parousia is not consciously promoted as a doctrinal issue but simply taken for granted. The real concern of contemporary Pentecostalism is how to succeed and prosper in life, making use of Spirit-given talents, abilities, opportunities, contacts and the like to achieve those 'destinies' to which God has called people. Much energy is expended in outlining 'the principles of success' in every field of human endeavour: marriage, finance, business, education, ministry and so forth.

The ultimate examples in these endeavours are the successes and prosperity of the various charismatic leaders who lead the new churches and movements. While classical Pentecostalism promoted personal piety through modest living, in contemporary Pentecostalism wealth is to be pursued because material wealth and prosperity glorify God. 'Money and success will chase you' is a familiar discourse in contemporary Pentecostal prayers over people. Money and physical wealth constitute signs of God's favour and goodness. The successful churches and family lives of the pastors constitute living testimonies for their followers, who must aspire to achieve the best they can in life.

---

[3] Amos Yong, *In the Days of Caesar: Pentecostalism and Political Theology* (Grand Rapids, MI: William B. Eerdmans, 2010), 5.

On account of its focus on power, empowerment and influence, Pentecostal prayer and preaching tends to be authoritative, passionate and aggressive. It has a particular focus on taking dominion over situations, for which a key biblical inspirational text is Paul's reference to Christians having been given the spirit of boldness and not of fear (Romans 8:15; II Timothy 1:7). In Pentecostal activity, words have a performative effect. It is permitted for people to rise up in church and physically appropriate words from a preacher by shouting, 'I receive it in the name of Jesus.' Prayer is articulated in a way that dispatches words to intervene in calamitous situations and terminate the activities of evil spirits by stopping them in their tracks. After all, Jesus spoke the word and the servant of a centurion was healed. Jesus' words of authority also brought the dead Lazarus from the grave, and by his command, a cripple who had been staying at the Pool of Bethesda for thirty-eight years returned home on his feet. Offerings also possess sacramental value. One can pray over one's money as it goes into the offering bowl that it returns to the 'sower of the seed' in the form of foreign currency or 'opens doors' to opportunity.

All this is to say that power and influence are vital elements in contemporary Pentecostal life in Africa. Influence flows from power and the understanding of power as outlined by Wright in the context of the work of the Spirit, which is very important as an entry point into the discussion: 'Power ... simply means the ability to do things. Power is needed if you are going to do anything good, as well as [being] used for evil. Power is the capacity to accomplish goals, or to influence the outcome of events and processes.'[4] In Pentecostalism generally, the presence of the Holy Spirit is always seen as the power of God in action. This power, which is also the power of the Holy Spirit, is never a theological abstraction. In situations in which the average Christian prays for the will of God to be done, the charismatic will command for things to change in the name of Jesus Christ. Liturgically ordered prayers are considered anathema in Pentecostal worship, for prayers that are read do not allow for proper authority to be exercised over situations in order for change to happen. In recent years there is a new development in which contemporary Pentecostal powers put together prayers and declarations in books for the membership, but the tone of the words carries the sort of authority that the believer is supposed to have in Christ.

The Jabez Prayer: 'Expand My Territory'

At the height of the development of Black Theology, James Cone noted that there is no truth for and about Black people that does not emerge out of

---

[4] Christopher J.H. Wright, *Knowing the Holy Spirit through the Old Testament* (Downers Grove, IL: Intervarsity Press, 2006), 34.

the context of their experience. Sermons, he noted, made clear that the Word and its proclamation in the Black Church were more than the 'conceptualization of theological doctrine'.[5] That principle underlying Black Theology is not dissimilar to the development of contemporary Pentecostal hermeneutics of dominion. The emphasis on breakthrough, success, enlargement, uplift and so on explains why the biblical story of Jabez in particular features prominently in contemporary charismatic preaching. The 'Jabez Prayer' in 1 Chronicles 4:9-10 reads:

> Jabez was more honourable than his brothers. His mother had named him Jabez, saying, 'I gave birth to him in pain.' Jabez cried out to the God of Israel, 'Oh, that you would bless me and enlarge my territory! Let your hand be with me, and keep me from harm so that I will be free from pain.' And God granted his request.

The critical points in the text for the new Pentecostals are the association of the name Jabez with pain, the request of 'blessing' from God in terms of the expansion of personal 'territory' and the granting of the 'request' by God that follows. In contemporary charismatic thought, the expansion of territory means the expansion of one's sphere of influence. It is thought that we are kept from experiencing that expansion by those things that tie us to our past.

In the African context, that bond to the past might be formed by an ancestral name, a generational curse or some relationship with a negative supernatural influence over peoples' lives. For contemporary Pentecostals, the story of Jabez directly addresses the question of how one can make a request to God for the enlargement of one's territory. The problems may also be practical because, as Otabil is wont to emphasise, the only way out of the quagmire of Africa's poverty is not just prayer but education, hard work and the application of God's principles of productivity. If you 'sow' time in education, money in investing, and other resources in ventures that bring returns, you can improve your lot in life.

Power to Make Wealth

In the previous chapters, we encountered Matthew Ashimolowo, founder and leader of the London-based Kingsway International Christian Centre. The titles of his books and sermons are very useful indicators of the issues that I classify under dominion theology. Writing on 'money' in the life of the Christian, he notes:

> Ignoring money is foolishness. You must learn to open your brains to creative solutions. Wealth as a target in itself is deceptive. You should rather pursue it in order to have enough to serve God, touch mankind, bless your community, and

[5] Cone, *God of the Oppressed,* 16-17.

enjoy the life God has given but in the end become a conduit through which God's great wealth can reach the world.[6]

The title of the book from which this quotation has been taken is an indication of the extent to which contemporary Pentecostalism has departed from classical versions of Pentecostalism in terms of teachings: The Coming Wealth Transfer: Believing the Prophecy, Applying the Principles, Preparing to Be a Millionaire for God. We have already noted that the absence of eschatological matters from the preaching of the new Pentecostals is a direct result of their emphasis on worldly prosperity. The logic is that it would be difficult to teach people to pursue the things of the world aggressively, almost as a divine mandate, and in the same breath preach a strong message that those mundane things need to be held loosely, because Jesus Christ will return like a thief in the night. The two emphases simply do not cohere, which explains why, in preaching about the Second Coming of Christ, classical Pentecostals had to judge carefully the weight they placed on wealth generally and on money in particular.

The shift in emphasis that has come with contemporary forms of Pentecostalism is a direct reaction to the views of those forms of Christianity that inadvertently ignored a theology of wealth and material prosperity through their concern with the end times and biblical teachings on the dangers of wealth and money. Thus Ashimolowo argues that the church, which is supposed to belong to the God of all wealth, has been consigned to poverty, with churches running on what he calls 'shoe-string budgets'. He goes on to explain how this happened, and his ideas are worth quoting in full:

> Part of this challenge stems from what the Church had taught in the past concerning finance and prosperity. In its attempt to divert people's attention from worldliness it has ended up creating an atmosphere where people shun any financial blessing, focus only on going to heaven, consider abundance as illegitimate and bad, and misinterpret statements of Jesus like when He said it is easier for a camel to go through a needle's eye than for a rich man to go to heaven … The experience of the Church does not add up because it does not sit properly with the promise of the scripture that says, 'He brought us out of our past experience and into a wealthy place' (Ps. 66:12).[7]

Much of this theology may make practical sense, but it tends to shoot itself in the foot by relying too much on the proof-text approach to biblical hermeneutics. One of the texts that Ashimolowo uses in support of his position that God wants the believer and the church to be materially

[6] Matthew Ashimolowo, *The Coming Wealth Transfer: Believing the Prophecy, Applying the Principles, Preparing to Be a Millionaire for God* (London: Mattyson Media, 2006), 164.
[7] Ashimolowo, *Wealth Transfer*, 10.

wealthy is 1 Peter 1:4. The King James Version, which most charismatic preachers prefer, reads, 'and into an inheritance that can never perish, spoil or fade, kept in heaven for you'. The context for the passage was formed by the challenges facing persecuted Christians of the Diaspora, and Peter was drawing their attention to the eschatological prize of being with Jesus if present sufferings were seen and embraced as one of the consequences of holding on to faith in the midst of persecution. If context is ignored in the interpretation of Scripture, passages can be made to serve the purposes of the interpreter rather than the purposes of the Spirit of God.

Having identified the fact that contemporary Pentecostalism is driven by dominion theology, we are now in a position to examine why the symbols of the dove, eagle and globe are selected to represent this theology. Through their experiential and renewal theology, Pentecostals remind us that the Holy Spirit who is associated with power in the New Testament – whether in the ministry of Jesus, or in the Luke-Acts narratives or in Pauline thought – is none other than the Spirit of the Lord God of Israel in the Old Testament.[8]

Symbolism of the Eagle

At the beginning of the contemporary Pentecostal movement in Ghana in the late 1970s, I wondered why the eagle featured so frequently in the daily discourses of this new stream of Christianity. The eagle is used as an illustration in many sermons; it is the subject of songs of inspiration; it is the name of young people's groups; some churches have the word 'eagle' in their name, and many charismatic conferences are designated 'eagle summits' or something similar. If the dove is representative of the calmer and gentler moves of the Spirit, the eagle represents his more aggressive and conquering side. The eagle can take dominion because it has the advantage in height, strength, endurance, longevity, vision and power over other birds. The critical text for many Pentecostals is Isaiah 40:27-31:

> Do you not know? Have you not heard? The Lord is the everlasting God, the Creator of the ends of the earth. He will not grow tired or weary and his understanding no one can fathom. He gives strength to the weary and increases the power of the weak. Even youths grow tired and weary, and young men stumble and fall; but those who hope in the Lord will renew their strength. They will soar on wings like eagles; they will run and not grow weary, they will walk and not be faint.

Contemporary Pentecostals apply this text in a variety of ways, including prayer. We encounter Bishop Charles Agyinasare, founder of the Word Miracle Church International, at various points in this book. In one of

[8] Wright, *Knowing the Holy Spirit*, 10.

his many publications, Power in Prayer, he applies the metaphor of the eagle in Isaiah as follows:

> The fact is that the eagle is the king of the birds. Scientifically, it has been proven that the eagle can spy its prey five miles away because it has very powerful microscopic eyes. It can also live for over thirty years ... [W]hen the eagle's feathers start getting weak, it goes among the rocks and uses its very sharp beak to remove all its feathers from its skin. After that, it uses its beak and talons to hit the rock till they fall off and the soft tissues come up. As a result of this the eagle is not able to eat for a number of days. It is also unable to fly for a while so it spends the time resting on the rocks. After it has gone through this period of fasting (waiting), fresh feathers come up and its beak and talons grow again. By this the eagle is renewed to a youth and is able to fly stronger than before. He does not get weary and is able to go after its prey better. The beak grows out stronger and the feathers and the talons are strengthened so it flies better and gets a better grip.[9]

Agyinasare compares the period of 'waiting' here to periods of 'fasting and prayer'. In his words, 'those who forsake themselves, make sacrifices and pay a dear price to wait on the Lord … will renew their strength, they will mount up with wings like the eagle.'[10] 'The more one waits upon the Lord', he continues, 'the more he breathes over you and the more his presence overshadows you and you renew your strength … As you wait on the Lord, God will infuse, inject and vaccinate you with his power and you will be energised to rise to fulfil your God-given destiny.' [11] The critical words in this exposition include 'breath', 'energy', 'infuse', 'inject' and 'vaccinate', which all indicate the presence of the Spirit of God upon and in people. The reference to 'hovering' in Genesis is even more relevant to the symbol of the eagle. According to Wright, 'wind blows it does not hover', so the text in Genesis suggests that 'the powerful Spirit of God was hovering, poised for action'. The word 'hovering' in Hebrew, he explains, is used of an eagle in the sky, poised, alert and watchful, ready for instant action to catch its fledglings.[12] The hovering of the Spirit of God over the waters therefore meant that God was in action bringing order out of the primordial chaos.

Those who are familiar with the rhetoric of charismatic Christianity in Africa will be aware that, in the beginning, much of that rhetoric was directed at the 'chaotic denominationalism' that had come to be associated with the historic mission churches. The young people in particular were

---

[9] Charles Agyin-Asare, *Power in Prayer: Taking Your Blessings by Force* (Hoornaar, Netherlands: His Printing, 2001), 11-12.

[10] Agyin-Asare, *Power in Prayer*, 12.

[11] Agyin-Asare, *Power in Prayer*, 13.

[12] Wright, *Knowing the Holy Spirit*, 14.

challenged to 'come out' of those churches on account of their dry denominationalism, moral permissiveness and staid liturgy, which did not engender supernatural encounters with the Holy Spirit. The theologically articulate but spiritually empty clergy were castigated for supervising and presiding over churches that were going nowhere. God's Spirit is the giver of life, and the Spirit was seen as having embarked on a mission of renewal with new churches. As Nicholas Duncan-Williams told me in an interview in 1991, 'God is on the move, but the older churches have not even sensed it.' The image of the Spirit of God as an eagle who hovers over chaos to make something out of it is in part responsible for endearing that symbol to contemporary Pentecostals.

The Spirit who hovers over the face of the waters is also the Spirit that is universal. The eagle has the ability to see farther than other birds; God too can see far, as the psalms articulate:

> Where can I go from your Spirit? Where can I flee from your presence? If I go up to the heavens, you are there; if I make my bed in the depths, you are there. If I rise on the wings of the dawn, if I settle on the far side of the sea, even there your hand will guide me, your right hand will hold me fast. If I say, 'surely the darkness will hide me and the light come right around me', even the darkness will not be dark to you; the night will surely shine like the day, for darkness is as light to you. (Ps. 139:7-12)

Here we have an articulation of what it means when we say God is omnipresent. The eagle, with its ability to soar to great heights and its powerful eyesight, sees what is below and therefore represents the power of the Spirit of God to be present, to see and to judge. Most importantly, however, the context of the Psalm is a context of a God who also cares, as Wright explains:

> So the truth of the universal sustaining, providing, caring role of the Spirit of God in creation is a heartwarming reassurance of our personal security and of provision for our practical needs. If God's Spirit cares this way for the whole creation, he can certainly manage to care for you. That is a wonderful thought, and we need to hold on to it in faith and confidence.[13]

This thought also informs much charismatic prayer, which emphasises faith and is offered in confidence, even aggression, with moving limbs, screams and loud cries, because, as this new Christianity often preaches, God gives the Spirit-filled believer a certain boldness that must be exercised in prayer. In charismatic Christianity, the believer learns to take authority over both the physical and spiritual circumstances of life and to put the devil in his place as a defeated foe. Not only does the eagle reflect

[13] Wright, *Knowing the Holy Spirit*, 22.

aspects of God's character, but God through his Spirit has also made the Spirit-filled believer an eagle: endowed with the ability to soar to great heights. Jesus, with his authority over both people and spirits, is the ultimate example. With this understanding in mind, Otabil's ICGC holds two annual meetings, one dubbed 'Greater Works' and the other 'Destiny Summit', which are meant to empower believers to take their Christ-mandated and Spirit-given authority and accomplish 'greater things' in life.

Contemporary Pentecostalism in Africa thus churns out a religious menu that focuses on empowerment and emancipation. The upwardly mobile youth that the movement attracts, the professionals, the unemployed and the poor are all inspired through 'motivational messages' to do something practical towards upward mobility. In the new type of pneumatic Christianity, there has been a complete shift from preaching that focuses on morality, the attributes of God, accepting your destiny in life and preparing for heaven, to a message that tells you to build houses, buy cars, travel abroad, expand your business, pursue wealth and improve your lot in this life. Several of its leaders, notably Mensa Otabil and David O. Oyedepo, have established universities to help people achieve these lofty aims, and there is much preaching on Black liberation and empowerment too. Here we see why the eagle is important in contemporary Pentecostal discourse, imagery and symbolism – it is empowered by its powerful wings to soar to admirable heights. This association translates into the provision of opportunities for higher education, self-improvement and empowerment seminars that have come to be associated with the new Christianity, which constitute the wings with which people are expected to soar to those heights.

Symbolism of the Globe

The globe is perhaps the most self-evident and vivid depiction of the expansionist mission agenda of contemporary Pentecostalism. We have noted in these pages that Pentecostalism is a movement that was tasked to be global from the outset. Jesus told the disciples that, when the Holy Spirit came upon them, they were going to be witnesses to him in Jerusalem, Judaea, Samaria and the ends of the world. Symbolic confirmation was given when people who had come from Europe, Africa, the Arabic world and the Semitic regions were all named as having participated in the outpouring of God's Spirit on the Day of Pentecost. The languages that were spoken declaring the wonders of God also broke linguistic barriers, making Pentecostalism an international movement from the beginning. Although the globe as a symbol does not appear in Scripture, I take it to be an apt representation of the expression 'ends of the earth'.

Thus it is not for nothing that a majority of the charismatic churches under study here have the words international, global, worldwide and, more recently, trans-continental in their names. In Ghana and Nigeria we have International Central Gospel Church, Global Revival Ministries, Perez Chapel International and Living Faith Church Worldwide. Prophetic declarations that people will have access to international opportunities have become part of contemporary Pentecostal discourse: 'I see some of you in London, Hamburg, Amsterdam, New York, Washington; receive your visa, receive your international travel; you will sign a bank-breaking cheque soon; you will live in your own house; your ministry is expanding; you have worked as an associate pastor for too long; you will have your own ministry and be in charge of a mega-size church.' These words are not a direct quotation but rather a summary of prophetic declarations that I have heard in charismatic prayer services in Ghana. The influence that is sought consists both of individuals breaking through in life by means of international travel opportunities, and of ministries being able to establish branches abroad. An international profile has become in important way for members, leaders and the movement in general to participate in the processes of globalisation.

The internationalism of contemporary charismatic Christ-ianity can be seen in the choice of names, establishment of overseas branches, symbolic representations, and the worldwide peregrinations of leaders within the movement. A useful example of this process can be seen in the work of the Nigerian charismatic pastor Sunday Adelaja, in the Kiev, Ukraine. His Church established in 1994 has a rather long name: 'The Church of the Embassy of the Blessed Kingdom of God for all Nations.' Each of these terms was chosen to reflect a certain transnational understanding of Christian mission:

> The Church is the representative of God on the earth – His 'Embassy'. Therefore, we – children of God – are the citizens of His Divine Kingdom and not citizens of this world! The Blessed Kingdom of God [is] a place of destruction of curses. At the head of every kingdom is a king. Our King is Jesus Christ! He is the Lord of all nations; … Jesus Christ is the Savior for everyone, irrespective of his age, color of skin, nationality and social status.[14]

An appropriate media image has been developed to reflect the philosophy of the name. The logo of God Embassy is a globe with Africa in the center. The globe, which symbolises the world as mission field, is capped by a golden crown with a Cross. Just below the crown is a light emanating from Ukraine, which remains otherwise unmarked. The light from Ukraine shines throughout Europe and the Middle East. Africa figures

---

[14] Stated in Church of the Embassy of the Blessed Kingdom of God for all Nations: 8th Anniversary Brochure (Kyiv, 2002), 5.

prominently, but the light and energy of the church emanate from Ukraine around the world.[15]

The Holy Spirit, Charismatic Symbolism and Empowerment

The relationship between the Holy Spirit and the symbolic representations in charismatic Christianity is not difficult to understand. I have argued consistently that this movement sees itself as empowered by the Holy Spirit to transform lives, to create upward mobility for individuals and to bring about change in society in general. According to Wright:

> Power … is effective action, making a difference, influencing events, changing the way things are or will be. It is not surprising, then, that the Spirit of God in the Old Testament is commonly linked with power, for the biblical God is nothing if not effective in action and in bringing about change! Indeed, when the Israelites spoke of the Spirit of Yahweh, it was often simply a way of saying that God himself was exercising his power on the earth, either directly or, more commonly, through human agents.[16]

The human agents referred to here would be those who, having been renewed by the Spirit, are moving Pentecostalism to a different level by emphasising the need to be engaged in public life. The dove is the symbol of the Holy Spirit who empowers God's children. The eagle shows the empowered at their best, in soaring above limitations into greater heights and achievements. The globe symbolises the birth of a movement that knows no limitations in terms of international reach, expansionism in mission and transnational networking.

Christopher Wright notes how we must take seriously the fact that good craftsmanship, artistic designs, embroidery and the abilities that go with them are said to be marks of the filling of God's Spirit. The text on Bezalel and Oholiab, he continues, 'encourages us to believe that the same Spirit of God who was at work in creation is also at work in that same wider sense, in all of those who, as human beings made in God's image, enrich our world with all kinds of creativity in art, music, colorful design, beautiful craftsmanship … and skillful speech and writing'.[17] Wright concludes, 'When we honor and admire such art, we give glory to the Spirit who empowers it.'[18] In emphasising the need for people to upgrade their skills, return to school, invest money and improve their lot in life, the new churches speak in tones that address what may be missing from the lives of

---

[15] Catherine Wanner, *Communities of the Converted: Ukrainians and Global Evangelism* (Ithaca, NY, and London: Cornell University Press, 2007), 214.

[16] Wright, *Knowing the Holy Spirit*, 36.

[17] Wright, *Knowing the Holy Spirit*, 39.

[18] Wright, *Knowing the Holy Spirit*, 39.

Africa's upwardly mobile youth, an engagement that is missing from the older churches at the moment. In church life, the sheep go where they can find pasture. Those who complain about sheep-stealing must therefore begin to water their dry grass, relying on the Spirit who is life-giver.

Chapter 4
Patriarchs in Pentecostalism: Jacob, Esau and Prosperity Hermeneutics

African pneumatic movements generally love the Old Testament especially, with its sacred places, manifestations of the power of God in prophetic dramas and, for the new Pentecostals in particular, the relationship between God's covenant and the material wealth of the Patriarchs. This chapter looks at a practical side to the theology of prosperity which focuses not on the simple name-it-and-claim it model but on the repackaging of the Jacob and Esau narratives. The weight of the discussion is on Jacob, who, according to contemporary Pentecostal hermeneutics, applies certain principles of negotiation to realise his God-given destiny of prosperity. For the new charismatic pastors, the lives of the Patriarchs and their experiences are paradigmatic of God's will and ways with those who trust in him. The idea of covenant tends to be strong within contemporary Pentecostal discourse, and biblical narratives are generally 'assumed to be historically factual'.[1] That Abraham was called by God and came into great wealth, and that St. Paul refers to the Gentiles as beneficiaries of the blessings of Abraham in Galatians 3:14, for example, is usually interpreted to mean that believers will also come into great material wealth and prosperity if they remain within the covenant.

The work of pastors Mensa Otabil and Eastwood Anaba provides the basis of the discussion in this chapter. These two authors stand out because their brand of prosperity gospel does not rely on the simplistic model, but rather emphasises hard work and the application of business principles to achieve success in life. That approach can be seen in Otabil's sermons, as Paul Gifford has noted:

> To those who ask 'God give me money', [Otabil] says 'God will not give you money … Where will he get it? But God can give you wisdom and with that you can go on his earth, you can [make] that thing.' … The proper prayer should be

[1] Paul Gifford, *Ghana's New Christianity: Pentecostalism in a Globalizing African Economy* (Bloomington and Indianapolis: Indiana University Press, 2004), 79.

> 'Give me wisdom', that he manufactures in abundance. Your God won't give you wealth; he gave you the power to create wealth'.[2]

The use of Scripture to prove how the Christian life ought to be lived to bring divine blessings to fruition is also considered in this chapter. In the new hermeneutics, as we shall see, prosperity involves more than mere positive confessions and the faithful discharge of tithing obligations. New lessons on how to prosper are drawn – especially from the life of Jacob and his dealings with his adversaries. In these alternative prosperity teachings, a person's adversaries may well provide 'opportunities for promotion',[3] as, inadvertently did Esau, who was Jacob's brother, and Laban, Jacob's uncle, when they opposed Jacob. Jacob outsmarted them because he had better principles of negotiation. The principles of negotiation are needed to achieve the ends that the new Pentecostals seek to make available to their followers. These are teachings that offer openings into a globalised world of opportunities and radical transformations not only of the self and empowerment of the Spirit, but also of economic and material circumstances: transformations that together reflect the glory of God. Neo-Pentecostals work the biblical text as hard as they can to counter traditional religious mindsets that equate poverty and deprivation with spirituality.

African Pentecostals and Scripture

In his study of Pentecostalism, Ogbu Kalu argues for the deployment of 'religious discourse' in place of the instrumentalist emphasis on deprivation, pathology, pessimism and externality. That religious discourse, he explains, recasts the story with a Christian idiom of hope, optimism, participation in Christ's victory, intercultural theology, anti-structure, racial nationalism and muscular evangelism. At the root of all these features, he notes, is how Pentecostals interpret and preach the Bible. Consequently he calls attention to the importance of looking at Pentecostal hermeneutics critically, as 'a specific lens for reading the Bible seriously'.[4] Kalu's explanation of why religious discourse should be taken seriously in the study of Pentecostalism provides a methodological understanding that drives my thoughts here:

> The religious discourse reaffirms that Pent-ecostalism is a pre-eminently religious movement and should be studied as such. The nature of its presence, self-understanding, what it says, does, and how it witnesses are important. People are

[2] Gifford, *Ghana's New Christianity*, 120.

[3] Gifford, *Ghana's New Christianity*, 55.

[4] Ogbu Kalu, *African Pentecostalism: An Introduction* (Oxford: Oxford University Press, 2008), xiii.

attracted by its message and by its hermeneutics of trust, its certitudes and claim to stand on the word. Therefore, we should study its theology and practices.[5]

In this chapter we see how contemporary Pentecostal readings and interpretations of the life of Jacob are made to reflect the belief in a gospel of success, upward mobility and achievement that bears fruit through the making of smart choices or better negotiations. In the material to be considered – Pastor Mensa Otabil's Buy the Future and Pastor Eastwood Anaba's The Quest for Supremacy – the life of Jacob is repackaged to speak to contemporary audiences.[6] The choices Jacob made, no matter if traditionally seen as morally wrong, are reinterpreted in terms of 'smart moves' or 'skillful negotiations' needed to succeed in today's turbulent, capitalist, consumerist and competitive world. Eastwood Anaba sets the tone with his observations on why Jacob should not be faulted for cheating:

Tradition presents Jacob as a trickster who subverted his brother's position. He is often misunderstood and misrepresented. His honesty has been questioned because of his shrewd business sense in dealing with his brother. … I believe that Jacob bought the birthright from an intelligent elder brother who was responsible for his actions. It was legitimate business they did. Secondly, the character of Jacob qualified him for the birthright above his brother Esau. Jacob was hard working. He was also disciplined and had his passions under control unlike Esau who could not handle a brief moment of hunger. Jacob possessed a very unusual sensitivity, which made him an ideal carrier of the birthright in the midst of hostile pockets of enemies. He gave spiritual things first place in his life. The bargaining power of Jacob was a strong factor in his accession to the top. He always knew what he deserved and he demanded it. His achievements were not the product of luck and sheer providence. Jacob was not a lucky man but a 'lurking man' who seized opportunities any time they showed up.[7]

The two publications listed are useful for this exercise because they are representative of the new hermeneutics offered on Jacob and Esau as I have heard them in Ghana and elsewhere in Africa. In the words of Eastwood Anaba the life of Jacob 'portrays vividly a quest for supremacy' because 'he outsmarted Esau and out-paced Laban to grab prosperity and wealth'.[8] Mensa Otabil pushes the argument further with an interpretation of the lives of Jacob and Esau as having much wider applications for the choices that peoples and nations make:

---

[5] Kalu, *African Pentecostalism*, xiii.

[6] Mensa Otabil, *Buy the Future: Learning to Negotiate for a Better Future than your Present* (Accra: Altar International, 2002); Eastwood Anaba, *The Quest for Supremacy* (Bolgatanga, Ghana: Desert Leaf Publications, 2004).

[7] Anaba, *Quest for Supremacy*, vi-vii.

[8] Anaba, *Quest for Supremacy*, 57.

> Some observe the various outcomes of life and conclude that it is all a matter of fate and destiny. That man has no control over what the final outcome will be. That is a very sad way to look at life. To think that God created man to just go through life like a robot pre-programmed without options, simply to act in certain predetermined ways is biblically flawed. ... There are those who work with a value system that is focused on short-term needs and tend to make decisions that seem beneficial today but become disastrous in the future. I call such people and nations, Esaus. On the other hand there are those who work with a value system that is focused on long-term benefits instead of short-term needs. They save what they have today and invest it for the future. I call them Jacobs.[9]

Pentecostalism, as André Corten and Ruth Marshall-Fratani point out, 'tends to have a surprisingly open and flexible approach to Biblical interpretation'.[10] In the particular story under study, this 'open and flexible' hermeneutics means that the mercies and graces of God, which may enable people to succeed in life in spite of their personal failures and potentially destructive choices, do not receive due attention. There is no reason to believe that any attempt is made on the part of our two interlocutors, Otabil and Anaba, to distort Scripture in their interpretation of this material. Their books, derived from sermon series, simply underscore the innovative attempts by new charismatic preaching to present a gospel that addresses contemporary challenges and speaks directly to the concerns of modern urban audiences. Any criticism should be read against the backdrop of the fact that the preachers use the material to serve particular purposes and Anaba seems very conscious of this, cautioning, 'Do not be too quick to read dishonesty into Jacob's acts. Many believers have specialised in identifying the wrong in people's acts instead of the vital productive lessons they can learn from the act.'[11]

Repackaging the Life of Jacob

In these works by Otabil and Anaba, Esau was not a vulnerable twin who was exploited; he simply made the wrong choices. Jacob, by contrast, made choices that led to successes and triumphs against the odds. According to those who read Jacob this way, life is about the application of biblical principles for the realisation of successes and prosperities that God has planned for his children. When the tales of the lives of Jacob and Esau are used in charismatic preaching and writing, the emphasis shifts from what grace and mercy can accomplish with the worst of sinners and truants, to reinterpreting Jacob's exploitative approach to life as principles of wisdom that culminate in success. The new reading is that life is about smart

---

[9] Otabil, *Buy the Future*, 5-6.

[10] Corten and Marshall-Fratani, *Between Babel and Pentecost,* 5.

[11] Anaba, *Quest for Supremacy*, 20-21.

negotiations. This position is illustrated by a picture of a hand shake – one black and the other white – on the cover of Buy the Future, by Otabil. In Quest for Supremacy, life is about 'wrestling' for one's place, illustrated by the two wrestlers in combat on the front cover of Anaba's book. Against the grain of conventional understanding of Jacob as a sinner transformed by grace from a deceiver to Israel, Jacob is presented by the two authors as one who made right and perceptive choices with the 'future' and 'supremacy' in mind. Otabil reinterprets Jacob thus:

> Most people see him as a trickster and a fraud who exploited his brother Esau. … Jacob did not spend his time scheming to take advantage of people. He developed a character that was very different from his name; he was an upright man. Later on in life, after a season of struggle for divine blessing, God rightly changed the name of Jacob to reflect his true heritage.[12]

A similar position appears in Anaba's book, with Jacob presented not as a cheat but one who simply had business sense:

> Jacob was not a dishonest person who subverted his brother Esau's position, to take away his birthright. As good men and women struggle to come out of the rubble of life it is not unusual to see them dented and distorted by the pressures around them; God concentrates on the good underneath the dents but man fixes his gaze on the dents.[13]

The references to 'struggles' in Otabil and to 'dents' in Anaba show that the two preachers do not take a simplistic approach to prosperity. The thought is that the road to our God-given destinies of abundance has many obstacles, but these obstacles are only transient if one stays focused and works towards a better future or supremacy. Thus, as Anaba explains, 'God turns the obstacle into a springboard to catapult you to another level of supremacy. Obstacles are not meant to obstruct you but to uplift you.'[14]

Wrestle and Negotiation Prosperity

In Buy the Future and The Quest for Supremacy, as we have seen, Jacob's life of deceit is repackaged and presented in terms of the pursuit of success. His eventual destiny-transforming encounter with God is upheld as an example to be emulated. 'Life is all about wrestling', Anaba notes, and 'Jacob was a wrestler.' For Anaba, Jacob wrestled with entities that were bigger than he was. He wrestled with an older brother, Esau; he wrestled with an uncle, Laban, for 'better conditions of service', and eventually he

---

[12] Otabil, *Buy the Future*, 28.
[13] Anaba, *Quest for Supremacy*, vi-vii.
[14] Anaba, *Quest for Supremacy*, 32.

even 'wrestled with God, the highest of all'.[15] What Anaba casts as 'wrestling', Otabil explains in terms of 'negotiation'. The two idioms cohere because wrestling an opponent to the ground may involve not just physical strength but also the wisdom to manoeuvre and outwit, which is what we find in Jacob. In the words of Otabil, people are where they are in life because they have chosen to be there:

> Human beings are not victims of circumstances; human beings are products of choices. You don't become who you are because circumstances made you so. You are where you are because of choices that you made yourself or choices that were made on your behalf.[16]

Thus, according to this understanding, Jacob and Esau got their just deserts for the choices they made. Esau was not exploited: he simply made foolish choices. Jacob was not a cheat: he knew how to choose well and at what time. The title and sub-title of Otabil's book virtually underscores the hermeneutical understanding that such readings introduce into the biblical narratives: Buy the Future: Learning to Negotiate for a Future Better than Your Present. The key expression here is 'negotiate'. In other words, Jacob 'bought the future' by learning to 'negotiate' for an improvement on his 'present' circumstances. Otabil writes in the preface: 'The thesis of this book is based on the principles gleaned from this Biblical story of the lives of Esau and Jacob.'[17] The book responds to a set of questions: 'Why does our future often so contradict our present?', 'Are there some things we do that make us prone to success and others we do that make us prone to failure?, 'Can we determine the outcome of our future today?'[18]

In response to these questions, Otabil explains that life ends up in success or failure due to choices made in life. That two people with the same opportunities can turn out differently is explained by 'two vital factors': first, the values they develop in their lives and second, the way they see life and respond to it. 'These two vital factors', he writes, 'ultimately, shape all the important decisions people make.'[19]

Destinies and Choices

Much in the interpretations of these two authors relates to destiny, a critical focus of contemporary Pentecostal discourse. In the African traditional context, what the Akan of Ghana refer to hyebere, destiny, also known among the Igbo of Nigeria as chi, is often invoked as causal explanation

---

[15] Anaba, *Quest for Supremacy*, 76-77.
[16] Gifford, *Ghana's New Christianity*, 121-22.
[17] Otabil, *Buy the Future*, ix.
[18] Otabil, *Buy the Future*, 3.
[19] Otabil, *Buy the Future*, 4-5.

when solutions to life's problems cannot be found. Pastor Otabil discounts this traditional understanding of the force of destiny as far as our God-given lives are concerned.[20] The Esaus of this life, Otabil explains, work with a value system that is focused on short-term needs and tend to make decisions that seem beneficial today but become disastrous in the future. Responding to the short-term need that is hunger, Esau exchanged the long-term benefits of the privileges of being a first born for something temporal: a bowl of pottage. The Jacobs, like their biblical paradigm, save what they have today and invest it for greater benefit in the future. That securing a better future depends on skilful negotiation is also present in Anaba's work. He notes that Esau negotiated badly and lost his birthright.[21] His principles of negotiation include not acting from a position of weakness: 'negotiate when your gifts and strengths are at their peak'. If you negotiate when you are vulnerable or when you are on the decline as Esau did, 'you may have to settle for less'.[22] Anaba concludes that 'you get the best deals only when your gifts are operating at maximum capacity'.[23]

That Jacob took undue advantage of Esau's temporal need for food to exploit him does not feature in the exposition. Vulnerability is simply interpreted as stupidity because the events are considered only from Jacob's point of view. Thus throughout Buy the Future, Jacob is presented as doing just what Esau failed to do. He clairvoyantly traded what was temporal for what was permanent. This approach to life, Otabil argues, is what determines success or failure, and not simply for individuals but also for nations and indeed for every endeavour of life:

> Although Rebecca was pregnant with twins who were just two individuals, God called them 'nations' and 'peoples'. The children of the womb were prophetic pictures of the characteristics of nations and peoples. There would be nations who would be modeled after the value systems of these children. There would also be people who would also model their lives and choices after the characteristics of these twins. Because God knows the end from the beginning, He gave Isaac and Rebecca a picture of their children's future.[24]

Thus Jacob and Esau are not simply individual characters whose lives have lessons for us but also they have what Otabil refers to as 'a wider trans-generational and trans-cultural reference'.[25] Otabil takes a different path from traditional interpretations, which tend to explain the different outcomes of the lives of Jacob and Esau in terms of God-given destinies.

---

[20] Otabil, *Buy the Future*, 5-6.
[21] Anaba, *Quest for Surpremacy*, 23.
[22] Anaba, *Quest for Supremacy*, 24.
[23] Anaba, *Quest for Surpremacy*, 24.
[24] Otabil, *Buy the Future*, 8.
[25] Otabil, *Buy the Future*, 8.

God, Otabil argues, did not pre-programme the brothers' choices for the future. All God did was to tell the parents through foreknowledge how the twins were going to turn out.[26] The rest came down to choices made during life's journey. What appears in popular Christian preaching and thinking as Jacob's life of deceits and lies, appears in Otabil's teaching – and, indeed, in charismatic hermeneutics generally – as 'principles' and 'opportunities' of success. Jacob, unlike Esau, knew how to go for what was enduring and he acted on that knowledge. The Esaus of this world simply operate with what Otabil refers to as 'faulty paradigms'.[27]

Challenging Africa to Think

In treating the material this way, Pastors Mensa Otabil and Eastwood Anaba apply the Bible in ways that speak to contemporary audiences, particularly young people looking for alternative means to succeed in life. They direct their messages not simply at individuals, but at Africans/Blacks in particular and their nations, attempting to use the Bible to inspire them to do something about the negative images and circumstances of privation that have bedevilled their peoples. Otabil definitely has Africa in mind when he writes that nations build their developmental paradigm after national values. Those values, he notes, will make them either 'Esau nations' or 'Jacob nations':

> Much as the practical realities of the worlds of Esau and Jacob differ vastly from what our generation has to deal with, the under-girding assumptions that shape our choices are all the same as what shaped theirs. ... The future is either bought or sold by the choices of today; and the choices of today are influenced by the paradigm you operate from.[28]

There is much wisdom in the lessons that are drawn from the text. According to Otabil, the main feature of the Esau paradigm is that it sacrifices the opportunities and potential of the future to fulfil the necessities of the present. Whereas Esau sells the future to buy the present, Jacob harnesses the resources of the present in order to 'acquire the opportunities and potential of the future.' Otabil concludes that people and nations 'cannot operate from an Esau paradigm and expect the blessings related to the Jacob paradigm'.[29] Esau is not absolved from blame, but Otabil does not blame individuals entirely for their predicaments in this life. He recognises that we are born into worlds in which wrong choices may already have been made by others, and the consequences of those

---

[26] Otabil, *Buy the Future,* 8.
[27] Otabil, *Buy the Future*, 10.
[28] Otabil, *Buy the Future*, 15.
[29] Otabil, *Buy the Future*, 16.

choices may affect us. However, even then, he explains, there is no justification for not working hard to alter unhappy destinies. God has given us the power of conscience and self-awareness to enable us to judge the rightness and wrongness of the different values and cultural options available to us.[30]

The Esau Paradigm

In Buy the Future and The Quest for Supremacy, Esau is not a vulnerable man whose situation was exploited by Jacob. His particular choice of the hunting profession led to his lack of achievement. Esau may have been a 'skilful' hunter but, according to Otabil, hunters tend to be too narrow in their focus, using their massive potential to pursue one type of game at a time. Hunters, he further argues, deploy great skills, abilities and strengths to achieve limited results. Sometimes the targets do not merit the levels of adrenalin released as the hunter chases an animal, and according to Otabil, the release of adrenalin overrides a person's power of reasoning and analysis. In other words, by choosing this profession, Esau was prone to the sort of failure that eventually came his way. Often the chases that hunters embark on do not yield any results, he explains. Applying this image to nations, Otabil notes that nations and people who manifest this tendency of hunters 'spend enormous national and personal resources focusing on largely insignificant and unbeneficial objectives'.[31] He concludes,

> When people operate from an Esau paradigm, they have the hunter's mentality and presume that what they have today will always be available and can also be accessed in the same way as they know it today. When we allow that thinking to shape our choices, we fail to plan and manage the life-cycle of our present achievements to cater for us in the future. We should always keep in mind that what we have today is not for the use of today. What we have today gives us the currency to purchase what will be tomorrow. Today's advantages must be used to buy tomorrow's opportunities.[32]

Pastor Otabil reads much into Esau's profession as a hunter in order to make his point that the choices Esau made in life were self-inflicted. The hunter has not mastered the art and science of nurturing what is needed, he notes, and so the hunter and his family do not have food security. Hunters have to go out every day to 'hunt' for their needs, but cultivators prepare for the day of scarcity and make provision for the emergencies of life. As a cultivator, Jacob had this advantage.[33]

---

[30] Otabil, *Buy the Future*, 17.
[31] Otabil, *Buy the Future*, 23.
[32] Otabil, *Buy the Future*, 25.
[33] Otabil, *Buy the Future*, 25-26.

The Jacob Paradigm

In both books more space is given to Jacob than to Esau because Jacob is representative of the principles that the authors seek to establish concerning how to succeed and prosper in life. As he does for Esau, Otabil also profiles Jacob based on the Genesis text. Jacob is described in the passage as a 'dweller in tents', which Otabil explains as having to do with his profession. 'Dwellers in tents' are cultivators, who are more productive than hunters.[34] Otabil does acknowledge that Jacob was not a perfect human being and so explains that his uprightness does not mean that he never sinned, but rather that 'Jacob stayed on the right side of God's principles.' In his words, 'Jacob worked with his mind, developed ideas and used his creative mind to solve his problems.' He proceeds to profile Jacob as a man of 'enormous vision, imagination and innovation'.[35] An earlier observation should be reiterated here: the exposition does not suggest that in dealing with Esau, Jacob used these powers of imagination and innovation to deceive or take advantage of his elder brother. That feature is completely lost in the desire to reinterpret Jacob's cunning ways as principles of success and prosperity. Thus, in a somewhat contentious interpretation of Genesis 25:27, Pastor Otabil states what he considers to be the difference between Esau and Jacob in their attitudes to life:

> Esau as a hunter operated from a productive paradigm and used much labour and physical energy to accomplish his tasks. He employed his great physical strength and athleticism as the main tool for his work. Jacob as a quiet and contemplative cultivator, operated from the productive paradigm of using the power and force of imagination and calculated planning in accomplishing his tasks.[36]

Here we see an attempt to place the power of the mind above the use of brawn and physical energy in the accomplishment of the tasks of life. Such thinking overlooks the principles of complement in the building of societies. The work of Esau as a hunter is presented as a waste of energy in the pursuit of limited game, but Jacob was productive because he employed the powers of the mind: 'whilst Esau ran with his feet after animals in the wild, Jacob run with his brains to discover a new and better way of husbanding and breeding the animals he had.'[37] People who observed Jacob may have thought he was not up to much, Otabil argues, because those who expend physical energy and sweat in the course of their work are considered productive. This thinking, he suggests, is erroneous. Jacob, unlike Esau, he explains, did not perspire much in the sun, running after

---

[34] Otabil, *Buy the Future*, 27.
[35] Otabil, *Buy the Future*, 28-29.
[36] Otabil, *Buy the Future*, 29.
[37] Otabil, *Buy the Future*, 29.

wild animals, but rather spent his time 'thinking about how to simplify the old procedures his society had inherited and functioned with'. Otabil reads into the text something that simply is not there and then concludes that Jacob was a man of dreams, imagination and innovation. His brain was always ticking with new ideas and possibilities. Jacob is thus presented as a man of ideas and, although Otabil does not say it in so many words, he presents Esau as one who, as a fool, expends his energies in unproductive ventures.

Esau, Jacob and Dominion Theology

In the rest of his book Buy the Future, Otabil very carefully and systematically draws out the implications of the choices that the twins Jacob and Esau made, and what they mean for our life's journey as we go through it as individuals, families and nations. Being a hunter meant that Esau was only a 'chaser' who was sorely disadvantaged when it came to applying what Otabil called the principles of nurturing in competitive situations. In effect, those with a hunting attitude to life, he claims, negotiate from a position of weakness and therefore are losers – a point similar to that made by Anaba when he noted that negotiations must take place when strengths and gifts are operating at their optimum levels.[38] Cultivators like Jacob are presented as nurturers who have options and are able to examine what they want at close quarters in order to make the best choices. The cultivator does not take off blindly into the wild in hot and frenzied pursuit of a target he cannot be sure of. He has the advantage of careful examination in making his choices, Otabil concludes. The two professions, lived out through the two characters, represent for Otabil what he calls 'two different productive value systems', and he poses the question, 'which of these systems was stronger?'[39] In effect, the idiom of 'wrestling' to secure a better future that Anaba employed is also found in Otabil's thoughts. And in turn, Otabil's idea that negotiating for better deals today has implications for our descendants, is also present in Anaba's work when he notes: 'Thousands of people in this generation are doing things others should have done in previous generations. Their predecessors were unwilling to pay the price and they have had to move backwards to do things which should have been done long ago.'[40]

Wrestling and skilful negotiations are meant to achieve a single end: to dominate peoples and systems. Contemporary charismatic theology is very much a 'dominion theology'. In this theology, as Corten and Marshall-Fratani explain, believers no longer retreat among themselves in order to

---

[38] Anaba, *Quest for Supremacy*, 23-24.

[39] Otabil, *Buy the Future*, 32-33.

[40] Anaba, *Quest for Supremacy*, 25.

maintain the purity of their beliefs and their moral rigor, salvation is resolutely this-worldly and the evidence of new life has become as much material as spiritual.[41] Dominion thinking underlies much of charismatic discourse and is found in the names of churches, titles of conferences and crusades, sermons themes, book titles and car bumper stickers. It also inspires much charismatic activity. Indeed Pastor Otabil's first book, The Four Laws of Productivity, is about the dominion that God has given humankind to 'subdue' the earth. International Central Gospel Church's yearly conference is dubbed 'Destiny Summit', with the 2007 event themed 'Emancipation'. Matthew Ashimolowo's television programmes are advertised as 'Winning Ways', which has also been the theme of a number of crusades in Africa. Christian Action Faith Ministry's Bible School is now 'Dominion University College'.

Dominion theology is about achievement and success, and so charismatic preaching tends to be very motivational, geared in particular to inspiring upwardly mobile young people to believe that they can make it. One of the important symbols of this type of dominion Christianity is the eagle. The eagle's dominion of the world of birds and its towering and soaring strength, to which Isaiah testifies, are cherished symbols in charismatic discourse. The impact of these messages on Africa's young people has been enormous. Testimonies tell of lives that were not going anywhere but have been turned around through applying the motivational messages of charismatic pastors like Otabil, Anaba and Ashimolowo. The best examples of dominion, success and prosperity are the charismatic pastors and their ministries. We are dealing here with a new generation of pastors who are incredibly gifted. Many of them are highly educated, although not necessarily in theology. Even without the theological resources and international networks originally available only to the historic mission denominations, charismatic church leaders have, within a generation, built some impressive mega-sized, dynamic and exuberant churches that have a positive impact on the lives of their patrons. Their innovative appropriations of modern media technologies in the cause of the gospel have stirred the older churches into emulative action.

Ephraim and Manasseh: Grace as 'Power in Weakness'

Against the backdrop of this dominion theology, Pastor Otabil notes from the lives of Esau and Jacob that 'it is desirable that we operate from a position of strength and not of weakness'.[42] He explains strength to mean the 'power and ability to accomplish a task'. This strength, he continues, is related not only to the application of physical force to get a task

[41] Corten and Marshall-Fratani, *Babel and Pentecost*, 7.

[42] Otabil, *Buy the Future*, 38.

accomplished, but also to all the abilities resident in a person that can be deployed at any time towards the provision of solutions to problems. If you operate from a value system that does not provide you with the strength to overcome the challenges you face, you will find it difficult to solve your problems. 'Your developed strength is your key to your ability to your viability on earth,' writes Otabil.[43] Otabil and Anaba teach their readers a number of very important lessons through the stories of the lives of Jacob and Esau. One of these lessons is found in their observation that life does not necessarily favour the one who started out first or has natural advantages. So, indeed, the Bible does not speak amiss when it says that 'the race is not for the swift' (Ecclesiastes 9:11). God was making a similar point when he told Rebecca, 'the older shall serve the younger' (Genesis 25:23). In effect the Gospel of Prosperity usually fails to employ a proper understanding of God's grace because it is sometimes driven by the presuppositions of the secular society to which we belong. That is how the Jacob and Esau narratives have been used in charismatic hermeneutics.

One clear example of the fact that things do not always work according to the so called principles of prosperity touted by preachers, is seen in the story of the blessing of Ephraim and Manasseh by their grandfather Jacob. In that story, Joseph received news that his father's health was declining and he wanted to bring his children for blessing before the old man passed away. Jacob's sight at this point had virtually failed him, so Joseph had to bring his sons close to his father for the blessing through the laying on of the old man's hands. In accordance with custom, Joseph positioned the older child, Manasseh, on the right and Ephraim, the younger one, on the left. At this point, the story as narrated in Genesis 48:14-19, reads as follows:

> But Israel reached out his hand and put it on Ephraim's head, though he was the younger, and crossing his arms, he put his left on Manasseh's head, even though Manasseh was the firstborn. … When Joseph saw his father placing his right hand on Ephraim's head he was displeased; so he took hold of his father's hand to move it from Ephraim's head to Manasseh's head. Joseph said to him, 'No, my father, this one is the first born; put your right hand on his head.' But his father refused and said, 'I know, my son, I know. He too will become great. Nevertheless, his younger brother will be greater than he, and his descendants will become a group of nations.'

The Bible does not explain why Jacob (or Israel) took this course of action. In his younger days Jacob had clearly deceived people around him, including his own father, in order to get what he wanted. We may never know for sure, but it is possible that having taken advantage of Esau, Jacob simply wanted to use that opportunity to justify the fact that the younger

---

[43] Otabil, *Buy the Future*, 39, 41.

could sometimes be placed over the older, as had happened to him. Whatever the reason, Ephraim was privileged against the paradigm of the day and made greater than Manasseh. And this is how God works sometimes. In so many instances, including the selection of Israel as God's chosen nation, God goes for the marginalised and underprivileged – non entities – in order to prove that his grace has no formula to it: 'my ways are not your ways neither are my thoughts your thoughts' we hear Isaiah saying to God's people (Isaiah 55). The same principle seemed to be at work in the parable of the prodigal son, in which the elder brother who stayed home and faithful to his father did not necessarily enjoy what he thought was due him. Jesus' parable of the workers in the vineyard makes the same point, where the workers who came late enjoyed rewards initially reserved for those who 'bore the heat of the day' (Matthew 20).

Nevertheless, the wisdom in this sort of teaching is undeniable, and it is the reason why so many Africans and African/Americans laud Otabil as one of the best Bible teachers of our generation. On the face of it, most of his teaching sounds practical, but several aspects of Pastor Otabil's understanding of the Jacob and Esau story come unstuck when placed within the bigger context of how God's grace works. The life of Christ and his choice of the Cross teach that God's power is often evident not in strength but in weakness. In our own day, the likes of Pastor Mensa Otabil are perhaps the best examples of how this grace works. Four decades ago there were no charismatic churches in Africa. When they emerged, everything about them was questioned by the mainline churches, with the newcomers referred to as 'mushroom' churches and their leaders castigated as theological illiterates. But through these seeming non-entities without any theological sophistication, God has raised a new breed of churches and church leaders who have taken Christianity to a completely different level. The historic mission denominations with all their intellectual capacities and resources are now working hard to emulate the methods of the new charismatic churches with their innovative and inspiring brand of Christianity. According to St. Paul, God takes the foolish things of this world to shame the wise. Those who look carefully will realise that it is because God's grace defies worldly wisdom and the principle of the 'first born' that Africa has in the twenty-first century become a major heartland of Christianity in the world. This progress has not been made through the application of any well-crafted principle of church planting and growth. God is proving that his grace cannot be formulaic. Hard work matters, but it is God who has the last word when one assesses 'promotion' in terms of Christian teaching and experience.

Conclusion

Gordon D. Fee has said that the problem of charismatic theology of prosperity or dominion is hermeneutical.[44] In seeking to use the Jacob and Esau narratives to challenge the contemporary Christian to apply the principles of wisdom, negotiation, hard work and perception choices in order to succeed in life, the hermeneutics fails, first, to put the proper weight on the deceptive lifestyle of Jacob and, second, to realise that sometimes it takes more than hard work to propel people into success. Zechariah prophesies in the same Spirit when he says, '"not by might nor by power, but by my Spirit," says the Lord' (4:6). Thirdly, it fails to take adequate account of biblical paradigms in which God's strength is found in weakness rather than in insistence on one's due and rights. So, for example, Jesus calls for 'turning the other cheek', and in one of his most important teachings on wealth notes that 'a man's life does not consist in the abundance of his possessions'. Most importantly, however, the perception that Jacob did not cheat but only asserted himself fails to read the story in the light of the 'life of Christ', who although he was in the form of God did not count equality with him a thing to be grasped, but 'emptied himself' and became human like us. Jesus Christ did not insist on his rights, and in fact his choice of the cross instead of the horse (which was a symbol of strength) was not considered a smart choice by Peter, who tried to persuade him not to proceed to Jerusalem. What brought Jacob, who started life as a conman, to be the symbolic figure of Israel was not his ability to deceive and outwit competitors, or even to negotiate or wrestle his way through life; it was rather the grace of God, which can lift harlots, publicans and thieves from the depths of destruction and place their feet on higher ground that they might reflect the glory of God.

[44] Gordon D. Fee, *The Disease of the Health and Wealth Gospels* (Beverly, MA: Frontline Publishing, 1985), 7.

Chapter 5
'Catching the Anointing': Aspects of Pentecostal Media Ministry

This chapter focuses on 'enchanted' texts and other audio-visual resources as deployed within African-led Pentecostalism. I use the expression 'African-led Pentecostalism' here because the chapter refers to the ways in which contemporary African Pentecostals and their leaders – both at home and in the Diaspora – use modern media as forms of ministry. The use of modern mass media in Christian ministry has developed as part of the self-definition of Pentecostal Christianity in particular. On the one hand, this extensive usage stems out of the inspiration to use media in the fulfilment of the divine mandate to make disciples of all nations. To that end, television and the internet, for example, expose ministries to large numbers of people across borders, whom the producers of religious commodities may not be able to reach physically. On the other hand, the international aspirations of Christian ministries make the use of mass media inevitable in the practice of religion. One needs to be in the media to be counted as important, a reality that is non-negotiable in a technological age. We see such a presence in the life and ministries of Dag Heward-Mills of the Lighthouse Chapel International in Ghana, Ukraine-based Church of the Embassy of the Blessed Kingdom of God for All Nations, led by a Nigerian, Pastor Sunday Adelaja, and other such contemporary Pentecostal ministries led by Africans. These contemporary Pentecostals deploy both conventional and new media extensively as tools for ministry.

In addition to whatever other purposes they serve, for contemporary Pentecostals, mass media resources tend to be seen by both producers and consumers as possessing a certain sacramental value. Books, cassette tapes, church magazines and other such resources, it is believed, could be embodied by the Holy Spirit and used for therapeutic and empowering purposes. As a result, the resources (including tapes and books) can be considered physical things that are conduits for ontological graces. African-led charismatic Christianity, including the older Spiritual churches, takes a sacramental view of life not simply because it is considered biblical to use visible items as carriers of anointing and power, but also because these worldviews resonate with those of traditional religious cultures. Radio sets, televisions, cell phones and other such devices have acquired the same sacramental values as blessed water, holy oils and handkerchiefs that may be blessed in order that they carry the power of the Spirit across to users. Testimonies speak of people receiving healing simply by touching a television set during preaching or prayer on the airwaves and others simply inhaling the prayer as offered on radio.

These occurrences must be understood against the backdrop of the fact that in the Bible, Jesus used sand to open the eyes of the blind and Peter the Apostle used aprons that had touched his person to heal. Generally, Africans take a sacramental view of the universe, in which the visible is a vehicle for invisible realities. Convictions that there are no sharp dichotomies between what is physical and what is spiritual tend to be stronger in African than in western thought systems. African cultures share this sacramental worldview with Pentecostals, whose pneumatic emphasis includes the ability of the Spirit to mediate God's power and presence through words and objects.[1] Because of its theological emphasis on unmediated access to transcendence, Pentecostalism has often been presented as a religion that de-emphasises ritual and the use of sacramental objects in the transmission of faith. The African-led Pentecostalism we discuss here refutes this paradigm. It innovatively utilises new media in fascinating ways to mediate the anointing of the Holy Spirit. Words and images of the anointed of God reduced to print or captured on various electronic storage systems are believed to possess the same powers that inspired their initial oral delivery. It is not uncommon in African Pentecostal churches for people who feel that particular prophetic messages have relevance for them to stand and shout, 'I receive it; I receive it; I receive' as a way of ritually appropriating the powerful effects of the word into their lives and circumstances.

Pentecostalism, Media and Religious Sensations

Birgit Meyer's theory of religious sensations is very apt for explaining the uses of the media resources under scrutiny here. 'Sensation', according to Meyer, encompasses 'feeling' and 'inducement' which is inspired by those 'sensational forms' that make what is transcendental 'sense-able', and, she notes, 'religious feelings are not just there, but are made possible and reproducible by certain modes of inducing experiences of the transcendental'.[2] The examples that Meyer gives resonate with my own understanding of sacramental objects in charismatic Pentecostalism:

---

[1] J. Kwabena Asamoah-Gyadu, 'Unction to Function: Reinventing the *Oil of Influence* in African Pentecostalism', *Journal of Pentecostal Theology*, 13, no. 2 (2005), 231-56.

[2] Birgit Meyer, *Religious Sensations: Why Media, Aesthetics and Power Matter in the Study of Contemporary Religion* (Amsterdam: Vrij Universiteit, 2006), 8.

> [The] notion of 'sensational form' can also be applied to the ways in which material religious objects – such as images, books, or buildings – address and involve beholders. Thus, reciting a holy book such as the Qur'an, praying in front of an icon, or dancing around the manifestation of a spirit are also sensational forms through which religious practitioners are made to experience the presence and power of the transcendental.[3]

My understanding of enchanted texts and audio-visual material has also been greatly helped by the work of David Morgan, particularly his two seminal publications, The Sacred Gaze and Visual Piety.[4] However, I use the work of Meyer extensively here, because much of her research has been based in Africa, and precisely on Pentecostal Christianity. Belief is mediated, and so it follows, as Morgan notes, that we must think about the media through which this happens. As he explains: 'Belief happens in and through things and what people do with them.'[5] My emphasis in this chapter is on those material media that serve to induce therapeutic feelings of religious excitement and hope in practitioners. Even when produced in Africa, sacramental media resources circulate freely among the faithful who live abroad. In dealing with their vulnerabilities and insecurities, African Christians living abroad find the media resources from Pentecostal leaders very helpful, and therefore these items tend to be popular in Diaspora religious cultures.

In the African Christian context, the ultimate sacramental material is the Bible, which has acquired a symbolic and ritual use in African revivalist Christianity. I discuss the sacramental use of the Bible in my work Contemporary Pentecostalism in Africa: Interpretations from an African Context.[6] In modern times church magazines, books and audio-visual materials have acquired similar status. Enoch Aminu of the Ghana-based Pure Fire Miracle Ministries specialises in praying for women with reproductive health problems – a key concern that makes women the chief clients of pneumatic Christianity in Africa. In December 2006, at a special service to pray for such women, Aminu encouraged participating couples to buy copies of the church magazine Pure Fire. Keeping that magazine on one's matrimonial bed, he explained, would induce the divine anointing required to make conception possible. In a traditional context in which diagnosis rarely rules out supernatural causality, the magazine, having

---

[3] Meyer, *Religious Sensations*, 8.

[4] David Morgan, *Visual Piety: A History and Theory of Popular Religious Images* (Berkeley, Los Angeles and London: University of California Press, 1998); *The Sacred Gaze: Religious Visual Culture in Theory and Practice* (Berkeley, Los Angeles and London: University of California Press, 2005).

[5] Morgan, *Sacred Gaze*, 8.

[6] J. Kwabena Asamoah-Gyadu, *Contemporary Pentecostal Christianity: Interpretations from an African Context* (Oxford: Regnum Oxford International, 2013).

acquired an enchanted quality following prayer, was expected to ward off evil and make effective God's miraculous power of conception and procreation.

Charisma and Sacramental Christianity

Charismatic Pentecostalism belongs to the category of New Religious Movements (NRMs) that emphasise charisma and the mediation of power. Such NRMs affirm the world and modernity and effectively appropriate sophisticated modern media technologies, creating formats that mediate experiences based on encounters with the Holy Spirit. Through the media and other sensational forms, NRMs manifest their presence within public space in order not simply to bring a message of transformation to the public, but also to establish a constituency for the charismatic personality at the centre of it all. The theology or religious orientation of charismatic Pentecostalism has a decidedly interventionist focus, and the charismatic individual at its heart is the human channel of the graces that the followers seek. Things associated with that person, including objects that he or she touches, acquire the required sacramental potency for serving various religious ends. Precisely this type of interventionist theology, served through an African pastor, has proved to be highly attractive to post-communist Eastern Europeans.

Thus Meyer is right in pointing to the need to investigate 'how all kinds of practices of religious mediation and the sensational forms produced and sustained by these mediation practices are situated in those broader structures that characterize neo-liberal capitalism'.[7] The adoption of new media, to return to Meyer's thoughts on religious sensations, does not happen in a vacuum. It is linked, she notes, 'with broader social and cultural processes'.[8] The collapse of the communist experiment left millions of people bewildered, disappointed and overwhelmed by the challenges of building personal and communal lives within new capitalist structures. The stress of negotiating one's way in nascent capitalist systems has led to social problems with increases in, for example, drug abuse, prostitution and armed robbery. The problems have exposed the deficiencies in state machineries that are supposed to deal with the social costs of adjustment. In their desperation many ordinary people have turned to religion for the means to navigate through the quagmires of life. In modern Eastern Europe, NRMs of both Christian and other religious persuasions, including various versions of Islam, have either been introduced or, where they were dormant, have found new leases of life in response to the desire for spiritual fulfilment. The dichotomy that the

[7] Meyer, *Religious Sensations*, 28.
[8] Meyer, *Religious Sensations*, 15.

western world created between sacred and secular realms of existence has thus not been sustained in the East European contexts under study. Denominational loyalties to Eastern Orthodox Christianity have also largely been eroded in the religious lives of many people. Significant numbers are seeking refuge in religions in which they have found new places to feel at home. Here they receive promises and assurances of divine solutions to social and personal troubles.

Embassy of God

Sunday Adelaja, a charismatic Pentecostal whose ministry is bringing hope to tens of thousands caught up in the capitalist experiment, has become an icon in Ukraine. Adelaja started the Church of the Embassy of the Blessed Kingdom of God for All Nations in 1994. It belongs to the Word of Faith movement and, indeed, that was the original name of the church until it was changed in 1992 to reflect its broader mission and desire to engage with the world. At its fourteenth anniversary, Embassy of God claimed a membership of 25,000 adults, who were distributed among its various branches, mainly within Eastern Europe but also with about six such branches in the United States. The central assembly in Kiev attracts upwards of 8,000 adults to its three services every Sunday. More than 90 percent of the membership is Eastern European. The current name of the church, as Catherine Wanner explains, 'signaled the church's new mission: to establish a public role for religion and to bring the faith to "all nations" through extensive missionising'.[9] In this stream of charismatic Pentecostalism, spoken words constitute sensational forms. Once spoken, they acquire lives of their own, a quality that is sustained when they come to be captured in print or as audio-visual material. At every Embassy of God event, much space is devoted to the marketing of Adelaja's books and tapes, and they are actively promoted as contributing to the positive destiny of consumers. Testimonies are invited from those who have experienced the relevant religious sensations simply by reading a book, listening to a recorded message or viewing an audio-visual version of Adelaja's sermons.

In charismatic Pentecostalism, words have performative force, an ontological quality that is not lost even when they are captured in print or on tapes. Thus book and tape distribution is a central part of charismatic Pentecostal media culture. Religion in the media has contributed immensely to the availability of these alternative resources of supernatural succour. Marleen De Witte perceptively captures this interface between technology and religion through the Weberian notion of charisma. Charisma refers to extraordinary gifts of grace 'denoting the gift of

---

[9] Catherine Wanner, *Communities of the Converted: Ukrainians and Global Evangelism* (Ithaca, NY, and London: Cornell University Press, 2007), 211.

authority, the power to capture people's attention, to evoke devotion, to make believe, to captivate and to enchant.' In the words of De Witte: 'Media technologies like television and film can make things and persons more beautiful and attractive than they really are, while at the same time presenting them as true and accessible. They give them a mystical kind of authority and make people desire to follow them.'[10] Adelaja is just that kind of 'mystic', his charisma not only evident through his personal presence and ministry but also mediated through the 'plurifold' media resources that he makes available to the public.

The media, in all its various forms, has been given a critical role in Embassy of God. Pentecostal Christianity, with its emphasis on what Meyer calls a 'mobile self' and a 'portable charismatic identity', is a religion that speaks to those with experiences of 'dislocation, fragmentation, and increasing mobility'.[11] The church has taken advantage of the opportunities that the collapse of communism and increasing engagement with the west have brought to countries like Ukraine. Thus, much of Adelaja's influence has come from this powerful media ministry. At the centre of it all is his own charismatic personality as the anointed of God who exudes the power of the Holy Spirit for the benefit of a following seeking various forms of intervention from God. Adelaja's sermons invariably come in a series that are eventually published as books or reproduced on CDs, DVDs and distributed across Eastern Europe. These days they go as far as the United States, increasing the transnational influence of such charismatic pastors as exporters of spiritual power. The impressive interactive website of Embassy of God offers the opportunity for the wider public to access the anointing available through Adelaja's ministry. He has developed a strong international network, with his books and their contents religiously appropriated by other pastors who work under his 'covering'.

I use 'covering' in the same sense that Ogbu Kalu uses 'Elijah's Mantle', signifying a process by which younger pastors read the books, listen to audio tapes and watch the video tapes of their mentors and imitate what they see and read.[12] The list of books available through the Adelaja stable is impressive. It includes The Road to Greatness (2006); Spearheading a National Transformation (2006); Kings and Judges of the Earth (2007); Mighty Warrior: How to Become Mighty Through Prayer (2007); Accessing Divine Wisdom: Wisdom is the Key to Reigning on Earth (2006); Victorious Despite the Devil: A Successful Christian Living

---

[10] Marleen de Witte, 'Altar Media's *Living Word:* Televised Charismatic Christianity in Ghana', *Journal of Religion in Africa*, 33, no. 2 (2003), 174.
[11] Meyer, *Religious Sensations*, 28.
[12] Ogbu U. Kalu, *African Pentecostalism: An Introduction* (Oxford: Oxford University Press, 2008).

in Spite of all Odds (2006); How to Hear the Voice of God (2007); Life and Death in the Power of the Tongue (2005); The Jesus You Never Knew (2006) and Pastoring without Tears (2007). Adelaja, by his own count, has produced close to seventy books since the ministry began. In Ghana the Lighthouse Chapel International's Heward-Mills has produced even more. I have three observations to make on these books, including those published in Russian and the electronic versions of his teachings. First, they all come from the ministry's own publishing house, Fares Publishing; second, there are pictorial representations in all of them that tell the story of Embassy of God and Adelaja's successes in particular as an anointed servant of God; third, the church members do not make a big distinction between whether they receive Adelaja's teachings live or, instead, in print or electronic format.

The reverence with which the materials, whether books or tape recordings, are received contributes to their sacramental value. Thus, an investment in these materials constitutes an investment in one's blessing and prosperity. At a 2007 Winter Fast in Kiev, much attention was paid to Adelaja's publications and tapes because he promoted them during preaching. Prayers were offered at every opportunity that the Lord would make a way for the publications to be accepted and accessed by the un-churched world. A whole session of the prayers on 5 December 2007 was devoted to this course. Members prayed, aggressively and fervently, that the Lord would help the books to gain acceptance and therefore influence the world outside the Embassy of God. The idea was that if the world was to be influenced by the Christian message then people should read 'such truths as written by Pastor Adelaja'. During one such prayer session the leader exhorted the congregation to recognise that the books contain 'revelations', 'anointing' and 'vision', and they were also 'inspired' by the Holy Spirit. The congregation was therefore urged to pray and even to repent of the fact that the books of the 'man of God' had not been handled as responsibly as they should. The subject 'books and influence' was a vital element of the meeting. Bose, Adelaja's wife, at one point came to the microphone and in a combination of glossolalia and plain language implored God to intervene and show 'us' ways in which her husband's books might be made accessible to the world, and made more and more influential through the anointing they bring.

Enchanted Media and the African Worldview

The prayers offered at the Winter Fast indicated that the pictures and images in the media materials are not of aesthetic value alone. Meyer has drawn attention to the expression 'aisthesis', understood as organising 'our total sensory experience of the world and our sensitive knowledge of it'.[13] In this type of charismatic Pentecostalism, the personal psychology and the perceived graces of the life of the leader, his charisma, drives the people. Wanner makes the important observation that the strategy that Adelaja has employed to bring non-believers under conviction, and to yield such impressive and rapid growth, trades on spiritually rooted understandings of illness and cure. The original and core membership of Embassy of God, as she rightly observes, is constituted by 'recovering addicts, and their grateful family members, who see the addict's cure and transformation as a 'miracle', testimony to 'God's grace'.[14] The understanding of the roots of social crises as fundamentally spiritual also determines the choice of therapy which, for a Christian charismatic movement, invariably means prayer and deliverance. This worldview, although part of western Pentecostal thought, is also present in African thought systems in a very central way.

Wanner notes that although there is nothing Nigerian, or even African, about the services that Embassy of God offers, the doctrine espoused by Adelaja draws on trends in theology that are well developed in Nigeria. Those familiar with the work of scholars like Birgit Meyer may be aware of the strong worldviews of mystical causality that are reflected through Ghanaian-Nigerian films. In these films the Pentecostal pastor, who is a charismatic, is above all else, an interventionist because of the anointing of the Spirit upon his life. The charismatic leader has the power to bless and curse, and the effect of such a personality in African prophetic religions cannot be underestimated. Being synonymous with the functional power of the Spirit, anointing has traditionally been associated with the 'spoken word' and 'touch' or the 'laying on of hands', a point to which we will return later in this volume. Thus it has been noted of the founder of an early twentieth-century African charismatic movement, the Nigerian Garrick Sokari Braide, who worked in the Niger Delta, that 'as his reputation for holiness grew, so too did a superstitious reverence for his person: people sought physical contact with him in order to receive healing or protection from danger. The water in which he washed was collected and dispensed as containing magical properties. His words were received as charged with spiritual force.'[15]

The key word in the process of mediating the supernatural here is 'anointing', which is understood in this stream of Christianity as the power of God in action and strongly present in the ministry of the prophet. Anointing has great emotional appeal when it comes to African religious

[13] Meyer, *Religious Sensations*, 18.

[14] Wanner, *Communities of the Converted*, 18.

[15] Lamin Sanneh, *West African Christianity: The Religious Impact* (Maryknoll, NY: Orbis, 1983), 182.

sensibilities because the indigenous religious context itself is one in which power determines the viability of religion. Thus the key concept of anointing is germane to our understanding of the popularity of contemporary African-led charismatic Pentecostal churches, such as those led by Sunday Adelaja in Eastern Europe and by Heward-Mills in Ghana. Adelaja's style of ministry and interpretation of social crisis and misfortune cannot be disconnected from his African background. Whether he consciously brings that background to bear on his ministry is a moot point.

Charisma and the Enchanted Word

In Visual Piety, David Morgan argues that, although language is a symbolic form that is generally shared, it should not be understood as an isolated or autonomous operator in the construction of reality. 'Language and vision, word and image, text and picture', he continues, 'are in fact deeply enmeshed and collaborate powerfully in assembling our sense of the real.'[16] With the introduction of new media into the ministries of contemporary African-led charismatic movements, anointing can now also be mediated through texts and tapes that contain the spoken words of the anointed. These words, like those of Braide, are believed to be charged with a spiritual force that can make things happen. Thus to 'catch the anointing', Dag Heward-Mills outlines in one of his books, 'you have to read my books and listen to my tapes'. Members and believers in the ministry of the leaders of charismatic Pentecostalism take this religious exercise seriously. What we have in these media resources therefore is not mere texts and tapes; these are enchanted new media that mediate supernatural power.

In his dated but still-acclaimed volume Religion in Essence and Manifestation, G. van der Leeuw discusses the importance of the written word in religion. Writing, he notes, could have magical connotations as a method of gaining power over the living word. The Muslim world is already familiar with the power of the printed word. The Qur'an is 'cosmic truth', which means that Muslims take a transcendent view of the holy book by looking at it as the verbatim word of God.[17] For Muslims, the Qur'an has been received as God speaking to humankind from all eternity, to every man and woman throughout the world – including the individual Muslim as he or she reads or recites the text or devoutly holds it, or vividly or dimly or even unconsciously remembers a passage or phrase from it. In the words of Wilfred Cantwell Smith:

---

[16] Morgan, *Visual Piety*, 9.

[17] G. van der Leeuw, *Religion in Essence and Manifestation*, trans. J.E. Turner (Princeton, NJ: Princeton University Press, 1986 [1938]), 435.

> [The Qur'an] represents the eternal breaking into time; the unknowable disclosed; the transcendent entering history and remaining here, available to mortals to handle and to appropriate; the divine become apparent. To memorize it, as many Muslims have ceremonially done, and even to quote from it, as every Muslim does daily in his and her formal prayers and otherwise, is to enter into some sort of communion with ultimate reality.[18]

That worldview means that the Qur'an as printed word is enchanted in a way that other sacred books may not be. Biblical examples of words that were communicated specifically to be written down include Moses and the Decalogue, Ezekiel and the words of prophecy in the book under his name, and Revelation, in which the glorified Christ asks John to write down his messages to the seven churches. As a result of the African belief in the power of words to bless and to curse, the Bible and Qur'an have been put to some innovative uses in popular Christianity. The Bible is holy and in the African imagination what is holy exudes power that could even be dangerous. In African hands therefore, the Bible has been received as something that is more than written text for academic study. Beyond the written text and its interpretations, the Bible quickly acquired new uses as a sacred book with inherent spiritual power. In one of the most popular Spiritual churches in Ghana, a copy of the Bible is kept perpetually on the table from which the prophet speaks. Sometimes it is tied to the ailing part of a person's body to mediate healing. The symbolic and talismanic uses of the Bible are therefore quite common, particularly in independent indigenous Christianity in Africa, because, for these local Christians, it is more than just text.

In contradistinction to western liberal positions, African Christians, particularly those belonging to the Pentecostal and charismatic streams of the faith, celebrate the divinity and supernatural status of the Bible. African Christian use of the Bible as a symbol of sacred power, however, does not in any way undermine its didactic uses. Thus, attention needs to be drawn to the inseparable link between the Bible as text and the Bible as a Holy Book in African Christianity. The African universe is one in which the supernatural is hyperactive. It is not uncommon for people to bury medicines, charms and amulets on their properties to secure such places against the presence of evil powers. Birgit Meyer illustrates from the Ghanaian context how people use dzo, medicine or juju, not only to cure bodily ills, but also to improve their trade or the growth of their plants, to become invulnerable in war or to be protected against evils inflicted upon them by others.[19] The physical media resources have acquired a similar status in African charismatic Pentecostalism. The primary use of these

---

[18] W. Cantwell Smith, *What is Scripture?* (London: SCM, 1993), 70.

[19] Birgit Meyer, *Translating the Devil: Religion and Modernity among the Ewe in Ghana* (Edinburgh: Edinburgh University Press, 1999), 70.

resources is not for talismanic purposes, and yet there is a strong connection between their perceived sacramental or talismanic power and how seriously their contents are regarded.

Conclusion

In this chapter, we have seen how contemporary Pentecostalism, standing in continuity with the older AICs, offers a prime example of the transnational nature of contemporary Pentecostalism and its innovative appropriations of modern media technologies. In the process, African sacramental worldviews have found a place in the hearts and lives of people going through challenges similar to those of Africans, as they attempt to find their way within the maze of capitalism and its numerous challenges. Belief occurs through the medium, which is the locus of religious sensations. The new African charismatic Pentecostal religion we have encountered here has taken the uses of the media to another level. In an Eastern European context in which religion is thriving within post-communist space and minds, the fascinating ways in which the media are being used defy the prevalent western thinking that capitalism and neo-liberal economic policies will succeed in edging religion out of people's lives.

Chapter 6
'I Declare': The Power of the Spoken Word

The title of this chapter, '"I Declare": The Power of the Spoken Word', captures the power of utterance in contemporary Pentecostalism. The focal point of the chapter is the TV advertisement for the July 2013 annual Destiny Summit, hosted by the International Central Gospel Church (ICGC) in Ghana. The advertisement began with a flying eagle – an important symbol of contemporary Pentecostalism, standing for the power of renewal. The eagle takes off into the sky, with its flight accompanied by the words, 'Rise up: move your life, ministry and business to new heights.' This advertisement also featured an array of international speakers, crowds of worshippers and the host, Pastor Mensa Otabil, with microphone in hand. With the rise of the eagle, we hear Mensa Otabil's voice in the background as he addresses listeners, inviting them to a destiny-changing experience. Mike Murdoch, the African/American prosperity preacher who was one of the guests, also speaks in the advertisement. He is shown saying: 'God reacts to my words not my thoughts.'

Power of the Word

The images – a flying eagle, microphone-wielding preachers, spoken word, internationally known charismatic televangelists and crowds signifying influence – were carefully chosen and packaged to reflect a certain contemporary charismatic cultural paradigm. The eagle as a pneumatic symbol for contemporary Pentecostalism has already been examined in this volume, but it is of relevance in this context too. Historically, it was by the word – through magazines, church newsletters and later radio and televangelism – that Pentecostalism became a global religion. At the beginning of his book To the Ends of the Earth, Allan Anderson gives a vivid description of how the global aspirations of Pentecostalism have played out down the centuries: 'The experience of the Spirit and belief in world evangelization are hallmarks of Pentecostalism, and Pentecostals believe they are called to be witnesses for Jesus Christ to the farthest reaches of the globe in obedience to Christ's commission.'[1] In a very

[1] Allan Anderson, *Ends of the Earth: Pentecostalism and the Transformation of World Christianity* (Oxford: Oxford University Press, 2013), 1.

instructive article, Waldo César describes Pentecostalism as a complex movement that combines biblical symbolism with modern forms of communication and global expansion.[2] The symbolic, he notes, 'functions as a language which blends what is immanent in the world with the transcendental; the "experience of the sacred" reveals itself in concrete situations in everyday life'.[3] One of the most common symbolic expressions of transcendental experience that I have observed is the use of the microphone to signify the performance effect of the spoken word.

The performance effect of the spoken word in African pneumatic movements is yet further evidence of the resonances between primal ideas and Christian innovation. In the traditional context words translate into action, and therefore the power of blessing and curse are very important, especially when coming from figures of authority. In the African Christian context, the authority of the believer is critical to contemporary Pentecostal self-perception. One does not come to God as a sinner begging for pardon, but as one granted authority in Christ and empowered by the Spirit to boldly claim his promises and declare others blessed or cursed as occasion may demand. After all, the Book of Proverbs states, 'Death and life are in the power of the tongue, and those who love it will eat its fruits' (18:21, English Standard Version). Belief in the power of the spoken word is not the sole preserve of African Pentecostalism. It stems from a general Pentecostal belief in the authority of the believer in Christ. In his book Blessings and Curses, for example, deliverance exponent Derek Prince writes that religious leaders have the potential to speak good or evil and see what they say become reality. Church leaders, he notes, can speak words that amount to curses on their members, such as when a pastor clashes with an associate who breaks away from his congregation.[4] The effects of blessings and curses, he explains, can last for generations and when uttered by servants of God are most effective.[5]

This power, which is believed to be inherent in the spoken word, is symbolised by the use of the microphone in Pentecostal media images and advertisements. In publicising upcoming events, Pentecostal churches make use of posters, handbills and other images on television, and always the favoured image of the speaker is with a microphone in hand. The microphone signifies many things, including the power of the word in preaching, ministration through singing and the ability to declare the word

---

[2] Waldo César, 'From Babel to Pentecost: A Socio-Historical-Theological Study of the Growth of Pentecostalism', in André Corten and Ruth Marshall-Fratani (eds), *Between Babel and Pentecost: Transnational Pentecostalism in Africa and Latin America* (Bloomington and Indianapolis: Indiana University Press, 2001), 22.

[3] César, 'Babel to Pentecost', 27.

[4] Derek Prince, *Blessings and Curses* (Kent, UK: Sovereign World, 1994), 39.

[5] Prince, *Blessings and Curses*, 40-43.

of God in tongues, prophecy, word of knowledge or narrative visions and revelations. It signifies the authority of the believer to cast out demons in the name of Jesus and pronounce blessings and prosperity on those with needs. By the word, the forgiveness of sins may be pronounced and evil cursed out of the lives of the troubled. The authority of the believer is demonstrated through the power of the spoken word. Thus in the Destiny Summit advertisement we hear Mike Murdock say, 'God responds to my words and not my thoughts.' That the Church of Jamaican American preacher Randy Morrison, in Minnesota, is called 'Speak the Word Church' says much about the importance of the spoken word in contemporary Pentecostalism.

Thus alongside space and time, César rightly identifies the spoken word as a vital component of Pentecostal spirituality. The spoken word, he notes, 'is the motor which drives this new spirituality, and oral performance is the most important aspect of the religious service'.[6] Pentecostal services, as César explains, unfold through various sounds transmitted through powerful sound speakers; oral performances here include, 'prayers, alleluias, songs, appeals, testimonies, more alleluias, offerings, confessions, casting out of demons, even more alleluias, biblical readings, sales of booklets and pamphlets, distribution of symbolic objects, miracles, and above all, speaking in "strange tongues".'[7] The spoken word is supposed to have the power of transformation. In this connection, Eastwood Anaba, a prominent charismatic leader in Ghana, writes, 'Impossibility should be ruled out of your vocabulary. ... We have the mandate to change our environment by speaking the word of faith. ... We have the mandate to set the oppressed free and our boldness in the exercise of our authority is crucial to the blessing of humanity.'[8]

In the words of César: 'The word moves hearts (emotion) and pockets (offerings).'[9] In addition to César's list, I add the preaching of the word, recounting of testimonies of God's goodness and more often than not blessing each other with some biblical benediction as people depart to their homes. It is not uncommon in contemporary African Pentecostal services to ask people to face each other and, holding hands, 'sow words of blessing' into each other's lives. Whatever the form it takes, the spoken word is considered to have a life of its own, and it materialises whether declared as blessings or curses. And indeed talk about curses, healing and deliverance usually includes 'refusing' or 'cancelling' curses spoken by others – known and unknown – against victims of spiritual oppression. When the Spirit

---

[6] César, 'Babel and Pentecost', 28.

[7] César, 'Babel and Pentecost', 28.

[8] Eastwood Anaba, *The Workability of Faith* (Bolgatanga, Ghana: Desert Leaf Publications, 2004), 38.

[9] César, 'Babel and Pentecost', 28.

descends at the highpoint of Pentecostal services, there are uncontrollable cries and screams, and sometimes there will be laughter and animal sounds, in line with the Toronto Blessing. Such audible sounds are closely associated with this form of expressive and emotion-laden spirituality.

The Spoken Word in Music

In Pentecostal services at which the power of the spoken word may be activated, an import place is occupied by the 'praise and worship' that involves celebration and submission to the power and presence of God in music. The lyrics of one of the most popular songs sung at worship services, Ancient of Days, read,[10]

Blessing and Honor
Glory and Power
Be unto the ancient of days
From every nation
All of creation
Bow before the ancient of days

Bridge:

Every tongue in heaven and earth
Shall declare your glory
Every knee shall bow at your throne
In worship
You will be exalted oh God
And your kingdom shall not pass away
Oh ancient of days

Chorus:

Your kingdom shall reign over all the earth
Sing to the ancient of days
For none can compare to your matchless worth
Sing to the ancient of days

Critical elements of these lyrics state, 'every tongue in heaven and earth shall declare your glory' and, from the chorus, 'sing to the ancient of days'. Praise of God is articulated in acknowledging what he does among his people. The verbalisation of the mysteries of God can even occur by 'singing in the Spirit': a term for singing in tongues.

---

[10] Title: Ancient of Days: Authors: Jamie Harvill and Gary Sadler; Copyright: Copyright 1992 Integrity's Hosanna! Music

Spoken Word: Prophetic Declarations and the New Christianity

Joel Osteen has been described as a 'smiling preacher' whose 'encouraging message of salvation and self-help' impacts upon millions across the world.[11] His global influence, as with that of several other members of the new category of motivational preachers, has come through media resources, notably, book publications, television ministries, internet websites and the circulation of CDs and DVDs of his messages and programmes. Unhappy with traditional Christianity, many have opted for the Osteens of this world, who preach motivational messages of positives and possibilities in this life, and that resonate with people who are disenchanted with denominationalism and traditional sermons that focus on eschatological issues of judgment, heaven and hell.

It is instructive that Joel Osteen took his theological cue from the ministry of his father, John H. Osteen, founder of Lakewood Church, in Houston, Texas. John Osteen first positioned himself within a network of prosperity and self-improvement preachers, and then embraced a gospel focusing on 'religious identity in Jesus Christ, speaking positive ideas in the midst of personal troubles … and a deep conviction that material well-being and divine healing are an integral part of the life of faith.'[12] John Osteen's 1972 publication There is a Miracle in Your Mouth outlines one of the fundamental principles of the gospel of positives and possibilities – the power of positive confession:

> Confession is made unto salvation! The miracle is there on your tongue. It is in your mouth. What do I mean? The promise of God is there. The God who cannot lie has given you many promises. The miracle is in your mouth. Dare to speak those promises out loud. Say them to yourself! Say them to yourself! Say them to the devil! Say them to the sickness! Say them to your mountain of trouble! Confess them in the face of all contrary evidence! Say them while you are so sick you can hardly think![13]

Prophetic declarations are made through various forms of print and electronic media, and although their origins are almost certainly North American, they have become part of the global charismatic culture. In his work I Declare: 31 Promises to Declare Over your Life, Osteen begins by noting:

> Our words have creative power. Whenever we speak something, either good or bad, we give life to what we are saying. … Here is the key; you've got to send

[11] Philip Luke Sinitiere, 'Preaching the Good News Glad: Joel Osteen's Tel-e-vangelism', in Pradip Ninian Thomas and Philip Lee (eds.), *Global and Local Televangelism* (London: Palgrave Macmillan, 2012), 88.

[12] Sinitiere, 'Joel Osteen', 91.

[13] Quoted in Sinitiere, 'Joel Osteen', 93.

your words out in the direction you want your life to go. You cannot talk defeat and expect to have victory. You cannot talk lack and expect to have abundance. You will produce what you say.[14]

The declarations that followers of these charismatic leaders are to appropriate for their lives are based on an unanimous interpretation of Proverbs 18:21, 'Life and death are in the power of the tongue', and Proverbs 6:2, 'We are snared by the words of our mouth.' The story of Jabez supports that position. Joel Osteen's 'Day One Declarations' sets the tone:

I declare God's incredible blessings over my life. I will see an explosion of God's goodness, a sudden widespread increase. I will experience the surpassing greatness of God's favor. It will elevate me to a higher level than I have dreamed of. Explosive blessings are coming my way. This is my declaration.[15]

The main theology of this movement is that Christianity is not merely a belief, but a confession. What we are today is understood to be the result of all that we have uttered or confessed in the past, and what we will become in the future will result from what we confess in the present.[16] Philip Sinitiere shows how Osteen has taken on this approach to the gospel by emphasising 'physical healing, encouragement, and positive confession'.[17] He explains,

Osteen encourages members to trust in God's supernatural intervention. He also focuses on personal agency by exhorting hearers to generate positive thoughts and to speak or 'confess' biblical passages that may provide a hopeful outcome to dire circumstances. At the core of Osteen's Bible confession is an evangelical emphasis on scriptural authority that informs a deeply personal spiritual transformation.[18]

Once a person catches the formula, the declarations are to be repeated as often as possible. Recently new material on prayers that are based on these declarations has also emerged. What God requires from one person may differ from what God requires from another, but these requirements have a common founding principle. In declaration 24, Osteen addresses a fundamental element of the charismatic culture of declarations: talking to the problems rather than talking to God:

---

[14] Joel Osteen, *I Declare: 31 Promises to Speak Over Your Life* (New York: FaithWords, 2012), v.
[15] Osteen, *I Declare*, 1.
[16] Sinitiere, 'Joel Osteen', 94.
[17] Sinitiere, 'Joel Osteen', 94.
[18] Sinitiere, 'Joel Osteen', 95.

> I declare I will speak only positive words of faith and victory over myself, my family, and my future. I will not use my words to describe the situation. I will use my words to change my situation. I will call in favor, good breaks, healing, and restoration. I will not talk to God about how big my problems are. I will talk to my problems about how big my God is. This is my declaration.[19]

Joel Osteen is North American, but he has many counterparts in the non-western world.

Speaking the Language of Success

Every year, Mensa Otabil develops his own creed, known as Prophetic Declarations. Making 'bold declarations is an important part of the Christian walk', Otabil notes. The declarations, he continues, are 'a medium for strengthening our faith and affirming our trust in God and his Word'.[20] According to his own statement, these declarations are received by waiting upon God, and he has 'led the church to make these declarations every week before preaching the sermon'.[21] These declarations are not empty and wild, Otabil suggests, because his church has received testimonies over the years about 'the power of these declarations as weapons of spiritual warfare'.[22] For the purposes of illustration, I give here part of the 2005 'prophetic declarations':

> You are my shield and my defense; My Lord in whom I trust. Today, I come into full agreement with your prophetic word for my life and declare that, 'this is my year of open heavens'. In this year, I receive special favor from the Lord. I receive abundant fruitfulness. I receive the fullness of God's goodness. I boldly declare that because the Lord has blessed me, no one can curse me. In the name of Jesus, I step into my season of favor ...[23]

My interest in these declarations as developed by the ICGC led by Otabil relates not simply to the effects that the spoken word is believed to have in pneumatic Christianity, but also to the fact that they have replaced the historic creeds traditionally recited in historic mission Christianity. The Apostles' and Nicene Creeds are outlines of the basic doctrines and theological teachings of Christianity. By contrast, these declarations are understood as appropriations of divine favour, including protection against one's enemies. In November 2013, Mensa Otabil completed a series, previously preached in his church, on twenty-one pathways to success on

---

[19] Osteen, *I Declare*, 125.
[20] Mensa Otabil, *Prophetic Declarations: 2005-2011* (Accra: ICGC, 2011), 3.
[21] Otabil, *Prophetic Declarations*, 3-4.
[22] Otabil, *Prophetic Declarations*, 4.
[23] Otabil, *Prophetic Declarations*, 7-8.

Ghana's TV 3 and other radio stations, including one of the most popular: JOY FM. Pastor Otabil, like the Osteens and others, preached that 'success is a product of your words':

> Along with embracing a new mindset, one must have the ability to speak with the language of success. Success has its own vocabulary. It speaks words which are positive and constructive. We have heard that said over and over, but its truth and relevance are unmistakable! You have to watch what you say! … The language of success is confident and creative.[24]

The prophetic declarations and the books in which these sermons are published are available for sale to the general public. They can also be accessed on the webpages of the churches involved, which tells again of the role of the media in these developments. Pradip Thomas and Philip Lee draw attention to the fact that televangelism is no longer limited to television, but is increasingly a new media phenomenon 'amplified and shaped on social media sites and accessed by mobile technologies in ever more complex circuits of production, distribution, and consumption'.[25] Once these messages were on television, they could also be accessed on websites, with mobile phones and, in almost every case, through CDs, DVDs and books. Wide media accessibility means charismatic messages are heard by many, as Thomas and Lee point out: 'these channels have placed religion in the public eye and, in doing so, have provided new opportunities for the mediation of religion, for a public articulation of intra-faith tensions, and for packaging religion for consumption in a globalized world'.[26]

In Ghana, Eastwood Anaba, founder of the Fountain Gate Chapel International, has also developed a whole theology, called Speak the Word. He has held large conferences around this theme, and the media resources from it – books, DVDs, CDs – circulate around the country and beyond. Christians must receive the Word of God and 'release' it against the forces of darkness. He writes, 'I sense it in my spirit that we have a command from God to Speak the Word.'[27] According to Anaba, the Word of God has an inherent power of self-fulfilment because it 'creates and forms things'.[28]

Inspired by this same understanding of the power of the spoken word, Daniel Olukoya has produced a book of written prayers, Prayer Rain, which contains set prayers for all circumstances of life. There are prayers for

[24] Mensa Otabil, *Pathways to Success: 21 Sure Steps on the Way to the Top* (Mansfield, TX: Blaze Publishing, 2008), 27.

[25] Thomas and Lee, *Global and Local Televangelism*, 1.

[26] Thomas and Lee, *Global and Local Televangelism*, 2.

[27] Eastwood Anaba, *Speak the Word* (Bolgatanga, Ghana: Desert Leaf Publications, 2013), xvi.

[28] Anaba, *Speak the Word*, 38.

spiritual growth, profitable sales, uprooting the tree of non-achievement, deliverance from evil inheritance, removing hindrances to advancement and demolishing stumbling blocks, and for obtaining profitable employment. In all, there are about 125 sets of prayers in the leather-bound book of 645 pages.[29] Exorcism and deliverance from spiritual affliction are very much a part of Pentecostal theological culture wherever the movement is found. Within an African context, however, with its ardent belief in spiritual causation, strategies have been developed to address local worldviews. Thus in Prayer Rain, Pastor Olukoya has a section on 'Deliverance from Foundational Pollution'. These are prayers intended to be said 'to release yourself from ancestral yokes and burdens' and 'to clean up unprofitable spiritual background militating against physical and spiritual progress'. Our 'foundation', Olukoya explains, refers to our background and the experiences we have passed through that have brought us to where we are today.[30] Much of the material builds on African traditional beliefs in ancestral curses as the cause of present problems.

Conclusion

The spoken word was part of the biblical Pentecost. The wonderful works of God were declared in tongues by those filled with the Holy Spirit. César draws our attention to the role given to that experience in the spread of Pentecostalism as a transnational movement today:

> The Pentecostal process of transnationalization starts with 'speaking in tongues'– the word – the culminating moment in the experience of the early church. The gospel extends throughout the Mediterranean world, breaks through religious, cultural and social frontiers … and reveals the new faith as anything but a mere Jewish sect. … Pentecostalism breaks down rigid traditional ecclesiastic structures and joins the secular, modern world, reaching out in all languages to all peoples and nations.[31]

[29] Daniel K. Olukoya, *Prayer Rain* (Lagos: Mountain of Fire Ministries, 1999).
[30] Olukoya, *Prayer Rain*, 306.
[31] César, 'Babel and Pentecost', 32.

Chapter 7
'Thus Says the Lord': Reinvention of the Prophetic

This chapter reflects on aspects of the interface between religious mediation, primal religion in Africa and African pneumatic Christianity by looking at how prophetic phenomena initially associated with the Spiritual churches were reinvented in contemporary Pentecostalism.[1] The re-emergence of the prophetic in contemporary African Christianity serves to illustrate the continuities existing between the Spiritual churches and the charismatic ministries. Included in what I have referred to in this volume as African pneumatic Christianity are the array of Christian religious movements ranging from older African Initiated Churches (AICs) to contemporary autochthonous Pentecostal/charismatic renewal and other para-church movements that emphasize the experiences of the Spirit in worship. We have learnt that all the movements or churches concerned – both traditional and contemporary – are founded and led by indigenous people. In the last two decades, the new charismatic churches or contemporary Pentecostals, as I have named them here, have become international. This internationalisation has occurred through the founding of churches in the African Diaspora, the wide distribution of media resources and the frequent travels of leaders and representatives of such movements to 'export' their spiritual power to those needing them. In the regions of the Diaspora, contemporary Pentecostals have retained their orientation as religious movements addressing concerns that resonate very deeply with African cosmological ideas.

The African churches and movements discussed in this volume, we have noted, can be classed together as revivalists or renewalists with ecclesiologies that emphasise the experiential presence of the Holy Spirit in ministry and worship. This pneumatic emphasis is seen both through the regular manifestations of the Holy Spirit in tongues, visions and prophecies, and also in a strong interventionist theology that gives attention to healing, prophecy, exorcism and deliverance. At the centre of these movements are mediators of supernatural power, people 'with eyes to see' into the invisible spiritual realm and who bring communication from that spiritual realm into the human/physical realm. These are the prophets. In a

11 Paper initially presented at the 'Primal Religion as the Sub-Structure of Christianity' Consultation, Lima, Peru, 29 July-10 August 2009.

sense they are charismatic figures who function as the Christian equivalents of traditional priests and diviners. The ministries of these Christian charismatic figures, although intended to be biblical, also very forcefully reflect the ways in which religious mediations occur within primal societies in Africa.

In the primal societies of Africa, as Ghanaian pastoral theologian Emmanuel Lartey points out, medicine has always been practised by traditional priest-healers, and therefore, to the traditional African, the most important activity of the priest is medical: the ability to diagnose correctly and to prescribe accurate remedies for various diseases.[2] The process of diagnosis usually requires consultation with spirits and 'reading' the spiritual realm. Such activity was initially associated with the AICs but is now also increasingly associated with the work of Pentecostal/charismatic Christian prophets. In the early 1960s Christian G. Baëta predicted its reinvention:

> [Prophetism] appears to me to be a perennial phenomenon of African life, and the basic operative element in it seems to be personal in character. Whether in relation to or independently of events or developments in society, the individual endowed with a striking personality and the ability to impose his own will on others, believing himself and believed by others to be a special agent of some supernatural being or force, will emerge from time to time and secure a following. Powers traditionally credited to such persons, of healing, of revealing hidden things, predicting the future, cursing and blessing effectually, etc., will be attributed to him whether he claims them or not … Such things as the above-mentioned endowment, inward illumination, a sense of divine vocation, spontaneous enthusiasm … are facts of life and have their effects on African society.[3]

Baëta's reference to the prophetic as something that has great appeal in African religious life is very instructive. Indeed another Ghanaian scholar, Joseph Quayisi-Amakye has in a recent volume discussed the reinvention of prophetism as a contemporary charismatic phenomenon.[4] The suggestion is that although the phenomenon is biblical, it is not unknown in African traditions. The ability to tell people what is wrong with their lives, pray for God's intervention for them and provide direction, popularly called in Ghana akwankyere, literally 'revealing to provide direction', is a critical feature of the African Pentecostal prophet. Such revelations, whether they occur within the traditional religious context or a Christian context, amount

---

[22] Emmanuel Y. Lartey, 'Healing, Tradition and Pentecostalism in Africa Today', *International Review of Mission*, 75, no. 297 (January 1986), 75.

[3] Christian G. Baëta, *Prophetism in Ghana: A Study of Some Spiritual Churches* (London: SCM, 1962), 6-7.

[4] Joseph Quayisi-Amakye, *Prophetism in Ghana Today: A Study on Trends in Ghanaian Pentecostal Prophetism* (Accra: Quayisi-Amakye, 2013).

to standing in the gap between the visible and invisible realms of existence in religious mediation. This chapter examines how the importance of religious mediation in Africa has led to a certain type of religious functionary whose activities include diagnosis, healing, prophecy and the reversal of unhappy destinies.

Christian Revivalism and the Bible in Africa

In The Next Christendom, Philip Jenkins makes the following observation, summarising the ways in which primal spirituality has been reinvented in non-western Christianity of the indigenous revivalist kind:

> Considering the central role of healing and exorcism in Southern churches, it is tempting to look for older pagan roots, and to ask just how the emerging congregations justify their ideas. Of course, Southern churches thrive because of their appeal to distinctly African or Latin American ideas – their ability to work within traditional culture – but these examples of accommodation do not amount to a betrayal of the faith, still less to syncretism.[5]

In other words the main intention of the African Pentecostal/charismatic movements under study here is to be biblical. In the process, however, the movements have also achieved contextual relevance by working within indigenous worldviews of spiritual causality and the use of supernatural force to interpret and counter the effects of extraordinary evil. If integrations into, or reinventions of, primal religious and cultural ideas do not amount to syncretism, then we are confronted with the question of how we are to understand these innovations that are said to be at work in the indigenous southern churches. One suggestion is that we should look at how the Bible is translated, interpreted and consequently understood and used in these contexts:

> The rising churches can plausibly claim to be following abundantly documented precedents from the founding ages of Christianity. The Bible itself so readily supports a worldview based on spirits, healing, and exorcism. When Jesus was asked if he was the Messiah, he did not give an abstract theological lecture but pointed to the tangible signs and wonders that were being done in his name ... When Paul took the Christian faith to Macedonia, the first known mission into Europe, he was responding to a vision received in a dream.[6]

Healing, visions and dreams are important religious categories in the sort of innovative Christianity under study here, and these phenomena have

---

[5] Philip Jenkins, *The Next Christendom: The Coming of Global Christianity*, rev. ed. (Oxford: Oxford University Press, 2007), 148.
[6] Jenkins, *Next Christendom*, 148.

long been recognised as central themes in primal piety as well. Jenkins concludes from these observations, as Christian Baëta, Andrew Walls and Kwame Bediako, for example, did much earlier, that 'in understanding what can look like the oddities of Third World churches, it is helpful to recall one basic and astonishing fact, which is that they take the Bible very seriously indeed'.[7]

Pentecostalism and African Religious Realities

We noted earlier that Christianity has within the last half-century grown to become a non-western religion.[8] In his writings, Walter Hollenweger traces the popularity of Pentecostalism to the primal nature of its spirituality, which he locates in the 'black roots' of the movement.[9] Harvey Cox shares this view in his theory that the 'resurfacing of archetypal modes of worship' in Pentecostalism helps explain the popularity of the movement.[10] The ability to take indigenous worldviews seriously and articulate a religious response to them within a Christian context has been a major strength of religious innovation in Africa, and has continued with contemporary Pentecostalism.

In recent times, I have been amazed at the way in which, while searching for breakthroughs in life (health, promotion, travel visas, employment opportunities and the like), African Pentecostals inveigh against their enemies and call upon the fire of God to destroy them. The truth is that, in libation prayer, cursing the enemies on the road to success has always been a part of indigenous religiosity. In taking that feature on, Pentecostalism simply invokes and works within familiar idioms and discourses. It does not suggest the fact that because this is religion that functions within primal worldviews everything done can be justified, it only provides reasons why Pentecostal spirituality connects very strongly with grassroots participants in Africa.

Prayer and Prophetism

The shortfalls of dominion or prosperity theology have generated renewed interest in the prophetic ministry, originally the trademark of the AICs. Prophets specialise in salvific goals not alien to primal thought. African

---

[7] Jenkins, *Next Christendom*, 148; Baëta, *Prophetism in Ghana*.

[8] Kwame Bediako, *Christianity in Africa: The Renewal of a Non-Western Religion* (Edinburgh: Edinburgh University Press, 1995).

[9] Harvey Cox, *Fire From Heaven: The Rise of Pentecostal Spirituality and the Reshaping of Religion in the Twenty-First Century* (Reading, MA: Addison-Wesley Publishing Company, 1995), chs 5-6.

[10] Cox, *Fire from Heaven*, 101.

salvific goals, for example, are often evident in libation prayers, as noted in Bolaji Idowu's Olódùmarè: God in Yoruba Belief:

The heart and center of prayers in the religion of the Yoruba is petition … The petitions are largely for what may be described technically as material blessings. They consist usually of asking for protection from sicknesses and death, gifts of longevity, children, prosperity in enterprises, victory over enemies, protection from evil spirits and of relatives near and distant, rectification of unhappy destinies, and abundant provision of material things; blessings on all well-wishers and damnation on all ill-wishers.[11]

These are the same ends to which much Pentecostal prayer is directed. Contemporary Pentecostalism is new only in the sense that it displays a more modern and socially sophisticated outlook than the older AICs. Theologically it shares continuities with its older compatriot. The Prayer Cathedral of Action Chapel International in Ghana, as I have discussed elsewhere, is virtually a reinvented sacred space for these purposes.[12] Every Thursday morning there is Jericho Hour, a period set aside for people to 'wrestle with God' in prayer and bring their problems down, just as the walls of Jericho crumbled under Joshua's leadership. Jericho Hour as a 'prophetic prayer service' started in Action Chapel in 1998. Today, the service attracts upwards of 4,000 participants, who attend to ask God to remove barrenness and sterility, barriers to employment and to academic achievements, and all other obstacles through which Satan, witches and demons may be frustrating their efforts. Requests for travel visas now rank next in popularity to prayers for physical healing at meetings such as Jericho Hour. In Accra, the capital of Ghana, Jericho Hour is replicated in prayers services variously dubbed Hour of Deliverance, Hour of Restoration, Hour of Grace, Hour of Divine Favour and Hour of Divine Intervention. These new prayer centres serve purposes that are not dissimilar to the 'mercy ground' and the 'garden' associated with the older AICs. They all function as sacred spaces where the power of the Spirit may be invoked to intervene in human affairs.

The early twentieth-century prophet William Wadé Harris took on the designation 'Black Elijah of West Africa' because, like his Old Testament model, he confronted people's ancient cult-figures or idols, which he combated by calling upon the fire of God as a demonstration of power. In Jenkins's explanation, legend tells how pagan shrines burst into flames as Prophet Harris approached, and their priests like those of Baal 'fled before

[11] E. Bolaji Idowu, *Olódùmarè: God in Yoruba Belief* (New York: Frederick A. Praeger, 1963), 116.

[12] For Jericho Hour, see, J. Kwabena Asamoah-Gyadu, *Contemporary Pentecostal Christianity: Interpretations from an African Context* (Oxford: Regnum Oxford International, 2013), ch. 3.

the coming of such supernatural power'.[13] Jenkins proceeds to illustrate that parallels between contemporary southern Christianity and ancient Christianity are just as clear when we consider prophetic leadership:

> The vitality of prophecy in the contemporary South means that the rising churches can read biblical accounts with far more understanding and sensitivity than Northern Christians can. In the book of Acts, prophecy was a sign of the true church. And if that was true two thousand years ago, why should it not be true of a man or woman of today, a [Simon] Kimbangu or [Isaiah] Shembe? Prophetic powers are exactly what Jesus promised his disciples, without any caveat that these gifts might expire with the end of the first century.[14]

A critical feature of the primal imagination is the belief in the existence of a separate supernatural realm of existence that constantly encroaches upon the natural order and engages with it through revelation, invocations and divinations. African Christians are generally in love with the Old Testament precisely because several parts of it, particularly the psalms, resonate with the primal imagination that associates the divine realm with salvation, strength and healing (Psalm 121).

In traditional libation prayer, for example, two types of audience from different realms are distinguished. The primary, but unseen, audience is of deities and spirits for whom the prayer is meant and who form the beneficent audience. The secondary audience is of the human realm and contains the potential beneficiaries of prayer. As the political and religious head of his people, the traditional chief (often represented by the linguist or priest) constitutes the link between the human and ancestral worlds. In his capacity as mediator and with eyes to see into the supernatural realm, the religious functionary has to invoke the help of the spirit world through libation prayers on festival days and at times of crisis. Thus, between the two realms of existence – natural and supernatural, physical and spiritual, seen and unseen – are those with the ability to invoke and communicate with the benevolent and powerful supernatural realm, in order to bring from there meaning, explanations, strength, health, protection, guidance and direction to those who stand in need of these salvific values.

Spiritual Causality and Religious Mediation

The religious functionary in the African context is, above all else, considered to be a person of sacred power, with supernatural ability to 'see' into and 'discern' developments within the realms of the supernatural. People repair to these functionaries for all kinds of medicine for protection against enemies and invulnerability within the physically and spiritually

[13] Jenkins, *Next Christendom*, 58.

[14] Jenkins, *Next Christendom*, 149.

precarious world in which life has to be lived. Anthony Ephirim-Donkor writes that primal preoccupation with mystical causality means that when death is believed to have occurred prematurely, for example, answers must be found regarding who might have been the cause: 'In consequence, the "reasons" for the cause of deaths are ascertained spiritually long before actual burials. To assist in their search for answers, the Akan seek out mediums, akomfo, because they are indispensable to pinning down the precise supernatural causality of deaths in order to reassure an otherwise anxious community to proceed with burial obsequies.'[15]

The belief in what Ghanaian philosopher Kwame Gyekye refers to as 'extraordinary evil', which is usually mystically caused through curses, witchcraft, ritual sin or mbusu and sometimes sheer hatred, drives many to the courts of indigenous shrines in search of remedies. Ephirim-Donkor explains that in Akan traditional thought, for example, the soul, okra, is a courier of Nkrabea, destiny. Destinies are divinely ordained courses of life that could be tampered with by supernatural enemies in order to change its direction and ultimately bring life to a disastrous end. This 'makes ethical existence tantalizingly challenging during adulthood'. He continues, 'Contextually, therefore, the anxiety over existential and metaphysical issues and their repercussions compelled individuals to seek mediumistic interventions for psychosomatic security and well-being.'[16] John D.K. Ekem has examined the nature of such mediumistic interventions in his work Priesthood in Context.[17]

In a very useful essay, Benjamin Ray explained the connections between the desire to rectify unhappy destinies within traditional Yoruba contexts and how these approaches to life are reinvented in African revivalist or Aladura (people of prayer) Christianity:

> Yoruba go to their shrines to seek cures for their ills, answers to their questions, and guidance to their lives. This pragmatic, ritually centered view of religion, characterized by Robin Horton's aptly chosen terms 'explanation, prediction and control', is not only fundamental to Aladura Christianity, it is fundamental to most other African independent churches as well. Given this pragmatic religious attitude, the pursuit of human well-being in the world requires considerable ritual effort. For the Yoruba, achieving full self-actualization means obtaining the

[15] Anthony Ephirim-Donkor, 'Akom: The Ultimate Mediumship Experience among the Akan', *Journal of American Academy of Religion*, 76, no. 1 (March 2008), 56.

[16] Ephirim-Donkor, 'Akom', 57.

[17] John D.K. Ekem, *Priesthood in Context: A Study of Priesthood in Some Christian and Primal Communities of Ghana and Its Relevance for Mother-Tongue Biblical Interpretation*, rev. ed. (Accra: Sonlife, 2009).

traditional 'good things' or 'blessings' (ire) in life: children, prosperity, health and long life.[18]

AICs in their various manifestations across the continent, whether as Spiritual, Zionist, or Aladura churches, remain the most intensely studied streams of indigenous Christianity in Africa since the turn of the last century. To this end, one of the leading players in the academic field of African Christianity, the late Professor Adrian Hastings of Leeds University, observed that scholars looking for interesting research topics in the field of African religion at the height of the popularity of the AICs in the 1960s, could hardly fail to be attracted by one of the almost innumerable new churches springing into vibrant existence in Africa. 'African Christianity', according to Hastings, suddenly became 'a popular subject indeed but almost entirely in terms of the independent churches'.[19]

Reinvention of the Prophetic

The movements that emerged through the evangelising and prophetic activities of prophets William Wade Harris of Liberia, Garrick Sokar Braide of the Niger Delta, Simon Kimbangu of the DR Congo and Isaiah Shembe of South Africa in the early decades of the 20th century took Christianity to a phenomenal level. Historic mission Christianity accomplished its bit by opening up sub-Saharan Africa to the Gospel of Jesus Christ. The translation of the Gospel into the vernacular ensured that Africans had access to the material in their mother tongues. It is more than three decades now since Christian Baëta's widely acknowledged seminal 'study of some "Spiritual" Churches' in Ghana was published. In a review of the book, Harold W. Turner, himself a leading scholar of African Christian independency, noted that 'there is no other work of such substance by an African scholar among the growing literature on African prophet movements and independent churches'. C.G. Baëta, Turner continued, 'has given us the first extended work on these phenomena in this whole area'.[20]

In spite of the seismic changes that have occurred within the field, Baëta's study remains one of the most informative, insightful and authoritative academic sources on Christian religious innovation in twentieth-century Africa in general, and in Ghana in particular. The findings of Prophetism in Ghana served as a point of departure for my own

---

[18] Benjamin C. Ray, 'Aladura Christianity: A Yoruba Religion', *Journal of Religion in* Africa, 23, no. 3 (1993), 268-69.

[19] Adrian Hastings, 'Christianity in Africa', in Ursula King (ed.), *Turning Points in Religious Studies: Essays in Honor of Geoffrey Parrinder* (Edinburgh: T&T Clarke, 1990), 204.

[20] Harold W. Turner, Review of *Prophetism in Ghana,* in *International Review of Mission,* 53 (1964), 94.

work on current developments within Ghanaian Christianity from the last quarter of the twentieth century.[21] Baëta was one of the pace setters in that field of study, and his works will remain important reference points for all those seeking an understanding of Christian religious innovation on the continent of Africa. In spite of some scathing criticisms of what he sometimes saw as a simplistic and shallow understanding of the Christian scriptures and theologies of the Spiritual churches, Baëta was on the whole sympathetic to the cause of the movements he studied. He did recognise in the Spiritual churches a major step forward in an attempt to make Christianity speak to African situations in more relevant ways than the historic mission churches were doing at the time. The encounter between Christianity in Africa and the African indigenous religions, with their ardent beliefs in myriads of supernatural powers for health, protection and survival, produced profound results, with many Africans clandestinely tapping from both resources in their quests for salvation. Baëta referred to the schizophrenic phenomenon of being a church member during the day while seeking protection from traditional shrines at night as 'belt-and-braces' Christianity, an attitude of religious syncretism quite common in Africa.[22]

The search for practical salvation, which he identified as a key source of attraction into the Spiritual churches, lives on in the modern manifestations of these churches. Prophetism in Ghana recognised in some of the Spiritual churches an attempt to put an end to such hypocritical Christianity in spite of any shortcomings they may have had. Based on his reading of 1 Thessalonians 1:9, Baëta considered the members of the Spiritual churches he observed at the time as representing African Christians who, like the Thessalonians of Paul's day, had turned away 'from these traditional resources of supernatural succour in order that help may be sought, for the same purposes, from the God of the Christian evangel'. This conversion process, according to Baëta, was 'the greatest positive step' that the Spiritual churches took. In his own words: 'The "spiritual churches" indeed have a very strong conviction that at long last the passage has been made from error to truth, from the wrong path to the right one, from darkness to light; and that, because this is so, the newly-found resource of helpful power cannot fail.'[23]

Major changes have occurred in the field of African Christianity since the height of the revivals initiated by the AICs at the turn of the twentieth

---

[21] J. Kwabena Asamoah-Gyadu, *African Charismatics: A Study of some Current Developments within Independent Indigenous Pentecostalism in Ghana* (Leiden: E.J. Brill, 2004).

[22] C.G. Baëta, 'Christianity and Healing', *Orita,* 1 (1967), 53.

[23] Baëta, *Prophetism in Ghana: A Study of some Spiritual Churches* (London: SCM, 1962), 135.

century. Some of the phenomena and religious orientations that Baëta identified have remained resilient in the face of these changes. For example, he saw in the Spiritual churches what he described then as 'a prodigious struggle to prove the reality of spiritual things in general and the Biblical promises in particular'.[24]

This idiom of 'power' from the Holy Spirit, identified in Prophetism in Ghana as a key underlying theme of independent indigenous spirituality, has also resurfaced as a critical aspect of the religion of the modern progenies of Ghana's Spiritual churches. These are the movements that Ogbu Kalu aptly refers to as the 'third response' to the missionary enterprise in Africa, following the nationalist churches of the late nineteenth century and then the AICs.[25] The new independent churches in question are popularly referred to in Ghana as the Charismatic Ministries (CMs), and they possess a physical look that is different from the classical AICs. They are made up of a more educated and younger following than the Spiritual churches, and also make use of more modern instruments of Christian expression, including, extensive use of media technologies. The contemporary Pentecostals have dropped uniforms and paraphernalia such as the African gourd rattle, which the Church of the Twelve Apostles, one of those studied by Baëta, believed was enchanted with the presence of the Spirit. Even though the new Pentecostals may be physically different from the older AICs, they are both African-initiated movements and, as Andrew Walls explains, the CMs share with their forebears 'a quest for the demonstrable presence of the Holy Spirit and a direct address to the problems and frustrations of modern African urban life'.[26]

In other words, some appreciation of the spirituality of the Spiritual churches may be needed for a fuller understanding of modern Ghanaian charismatic Christianity. Baëta's work provides the key background text for this endeavour. The very designation of 'Spiritual churches' that Baëta used for Ghana's version of the older AICs, against such other terms and expressions as 'separatist', 'messianic' or 'syncretist' cults, underscored their pneumatic orientation. Against the backdrop of accusations that the incorporation of elements from traditional African religious rituals into AIC spirituality represented aberrations of the Christian church and of the gospel of Jesus Christ, Baëta became one of those scholars who firmly and sincerely believed in their decidedly Christian orientation. The new charismatic churches are among the ardent critics of the Spiritual churches because of the perceived proximity of their healing rituals to those found in

---

[24] Baëta, *Prophetism in Ghana*, 135.

[25] Ogbu U. Kalu, 'The Third Response: Pentecostalism and the Reconstruction of Christian Experience in Africa', *Journal of African Christian Thought*, 1, no. 2 (1998), 3-16.

[26] Andrew F. Walls, *The Missionary Movement in Christian History: Studies in the Transmission of Faith* (Maryknoll, NY: Orbis, 1996), 93.

the African traditional shrines. Yet, in several respects, the theologies of the two movements, especially their insistence on reliving biblical Christianity, means that they are not as discontinuous as the new churches may want the world to believe. In a recent study of charismatic Christianity, Paul Gifford points out that more than 90 per cent of the sermons in the new churches centre on the Old Testament.[27] Baëta had made a similar observation of the Spiritual churches much earlier, noting that in the Spiritual churches, where reversions to African traditional practices had taken place, they were attributed to 'the authority of the Old Testament rather than the fact that the customs were African'.[28] The contribution of Ghana's Spiritual churches to African Christianity is evident in the enculturation processes they initiated. Some of the changes that have occurred in Ghanaian Christianity since the publication of Prophetism in Ghana are also noteworthy because they enable us to appreciate the sharpness of Baëta's prophetic insight as articulated in his study.

First, from the late 1960s and under pressure from the forceful impact of the AICs, the historic mission churches, started incorporating elements like handclapping, dancing, locally-composed Christian choruses, prayer vigils and healing into their otherwise ordered and formalised worship services and liturgical structures. Historic mission churches also started tolerating charismatic renewal movements within their own churches, in an attempt to respond to the challenge of the presence of the AICs, and to stem the steady drift of their members to the new African churches as places 'to feel at home'. The Presbyterian Church of Ghana in 1965 and the Methodist Church, Ghana in 1969, specifically discussed the challenges that the presence of the Spiritual churches brought to their own ministries, and established committees to study them: to evaluate for emulation what benefits they could derive from the popular worship services and interventionist theologies of the independent churches which they had previously despised. The changes have come full circle with the tolerance of renewal movements within historic mission denominations, the rise of new Charismatic churches, and the transformation of some AICs into CMs being a way to ensure their own survival in the midst of modernity and change. The benefits of the renewal initiated by the Spiritual churches have thus been mutual.

Second, except for South Africa's Zionist churches, the AICs have been on the decline since the 1970s. At a time when several scholars and theologians were considering whether the AICs were the future of African Christianity, Baëta had already noticed the 'approaching fatigue' in these churches and virtually predicted their demise. That prediction has also

---

[27] Paul Gifford, *Ghana's New Christianity: Pentecostalism in a Globalizing African Economy* (Bloomington and Indianapolis: Indiana University Press, 2004), 71-82.

[28] Baëta, *Prophetism in Ghana,* 128.

come to pass, as evidenced by two Ghana Evangelism Committee surveys conducted in 1986 and 1991. Within the five-year period between the two surveys, attendance at the services of both the Apostles Revelation Society and the Musama Disco Christo Church had declined by 17 per cent. Attendance at the Sacred Order of the Cherubim and Seraphim declined by 24 per cent, in the African Faith Tabernacle by 23 per cent, and the Church of the Twelve Apostles by 22 per cent. The reasons for the dwindling fortunes of the Spiritual churches include the incapacitation – and even deaths – of their charismatic prophetic leaders, around whose personalities and gifts the churches revolved; the lack of ecclesial structures like youth and children's ministries that would have ensured the natural supply of members; the focus on healing and prophecy at the expense of Christian discipleship through serious evangelism, expository preaching and theological education. Reference has already been made to the metamorphosis into contemporary Pentecostals in an attempt to adopt a more modern outlook. The problem-solving orientation of the ministries of the Spiritual churches meant that they attracted large numbers of floating members, who kept moving from prophet to prophet in search of solutions to their problems. A number of Spiritual churches have also split up for reasons ranging from lack of accountability to succession-related acrimonious conflicts at the deaths of the founders of these churches. For instance, the African Faith Tabernacle popularly called 'Nkansah' after its leader Prophet James Kwame Nkansah, was one of the churches studied by Baëta. Since the death of the prophet in 1987, this church has experienced a succession of problems that have led to its splitting into at least five factions.[29]

Third, and most importantly for our purposes, since the publication of Prophetism in Ghana, the ministry of the prophet as a key religious functionary has re-emerged within modern forms of indigenous Pentecostalism represented by the new Charismatic churches. Gifford discusses the nature and ministry of the new prophets in his book Ghana's New Christianity.[30] This new manifestation of prophetism within modern Ghanaian Christianity is remarkable when considered in the light of the predictions made by Baëta more than three decades ago. That Prophetism in Ghana has remained relevant in the midst of the changes discussed is a result of the very prophetic insights that Baëta brought to his study. He wrote with clairvoyance, guided by a unique ability to look at the Spiritual churches and predict what the nature, impact and future trends in the development of these movements were likely to be.

The Spiritual churches may be declining numerically, but their diminishing physical presence has not erased their unique contribution to

---

[29] Asamoah-Gyadu, *African Charismatics*, ch. 3.

[30] Gifford, *Ghana's New Christianity*, 89-112, 186.

African theology. In fact, their qualitative impact on Ghanaian Christianity continues through an enduring religious and theological heritage. This heritage is evident through the initiation of an effective enculturation process, the normalisation of charismatic experiences in Christian expression and worship, a more practical view of salvation, the use of oral theology and an innovative gender ideology in which, for the first time, women have become founders and leaders of Christian churches in Africa. Perhaps the greatest contribution of the Spiritual churches to Christianity in Ghana is that they have bridged the gap that formerly existed between primal spirituality and Christianity. In contrast to western Christian theologies that seem on the whole to be a system of ideas, primal religions, according to Ghanaian theologian Kwame Bediako, are generally conceived 'as a system of power and of living religiously as being in touch with the source and channels of power in the universe'.[31] In primal religiosity, finite human beings stand in need of the powers and blessings of benevolent transcendent powers, and draw on such sources for protection from evil forces through appropriate covenant relationships with such transcendent benevolent helpers.

The Spiritual churches became popular in African countries like Ghana because they affirmed the reality of God and other supernatural entities. Destructive and malevolent powers seeking to destroy people, and angels representing the Christian equivalent of transcendent benevolent powers, both featured prominently in the worldview of the Spiritual churches. Into the twenty-first century the theology that seems to have become characteristic of the African church is that which takes seriously the pneumatic experiences of the Bible in general and the New Testament in particular, underscoring many of Baëta's findings. The renewal occurring within Ghanaian Christianity has been such that even those churches that stand in historic continuity with western missions, and which have inherited their rationalistic, systematic and creedal forms of Christianity, have been forced to take charismatic renewal seriously. The process has involved a rethinking of traditional church pneumatologies that includes a practical articulation of a response to the reality of evil, a non-negotiable element in the religious consciousness of all Christians who are alive to the world of the Bible. In this way, Africa, through the ingenuity of the African independent church movement and typified by the Spiritual churches, has emerged as the new centre of theological creativity: 'a laboratory' as Bediako calls it, where 'Christian answers to African questions are hammered out'.[32] We owe our understanding of African-initiated

---

[31] Kwame Bediako, *Christianity in Africa: The Renewal of a Non-Western Religion* (Edinburgh: Edinburgh University Press; Maryknoll, NY: Orbis Books, 1995), 106.

[32] Kwame Bediako, interviewed by Kim A. Lawton, 'Faith without Borders: How the Developing World is Changing the Face of Christianity', *Christianity Today* (19 May 1997), 44.

Christianity to scholars like Baëta, who drew attention to the Spiritual churches and affirmed them as truly indigenous Christian movements whose innovative Christianity had much to teach about what it meant to be African and Christian at the same time, yet without undermining either of these twin identities.

Religious Mediation and the Primal Imagination

There are various categories of traditional medical persons in the traditional contexts. Some practise as plain herbalists without supernatural discernment. Others who possess that power of discernment especially in perceiving the spiritual forces at work in the lives of clients, are widely respected as religious functionaries who have 'eyes to see' beyond the physical. The one with eyes to see would fit the category of diviner or okomfo, priest or priestess in the Akan conceptual scheme. The processes leading to the calling, making and operations of akomfo are particularly important for understanding religious mediation in Africa and why religious innovation in both its older Aladura and newer Pentecostal/charismatic forms have attracted Africans in such significant numbers. In the primal context, as we have just learnt, what is primarily real is the spiritual. As Kwame Bediako points out, in the west the Christian faith encapsulated a system of doctrinal ideas, but, in such primal contexts as those of Africa, it has been conceived as a system of power.

Thus the okomfo (priest) is always a person of 'sacred power' with eyes to see into the supernatural realm, and the ability to communicate with supernatural reality: he can secure meaning and help from there for people and communities in their search for answers to the uncertainties, enigmas and perplexities of this life. The calling of an okomfo first involves the seizure of the personality by the deity, who alights upon the candidate in order to call him or her into its service. Ephirim-Donkor defines akom as a 'mediumistic state' and explains it in terms of 'a unique extrinsic phenomenon whereby an invisible agent acts unilaterally on a human being in order to bring the subject under its dictates'.[33] A person who gets possessed, or on whom a deity alights – if it is discerned that the experience is a call into priesthood and not the onset of insanity – is then sent out to be trained as a religious mediator or functionary. In a study among the Edo of Benin City, Nigeria, Paula Ben-Amos was informed that when the god comes down on a person's head 'she can see everything' and 'anything she says is directly from Olokun', the deity.[34]

The relationship between the deity and the okomfo is considered by the Akan to be very intimate because, after the initial experience of possession,

[33] Ephirim-Donkor, 'Akom', 55.

[34] Cited in Ephirim-Donkor, 'Akom', 55.

the priest, irrespective of gender, is regarded as the wife of the priest. Indeed, as we saw in Chapter 5, the act of possession is conceived in terms of sexual intimacy, and so the expression akom afa no (he or she has been possessed by a deity) signifies the invasion of the privacy of an individual by the deity. The expression afa no is employed when a man has sexual intercourse with a woman against her will. Thus what the Akan refer to as akom is 'a unique extrinsic phenomenon whereby an invisible agent acts unilaterally on a human being in order to bring the subject under its dictates'.[35] It is the intimacy with the deity and the 'years of austere professional training' leading to the attainment of 'the highest socio-religious and spiritual state' that enable the religious functionary to hear from the gods, and bring communication and direction from them to religious seekers. John Ekem shows why this mediatory role would ensure the survival of such an institution:

> Precisely, akomfo are who they are because of their mediating role in the fight against different forms of evil in Akan communities. Their rigorous training prepares them for this important role as mid-persons between the empirical and meta-empirical worlds. Apart from invoking the supernatural through their akom, Akan traditional priests and priestesses bring supplicants closer to the spirit world by means of their role in sacrificial rites ... It is reasonable, therefore, to argue that as long as needs of the above nature remain in Akan communities, traditional priesthood will hardly lose its value for many Akans.[36]

Ekem gives two meanings to the word okomfo: in secular language, the word kom refers to 'hunger', but in religious discourse it refers to the act of cultic or spirit-inspired 'dancing'. When any music and dance forms are set aside as something sacred to the gods or divinities, they assume ritual value. They are cultivated not only to provide the atmosphere and emotional conditioning required for sustaining a ritual occasion, but also as a medium for reaching the unseen. In other words they are invocatory. Many divinities, like their worshippers, can be deeply affected by music and dance. Indeed, the most common situation in which some of the gods manifest themselves is when music set aside for them is performed. Among sections of the Ga communities of Accra, the nature of the dance form tells the informed observer which deity is at work in a medium. The deities descend to the people through their human mediums and participate in the music and dance.[37] Thus, as Ephirim-Donkor notes, in public the 'akom is conjuration in a state of trance, which includes unique dances in response to unique musical dictates of deities'.[38]

---

[35] Ephirim-Donkor, 'Akom', 55.
[36] Ekem, *Priesthood in Context*, 177-78.
[37] Nketia, 'African Spirituality', 18.
[38] Ephirim-Donkor, 'Akom', 59.

Akom, in the senses of both 'hunger' and 'cultic dancing' to ritual music, is applicable to traditional priesthood for it is through the spiritual disciplines of 'fasting' and deliberate abstinence from 'pleasure' that the religious functionary achieves the 'spiritual alertness' and 'heightened sensitivity' to supernatural communication that enables religious mediation to occur in the context of power. Ritual music creates the appropriate atmosphere for the gods to descend among the people, possess the priest or priestess and then deliver the required messages through them as mediums. Thus akom refers to the act of 'prophesying' under the influence of a possessing deity, and it mostly (though not always) occurs during a period of trance. When the religious functionary keeps spiritually alert to physical, spiritual and ritual purity, it makes it easier for the spirit of the deity to descend or alight upon him or her and bring word to the confused and troubled world of humans:

> The akomfo possess a repertoire of secret herbal knowledge, which they draw upon to aid the treatment of all kinds of illnesses. Before applying their medical skills, however, they divine the diagnosis thus ensuring that holistic healing was psychosomatic. In this way, the spiritual causation of an otherwise physical affliction is first mitigated ... On matters of state, the akomfo are consulted regularly, especially during exigencies in order for them to make known the will of the ancestors and deities to their earthly representatives, the rulers. Thus the akomfo are prophetic voices who promulgate future events to society through traditional rulers.[39]

Thus akom 'is wholly and ritually meaningful, as it entails acquiring a repertoire of spiritual and medical knowledge needed to address magico-medical, psychosomatic and spiritual welfare of society'.[40] Spiritual alertness also means the ability to 'see' beyond the ordinary, and that is the capacity that the second herbalist/diviner in our case study displayed. Indeed, we learn from Ephirim-Donkor that the process of graduation from shrines after training for the okomfo includes swallowing the eyes of a dog, in order to increase the power of supernatural visibility which that animal is believed to possess.

Religious Mediators as Persons of Sacred Power

The calling, role and modus operandi of the okomfo, babalawo or nganga, as these religious functionaries may be designated within various African traditions, presents a particularly striking example of how the resonance between primal piety and indigenous revivalist Christianity works out in practice. When the okomfo comes under the possessing influence of the

[39] Ephirim-Donkor, 'Akom', 58.
[40] Ephirim-Donkor, 'Akom', 59.

deity, he or she speaks not in ordinary human language, but in the language of the gods. The gods do not communicate in human languages; they use 'primal tongues' as a sign of their existence and presence. It lies in the power of religious functionaries with access to the language of the supernatural realm to then relate to suppliants what the gods may be saying.

Harvey Cox points to the meaning of Pentecostal tongues in the light of a phenomenon that has always been known within primal traditions. He explains why the phenomenon of glossolalia constitutes a profound transcendental experience or a form of vital participation in the life of transcendence:

> Now tongue speaking was viewed as the Spirit mercifully providing the sounds by which a stammering soul could speak to God. … It was understood not primarily as a supernatural tool for world mission but as a deliverance from the iron cage of grammar and a graceful provision to those who did not have the strength or the fluency to pray with their own words. … It has persisted, I believe, because it represents the core of all Pentecostal conviction: that the Spirit of God needs no mediators but is available to anyone in an intense, immediate, indeed interior way.[41]

It is within this context of the human inability to adequately capture and express the deep things of the spirit, that Paul describes Pentecostal tongues as 'groans' or 'sighs' that are 'too deep for words' (Rom. 8:26). His reference is not to silent prayer, as popular interpretations have generally cast it. Rather as Pentecostal New Testament scholar Gordon Fee suggests, 'sighs too deep for words' refers to communicating languages that are humanly incomprehensible because 'we do not know how to pray'. Human languages are limited in their ability to articulate what lies deep within the human psyche. Interpretations of Pentecostal tongues are given to those to whom the Spirit grants the required ability. In the traditional shrine, it is left to the Osofo, who is the mouthpiece of the deity, to interpret what the okomfo, who assumes the position of the deity under possession, may be saying to suppliants.

Religious Mediation and African Christianity

It is instructive that the Yoruba designation of the diviner, babalawo, literally means 'father/custodian of secrets'. The functions of both okomfo and babalawo include diagnosis, the prescription of appropriate remedies and, when needed, a prophetic function that reveals the minds of gods and deities to peoples and communities. Understood in this way, the re-emergence of the prophetic in African Independent and Pentecostal

---

[41] Harvey Cox, *Fire from Heaven: The Rise of Pentecostal Spirituality and the Reshaping of Religion in the Twenty-First Century* (Reading, MA: Addison-Wesley Publishing Co., 1995).

Christianity takes on a particular significance. Jenkins correctly refers to the independent churches as demonstrating the real spiritual hunger that Christianity encountered, and sought to satiate, within its African converts.[42]

These particular types of Christianity constituted paradigmatic shifts from the rational and cerebral expressions of the faith associated with the historic western-mission–related denominations because they offered more reasonable and experiential forms of faith that were especially able to cater to the tensions that exist within people and communities as they sought to make sense of their physically and spiritually precarious African worlds. Rijk van Dijk explains how this occurred when Pentecostalism in Ghana came under indigenous leadership:

> When the mission Pentecostal churches were placed entirely in the hands of African leadership in the 1930s and the 1950s, the leadership accommodated to notions of the spirit world, the ways in which individual subjects were affected by such influences and forces, and it developed distinct ideas on how such afflicting forces could be counteracted in prayer-healing, speaking in tongues and similar rituals.[43]

The sense of the supernatural and the need to anchor one's destiny in it has not declined for Africans; rather, the need for powers of protection and salvation has increased. The 'spiritual allies' of Aladura Christians, as Ray refers to them, include God, Jesus Christ, the Holy Spirit and the angels.[44] Globalisation, modernity, emigration to western countries and economic development have created new fears, anxieties and challenges. This has made resorting to supernatural solutions to problems even more important for many Africans. The 'spiritual allies' of the African Christian reside in the supernatural realm and their powers are mediated by the ministers of the church, i.e. prophets, dreamers and visionaries. Thus, as Ray observes, prayer influences both heaven and the world in a positive way, because in governing one's relation to 'heaven', prayer simultaneously makes one's 'world' prosper.[45]

It is thus not surprising that even in the African Diaspora in the west, a majority of the churches that are proliferating belong to the Pentecostal/charismatic type. People seek God's face through his powerful men and women, attending church with concerns about the regularisation of immigration papers, employment and the general socio-economic dislocations that accompany life in foreign lands when people are

---

[42] Jenkins, *Next Christendom*, 54.

[43] Rijk A. van Dijk, 'From Camp to Encompassment: Discourses of Transsubjectivity in the Ghanaian Pentecostal Diaspora', *Journal of Religion in Africa*, 27, no. 2 (1997), 140.

[44] Ray, 'Aladura Christianity', 271.

[45] Ray, 'Aladura Christianity', 272, 273.

categorised as 'aliens'. Although the intention is not specifically to be African, the reinvention of the religious mediator as a person of sacred power has never been alien to the primal imagination, as Ephirim-Donkor explains:

> The reason for their [akomfo's] indispensability is simple: the Akan have a deep-seated desire, even an obsession about the future. But not any future event – they have an intrinsic desire to know, receive answers and affirmation from the ancestors and deities about existential metaphysical and existential conditions … Nevertheless the hard economic and existential conditions, spurred on by the psychological pangs of ancestral affirmation are sufficient to cause people to act in ways that are contradictory to their non-African medical and religious beliefs, as they ritually attempt to order their lives meaningfully, using the only recourse available to them traditionally, akomfo.[46]

Two Akan words stimulate my thoughts regarding the manner in which primal ways of being religious and dealing with traditional religious functionaries have been reinvented in African revivalist Christianity: ebisa, which means search or seek, and akwankyere, which means direction. Ebisa relates to the ways in which people seek explanations about their destiny from indigenous prophets, and akwankyere is the direction that people may receive with regard to, for example, their domestic, political, family, business, relationship, marital, health, reproductive health and economic conditions, for which they may be seeking divine intervention. In both its older Aladura and new Pentecostal forms, the ministry of the prophet exists.

There are those who give inspired messages during worship services, but these individuals can be distinguished from those with the gift of prophecy. The former may be found in any Christian church, but the latter, which is the institutionalised form of the prophetic office, is certainly a Pentecostal phenomenon. In the older independent churches of Africa, most founders or those in leadership were prophets of the second kind, and this form has re-emerged in contemporary Pentecostalism in Africa. Healing, broadly understood here to mean divine intervention in those concerns with which people would normally have sought help from traditional shrines, is the most important function of these prophetic figures. The Pentecostals in particular distinguish between vocal gifts such as prophecy and words of knowledge, on one hand, and revelation gifts, such as visions and dreams, on the other. The two sets of divine grace are not mutually exclusive because they both relate to the giving of appropriate guidance for those seeking direction for the course of their lives. The gift of 'discernment', for example, refers to the supernatural ability to determine the extraordinary source of an issue and offer appropriate guidance on how to deal with it.

---

[46] Ephirim-Donkor, 'Akom', 71.

This ability to discern the future explains why some modern African Pentecostal prophets have even taken the official Old Testament title of 'seer'. These revelatory abilities and directions, as with the akomfo practices, are sharpened by prayer, fasting and moral purity. Interestingly, the Akan words nkomhyeni and odiyifo, used interchangeably for 'prophet' in the translated scriptures of the Akan, relate to the acts of 'prophesying' and 'seeing' or 'revelation'. On occasion these graces may be activated in an atmosphere of loud music and dance, which are characteristic features of Pentecostal worship. One Ghanaian Pentecostal prophet is quoted as acknowledging that 'music invokes the supernatural presence into the midst of worshippers', and to that end, 'it is not uncommon in a Pentecostal prophetic service to find a singer called upon to prepare the ground and charge the atmosphere with powerful worship songs before a prophet speaks'.[47]

Conclusion

The Christological implications of power wielded by the new prophets can be very profound because Jesus, as the ultimate High Priest, embodied in his person and ministry several, if not all, of the positive functions attributed to those in charge of religious mediation. It was Baëta who noted in his study of African independent churches in Ghana that the rise and development of Spiritual Churches, as they are called in Ghana, help to explain the relation of African Christianity to culture. The Spiritual Churches, he contended, throw up a number of clues in the whole problem of adaptation and syncretism in the world mission of the church.[48] Through a comparative examination of the roles of the traditional religious functionary and the Christian functionary, I have sought to illustrate how, in seeking to remain biblical, the church in post-missionary Africa unconsciously expresses her faith through phenomena that lie deeply embedded in the primal imagination. Perhaps African Christianity, and the Christianity of the Third World generally, constitute better reflections of the faith in its biblical forms than the historic western patterns that, for centuries, the world has been made to accept as representing what Christianity was meant to be.

---

[47] Joseph Quayesi-Amakye, 'Let the Prophet Speak: A Study of Trends in Pentecostal Prophetism with Particular Reference to the Church of Pentecost and some Neo-Pentecostal Churches', unpublished MPhil thesis (Accra: Central University College, 2009), 108, 110.

[48] Baëta, *Prophetism*, 5.

Chapter 8
'His Banner Over Us Is Love': Transdenominational Renewal

Rev. Dr. Maxwell Aryee is an ordained minister of the Methodist Church Ghana and, until 2012, worked as the Director of the medical facility at Ghana's Atomic Energy Commission. Prior to that appointment, he worked as a medical officer at Ghana's Korle Bu Teaching Hospital where he was better known not for his professional competence, but as an alcoholic. There are many senior medical officers who describe Dr. Aryee's conversion to Christ as nothing short of a miracle that could only have happened by the power of God. He was Born-again in 1986 at a meeting of the Full Gospel Businessmen's Fellowship International Breakfast Meeting (FGBMFI) at the then Ambassador (Movënpick) Hotel in Accra. Rev. Dr. Maxwell Aryee who has shared his testimony on many FGBMFI platforms and in churches, tells of how he started drinking as a final year medical student because he was referred in one subject.

The shame that comes with such perceived failure in Ghana medical schools led him to start drinking to deal with some anxiety disorder that developed in his life as a result. 'I graduated from beer to hard liquor and by the time I started practicing, I was on sedatives and tranquilizers. I used my medical knowledge in a self-destructive way and it was only by the grace of God that I was not dismissed from my job and my license withdrawn. My teachers were ashamed of me.' He recounts how he was invited to a FGBMFI Breakfast Meeting by a female patient of his, and in fact how he thought that the invitation was for the woman to repay his medical services with some sexual favours. 'Instead, we ended up at a FGBMFI meeting where I gave my life to Christ, became a member and rose through the ranks to become President of the Accra Premier Chapter in the early 1980s.' In the mid-1990s, Dr. Maxwell Aryee was ordained by the Methodist Church Ghana.

This chapter discusses the rise of lay transdenominational charismatic and evangelistic movements within the Ghanaian Christian landscape. It provides an overview of the historical development of FGBMFI and Women's Aglow in Ghana, and identifies the impact of these two Pentecostal movements on Christianity and society in the country. Scholars who track and interpret the historical development of Christianity in Africa typically highlight the phenomenal growth in numbers, the diversity of fellowships and denominations, and the impact that the faith is having on the peoples of the continent. Paul Gifford, for example, notes the impact of Christianity on Africa when he quotes Adrian Hastings: 'Black Africa today is totally inconceivable apart from the presence of Christianity, a presence which a couple of generations ago could still be not unreasonably dismissed as fundamentally marginal and a mere subsidiary aspect of colonialism.'[1]

It is pertinent to reiterate our earlier point that, although there has been a general upsurge in Christian activity, especially in the two-thirds world, the growth has been most noticeable within the Pentecostal/charismatic strand of Christianity. In 1986, Walter Hollenweger drew attention to this growth when he observed that by the year 2000 the population of Pentecostal Christians would number as many as all other Protestant groups put together. He stressed the implications of this growth:

> It reveals that the overwhelming part of this Christianity belongs either to the indigenous non-white or to the Third-World Pentecostal churches. Taken together with the general trends in the Roman Catholic and Protestant churches, this indicates that the numerical and perhaps also the spiritual centre of Christianity will shift away from white Western forms to this new type of Christianity. Christianity as a whole will no longer be a predominantly white person's religion.[2]

We live in an age when chapels in Europe are being converted into warehouses, bars, restaurants, museums and, in not a few instances, Buddhist and Hindu temples or even strip clubs. Yet churches in my native Ghana are struggling to find places to meet. Cinemas and other property originally built for commercial and secular purposes have now been converted into meeting places for transdenominational charismatic fellowships and places of worship for churches of that orientation. If the growth continues at the present rate, many countries in sub-Saharan Africa could become strong Christian nations with the church as their conscience.

Two of the primary influences of Pentecostalism on Ghanaian Christianity have come through the lay-oriented fellowships of the FGBMFI and Women's Aglow. The motto of FGBMFI reads, 'His Banner over Us is Love' and that of the Women's Aglow exhorts, 'Be Aglow for Jesus'. This chapter shows how Christian revitalisation has worked historically within the African Christian context through movements of renewal such as FGBMFI and Women's Aglow fellowship. The reverse of

[1] Paul Gifford (ed.), *The Christian Churches and the Democratization of Africa* (Leiden: E.J. Brill, 1995), 2.

[2] Walter Hollenweger, 'After Twenty Years' Research on Pentecostalism', *International Review of Mission*, 75 (January 1986), 3. Emphasis added.

what the President of FGBMFI in Ghana said during a 2011 national convention of their efforts over the years is equally true of Women's Aglow. He noted,

> Full Gospel Business Men's Fellowship International Conventions have played a very important role in fulfilling the vision God gave to our founder Demos Shakarian of Blessed Memory. Over the years … many businessmen, professionals, indeed men from all walks of life, their wives, and families have experienced the power and reality of God, and have been equipped, energized to go into the market place and draw men [and women] to God.[3]

One cannot go far in the study of the wide-ranging and manifold phenomena found in the modern religious life of Africa without some system of classification.[4] The variety of theological, liturgical and behavioural expressions in Pentecostalism in Ghana, even when they hold ideals in common, gives rise to an extensively heterogeneous movement. When it comes to categorising the different types of Pentecostalism, however, I hesitate to use strict typologies, preferring to see them rather as waves of the same movement whose emergence and existence, although occurring at different times, dovetail into each other.[5] Certain aspects and versions of the movement may wane but are unlikely to perish without trace because previous Pentecostal movements tend to influence subsequent ones, especially if they emerge within the same cultural context.

FGBMFI and Women's Aglow are included in the variety of churches and movements that emphasise the active presence of the Holy Spirit, with manifestations of power in 'signs and wonders' in the lives of people who have experienced the Spirit. The establishment, presence and ministry of these fellowships give contextual expression to two texts from the gospels. The first text is Jesus' commission of the Gerasene demoniac following that man's deliverance. When, following his recovery through Jesus' intervention, he asked to be a disciple, the man received this alternative suggestion, as recorded in Mark's gospel: 'Go home to your family and tell them how much the Lord has done for you, and how he has had mercy on you' (Mk. 5:19). The second text highlights the witness of the Samaritan woman after her encounter with Jesus at the well and the response of her

---

[3] Timothy E. Ati, 'Welcome Address' as printed in Full Gospel Business Men's Fellowship International 2011 National Convention Brochure (31 August-3 September 2011 at the Accra International Conference Center), 1.

[4] Harold W. Turner, *Religious Innovation in Africa: Collected Essays on New Religious Movements* (Boston, MA: G. K. Hall, 1979), 79.

[5] This hesitation does not mean that typologies are not useful. In spite of their limitations, they help to give a general impression of categories of religious movement in various contexts. For an example of a useful typology of Pentecostal movements in Ghana, see Cephas Omenyo, 'The Charismatic Movement in Ghana', *PNEUMA: The Journal of the Society for Pentecostal Studies*, 16 (Fall 1994), 169-85.

countrymen and women to her testimony. We read in John's gospel: 'Many of the Samaritans from that town believed in him because of the woman's testimony. "He told me everything I ever did ..." They said to the woman, "We no longer believe just because of what you said; now we have heard for ourselves, and we know that this man really is the Saviour of the world"' (Jn. 4:39, 42).

Testimony as an Oral Theological Form

We encounter in these passages, and in the experiences recounted in the Acts of the Apostles, the use of personal testimony emanating not from written theology, nor even from those in holy orders, but from the personal experiences of ordinary laypersons who have a salvation story to tell. Oral theological discourse, confirming acts of the Spirit, is a powerful missionary tool used by the FGBMFI and Women's Aglow fellowships, which are made up of laypersons who share their personal testimonies with others to inform them of the transforming power of the Holy Spirit. They give expression to Paul's expectation of the Corinthians: 'You yourselves are our letter ... known and read by everybody ... written not with ink but with the Spirit of the living God, not on tablets of stone but on tablets of human hearts' (2 Cor. 3:2-3).

The role of oral theology as an effective tool in mission was first provided by the African Independent Churches. Recounting publicly one's own experience of miraculous redemption through God's intervention – relating dreams and visions and 'witnessing' – has always been an essential part of their worship. Members of the AICs have a vibrant active faith with a strong sense of mission. Their faith is expressed not in written theology but in the form of a story depicting the mighty acts of the Holy Spirit. They share testimonies of the manifestations of the power of God in healing, deliverance from 'principalities and powers', and the gifts of glossolalia – gifts that Christ freely gave to his church but that are somehow stifled in the ministry of established, mainline Christianity.[6] These personal testimonies are viewed by members of the AICs as 'proofs' that they serve a living God.

As Walter Hollenweger points out, oral theology, with its use of the descriptive categories of the story, the witness and the vision, is biblical and lies at the roots of Black spirituality. Its usage helps explain why the neo-Pentecostal movement has flourished in the two-thirds world. Hollenweger writes: 'In these preliterate, semi-literate, or post-literate cultures the medium of communication is – just as in biblical times – not

[6] I use the term *mainline Christianity* with reference to Christianity as passed on by traditional western mission churches like the Methodist, Presbyterian, Anglican and Roman Catholic Churches, who were the pioneers of the Christian gospel in West Africa.

the definition but the description, not the book but the parable, not a systematic theology but a song, not the treatise but the TV programme, not the articulation of concepts but the celebration of banquets.'[7]

In keeping with the features of oral theology, FGBMFI and Women's Aglow – both non-denominational fellowships of charismatic laypeople – also use their personal conversion testimonies, healing by prayer, the ministry of song, glossolalia and exorcism to evangelise others, particularly business colleagues and associates. They hold monthly gatherings over breakfast, luncheons or dinner where selected speakers share without apology their experiences in the 'world' and subsequent conversion to the Lord. The testimonies often depict divine intervention in the sharer's life, resulting not only in a change of life but also in baptism of the Holy Spirit with the manifestation of speaking in tongues.

Manifestations of the Spirit

Given the prior use of testimony by the AICs, it is not surprising that the method has caught on so effectively. The speaking of tongues is central to the identity of these fellowships. Article 8 of the doctrinal statement of FGBMFI, for example, states unequivocally: 'We believe in the baptism of the Holy Ghost, accompanied by the initial physical sign of speaking with other tongues as the Spirit of God gives utterance ... as distinct from the new birth, and in the nine gifts of the Spirit, listed in 1 Corinthians 12, as now available to believers.'[8] In keeping with this position, eligibility for executive positions requires one to have been Spirit-baptised with the evidence of 'speaking in tongues' or to be aspiring to that experience.

Meetings are characteristically Pentecostal, with an invitation for people to 'give their lives to Christ' following the testimonies for the day. Responses are normally overwhelming, and time is dedicated to prayers for healing and deliverance from demonic powers, and to prayers for God's intervention in the various endeavours of life. The fellowships have a high regard for people in full-time Christian ministry. The presence of such people at meetings would normally be acknowledged and prayers would be said for them. Full-time ministers, however, although they may apply for membership, are not permitted to serve on executive committees.[9]

These fellowships are therefore entirely lay-initiated and organised, and are committed to breaking the pneumatological silence that has recently characterised the mission of the mainline churches. The use of lay initiative

---

[7] Walter J. Hollenweger, 'Charismatic Renewal in the Third World: Implications for Mission', *Occasional Bulletin of Missionary Research*, 4 (April 1980), 69.

[8] Full Gospel Business Men's Fellowship International, *Constitution and By-Laws and Articles of Incorporation*, revised version July 1985, 7.

[9] FGBMFI, *Constitution*, 7.

in mission has long been a feature of Christianity in Africa. The history of the older historic or mainline churches is replete with examples of such laypersons in the spread of the gospel across West Africa. For instance, recalling a 'survey of how the numerous congregations within one densely populated region of Nigeria had come into being', Andrew Walls notes:

> Time after time the seminal figure was a new court clerk who was a Christian, or a worker on the new railway, or a tailor, carrying his sewing machine on his head, or some other trader. Some such stranger, or a group of strangers, had arrived and had started family prayers, stopped work on Sunday, and sang hymns instead, and some local people got interested. Or perhaps the initial impetus came from people from that village who had gone elsewhere – to school, to work, to trade, in more than one case to jail – and on return home sought the things they had found in their travels.[10]

What is new in the ministries of FGBMFI and Women's Aglow, then, is neither the emphasis on personal testimony nor the emphasis on lay ministry; rather, it is their commitment to remain non-denominational fellowships of charismatic laypeople who stay in their respective churches or denominations serving as agents of renewal. They are 'missionaries without robes' whose impact on the Christian church has been profound.

Full Gospel Business Men's Fellowship International

FGBMFI was founded by Demos Shakarian (1913–1993), a millionaire dairy farmer from California whose ethnic background was Armenian. He felt God asking him to start a fellowship of businessmen drawn from diverse denominations to share their faith in Christ. In 1926, at the age of thirteen, he received the glossolalic experience through the baptism of the Holy Spirit while sitting through a normal Sunday Pentecostal service. This experience proved to be a decisive event in his life. A strong believer in biblical prophecy, Shakarian describes a revelation the night immediately following his Holy Spirit baptism experience that also brought him partial healing from a hearing impairment:

> I felt a surge of superhuman energy – as if I could float right out of the house and sail the heavens in the power of God. I felt as if I could look down on earth from God's perspective, see all human need from the vantage point of his supply. And

[10] Andrew F. Walls, *The Missionary Movement in Christian History: Studies in the Transmission of Faith* (Maryknoll, NY: Orbis Books, 1996), 87.

> all the while He was whispering to my heart, Demos, power is the birthright of every Christian. Accept power, Demos.[11]

His immediate response following this dramatic divine experience in healing and revelation is reminiscent of Paul's experience on the road to Damascus: his words were 'Lord, I said, I know that when you heal people it's because you have work for them to do. Will you show me, Lord, the job you have for me?'[12]

The first chapter of FGBMFI was started in 1951, with Oral Roberts as the main speaker. Roberts encouraged Shakarian in his efforts. At the preliminary meeting, Roberts prayed: 'Lord Jesus ... let this fellowship grow in your strength alone. Send it marching in your power across the nation. Across the world. We give You thanks right now, Lord Jesus, that we see a little group of people in a cafeteria, but that You see a thousand chapters.'[13]

The fellowship began to grow at a remarkable rate, and by 1988 it had 3,000 local chapters and had spread to eighty-seven countries. From the outset, Demos and his wife, Rose, stressed two principles. First, they emphasised that members should not leave their churches even if the denomination did not know the power of the Spirit. Second, they urged each member to serve as a missionary to his own church.[14] On his initial contact with the fellowship as a speaker, David du Plessis described it as a 'worldwide fellowship of ordinary businessmen filled with the Holy Spirit! Each man a missionary to the people he works with every day'.[15]

FGBMFI in Ghana

The movement was introduced to Ghana in 1976 by Joseph Kwaw, a private businessman who doubled as an import/export merchant. He had helped a Nigerian friend, Daniel Wardieh, to clear some goods from one of

---

11 Demos Shakarian, *The Happiest People on Earth: The Long-Awaited Story of Demos Shakarian as Told to John and Elizabeth Sherrill* (Chappaqua, NY: Steward Press, 1975), 37.

12 Shakarian, *Happiest People*, 37.

13 Shakarian, *Happiest People*, 120.

14 Shakarian, *Happiest People*, 121.

15 Cited in Shakarian, *Happiest People*, 122. Emphasis added. David du Plessis is presented in the literature as the person who has had the most influence on neo-Pentecostal growth. He is a South African who served as a pastor with the Apostolic Faith Mission. He migrated to the United States in 1948 and became an Assemblies of God pastor in 1955. From 1951 he championed ecumenism by initiating dialogue with the World Council of Churches (WCC) and was invited to attend the second WCC assembly, in Evanston, Illinois, in 1954. He participated as a Pentecostal observer at the third WCC assembly, in New Delhi, India, in 1961. His ecumenism cost him dear: in 1962 he was disfellowshipped by the governing board of the Assemblies of God for his contacts with the WCC.

Ghana's ports, and Wardieh, who was then the president of FGBMFI in Nigeria, passed on some literature about the fellowship to Kwaw, with the intention of encouraging him to start a branch in Ghana. Kwaw told me in an interview: 'I caught the vision because the literature spoke about a group of businessmen who will witness to their colleagues.' The first breakfast meeting was held in 1978 at the Ambassador Hotel in Accra. The speaker was Deacon G. K. Abankwa of the Accra Calvary Baptist Church. Disappointingly, the meeting attracted only five people. During that same year, however, the tide turned somewhat when the Nigerian charismatic evangelist Archbishop Benson Idahosa was holding a crusade in Accra. Kwaw, who had served as a member of the crusade planning committee, asked Idahosa to announce the formation of a Ghana branch of FGBMFI, which he did. The exposure increased awareness of the fellowship, and appeals were made to some well-known Christian businessmen for financial support. One of those business leaders, Simms Mensah, who then belonged to the Assemblies of God Church, subsequently became the first president of FGBMFI in Ghana.

Things did not go well for the fledgling organisation. According to Kwaw, 'after a while things started falling apart ... People stopped responding to invitations with all kinds of excuses. We later discovered that a lot of our members were in various lodges and because the testimonies challenged such things they refused to come.' Things got so bad that at one meeting, in spite of elaborate preparations, Kwaw recalls, 'there was no one to eat the food besides me and my son! ... We took courage in the promises of Scripture.' Kwaw cited the words of the prophet Habakkuk: 'For the revelation awaits an appointed time; it speaks of the end and will not prove false. Though it linger, wait for it; it will certainly come and will not delay' (Hab. 2:3).

Demos Shakarian recounted similar experiences at the start of the fellowship in the United States. Because Kwaw held the firm conviction that the fellowship in Ghana was being established under divine leadership, he assured himself that it would certainly succeed. 'One day my son told me he had had a dream that the FGBMFI had become a big organisation and that the Africa office had been moved to Ghana!' The following Christmas, Kwaw gave to selected friends as Christmas presents copies of Voice, the official mouthpiece of FGBMFI.

This strategy of literature distribution among lay businessmen worked, and in 1983 the fellowship took off. Nana Kwesi Amoakohene II, one of the recipients of the magazine who responded, became the national vice-president of FGBMFI in the 1990s. Kwabena Darko, Ghana's most celebrated poultry farmer and a former presidential candidate, also became involved. A surge of fresh leadership gave a second life to the movement. Today, FGBMFI boasts more than two hundred chapters with a registered membership comprising people from every profession in the land. The

Africa office has been moved to Ghana, and Kwabena Darko, who previously served as Africa president, now serves on the international executive board.[16]

Women's Aglow

The Women's Aglow fellowship began in 1967 with a luncheon meeting in Seattle. A FGBMFI meeting had just ended, but, as people dispersed to their homes, four Seattle women – Joyce Doefflein, Virginia Blankenship, Ruth Gothenquist and Rose Collins – stayed behind. They joined hands and prayed that God would raise a full gospel fellowship for women 'where those coming could meet to pray, have fellowship, and listen to the testimonies of other Christian women'. The women called a meeting in the summer of 1967, and by the autumn of that year they had been able to hold a breakfast meeting modelled on FGBMFI. By 1990, the global strength of Women's Aglow stood at 2,600 fellowships in over eighty-eight countries spanning six continents. Part of the mission statement of Women's Aglow reads: 'Women's Aglow Fellowship provides support, education, training, and ministry opportunities to help women worldwide discover their true identity in Jesus Christ through the power of the Holy Spirit.'[17] In line with the Pentecostal persuasion of Women's Aglow, Article Five of the organisation's statement of faith affirms: 'We believe in the baptism of the Holy Spirit with the evidence of speaking with tongues as the Spirit of God gives utterance; that all the gifts of the Spirit are valid and operative today and that the fruit of the Holy Spirit should be increasingly evident in a Christian's life.'[18]

The fellowship in Ghana began in 1983 in the midst of a severe economic depression and famine. The country's plight had been worsened by the repatriation from Nigeria of scores of Ghanaians who had travelled to that country at the height of its oil boom in search of better financial prospects. The hardship was so severe that people gave the name 'Rawlings's chain' (i.e., necklace) to the protruding collarbone resulting from malnutrition.[19] A group of Christian women started a prayer fellowship, meeting daily for three months to intercede for the nation, asking for God's intervention in Ghana's plight. During the time of this

---

[16] This account of FGBMFI is constructed largely on personal observation and on interviews with Joseph Kwaw.

[17] Women's Aglow Ghana, *Mighty Women of Valour of Our Generation*, 10th Anniversary Handbook, 25-27 November 1993, 18.

[18] Women's Aglow Ghana, *Mighty Women*, 23.

[19] The then flight lieutenant Jerry John Rawlings, who had taken power through a military coup in 1981, was the chairman of his ruling Provisional National Defence Council. He had promised the country better times, so this name was the Ghanaians' way of showing how his intervention in the affairs of state had made them worse off.

prayer vigil, American evangelists T.L. Osborn and Daisy Osborn, who were visiting West Africa, were in Nigeria. The group of women sent a letter requesting Daisy to 'come and encourage us in our plight'. Daisy Osborn responded to this call, and her visit culminated in a four-day crusade at the Kwame Nkrumah Conference Center in August 1983. One of the women reported:

> In our forlorn state, God made His presence felt among us. Many souls were won for Christ, and many were set free from diverse ailments. Indeed during those few days of the crusade, God worked mightily in our lives. At the end of the crusade, ten of us were invited to the castle by the Head of State ... to have an audience with him.[20]

As a result of the encouragement of Daisy Osborn, the women decided not to disband but to maintain the group as a women's fellowship, calling it the Christian Women's International Fellowship and choosing the dove as a symbol. Later that year, they discovered with excitement that there existed in the United States an international fellowship for women that was called Women's Aglow and had the same symbol. The name of the fellowship was subsequently changed to Women's Aglow [21] and through Christina Darko (the wife of Kwabena Darko) they sought and obtained affiliation with the international body.

Today, like FGBMFI, Women's Aglow in Ghana has more than two hundred chapters registered with the international office. The chapters are spread across the length and breadth of the country and are increasing in numbers through breakfasts and other meetings held for women. Women's Aglow also holds a monthly prayer service at Ghana's Independence Square in Accra to 'intercede' for the nation. This programme attracts upwards of 10,000 women at a time, and speakers come from both FGBMFI and within the Aglow movement itself.

The Impact of FGBMFI and Women's Aglow on Ghanaian Christianity and Society

The specific impact of FGBMFI and Women's Aglow on Christianity and social life in Ghana needs to be charted. My brief analysis will focus primarily on the influence of these Pentecostal lay organisations on Ghanaian Christianity and will allude only in cursory comments to their impact on the broader society. Seven areas of Pentecostal influence on Ghanaian church and social life can be identified.

---

[20] Women's Aglow Ghana, *Mighty Women*, 9.

[21] The change of name had been planned a little earlier because the women had discovered that their previous name clashed with that of the women's fellowship of the Redemption Hour Ministry.

1. Emphasis on Dreams and Visions

In keeping with Pentecostal spirituality, one might anticipate the very significant role that dreams and visions have played in the calling of people into the leadership of FGBMFI and Women's Aglow fellowships. Demos Shakarian claimed that his own calling and commitment to the fellowship came through these means of revelation, and the testimonies of other leaders across the globe are replete with stories of God's call to them through dreams and visions. The same Pentecostal claim is found in Ghana.

The reference to dreams and visions has to do first with a claim of divine revelation that comes through trance-visitations, as seen in the experiences of Isaiah the prophet and of Peter and Cornelius in the Acts of the Apostles. Secondly, dreams and visions can provide inspired insight and strong conviction about a course of action to which God is directing the recipient. In such cases, whatever the challenge, the endeavour can be undertaken because that is the direction in which the Spirit seems to be leading. Dreams and visions are very much a feature of Pentecostal Christianity, and they help explain why Pentecostals engage in giving and evangelism with such a strong sense of commitment and purpose.

Nana Kwesi Amoakohene II shared with me how, prior to his involvement in FGBMFI, he dreamed of having a party:

> I used to have good parties you know ... In this particular party, instead of the booze we were sharing the word of God. I shared it with my pastor ... and he said we should pray about it. It was after this that I had the Christmas present of the Voice magazine from Brother Joseph Kwaw. I told him about the dream and apparently he had been struggling with the vision and praying somebody would come with the resources ... and I had the resources so I said, 'Let's begin.'

For many of these people, the encounter with God is experienced as so dramatic, and the conversion experience is so powerful, that they lead to a deep spiritual yearning to do something for God in order to make up for lost years in the pursuit of worldly gain or pleasures. For others it may be the experience of healing or deliverance from some ailment or hopeless situation that creates the deep desire to put everything at the disposal of the God who 'makes all things possible'.

Every experience from that point in the life of the believer becomes subject, in Pentecostal parlance, to an interpretation of 'what God is saying', 'where God is leading' or 'what God wants me to do'. This interpretation is supported by an appeal to the stories in the gospels of two people we have already encountered, the Gerasene demoniac and the Samaritan woman who wanted everybody to 'come and see a man who told me everything I ever did'. Zacchaeus was even more forthright in his response: 'Look, Lord! Here and now I give half of my possessions to the poor, and if I have cheated anybody out of anything, I will pay back four times the amount' (Mk. 5:18, Jn. 4:29, Lk. 19:8).

2. An Expression of Unambiguous Christianity

The impact of the historic mission churches, as pioneers of the Christian evangel in West Africa, has been truly remarkable. For instance, in Ghana these churches not only penetrated the country with the gospel, but over the years they have also made their mark through the provision of schools, medical and other useful facilities upon which Christian bodies coming later continued to build. However, after more than a century and a half of their existence in Ghana, coupled with their links with colonial power and the advantages provided by their schools, hospitals and clinics, the mainline historic churches had begun to take their constituency for granted. Post-first-generation Christian young people[22] became 'Christians' not by conscious choice, but as a matter of course, by inheriting the tag 'Christian' from their parents and enrolling into church membership by producing infant baptismal certificates and learning by rote church creedal formulations to be recited during confirmation.

The result of this post-first-generation Christian phenomenon has been that the mainline churches have become packed with scores of people with 'a form of religion but who denied its power' (2 Tim. 3:5). The rate of nominalism is high, and, in a world that has become religiously pluralistic, 'Christians' have become the proselytising target of other faiths, 'reeds shaken by the wind' and blown to and fro by every wind of doctrine.

While not denying the Christian impact of the mainline churches, it must be pointed out that one of the greatest contributions of Pentecostalism to Christianity has been to make faith a matter of deliberate choice. In the particular cases of FGBMFI and Women's Aglow, every breakfast meeting concludes with an Altar Call, where people consciously 'hand over' the affairs of their lives to God and which is followed by months of teaching in the demands of Scripture on the lives of Christians. In the FGBMFI and Women's Aglow versions of Christianity, there are no ambiguities as to what it means to be a Christian, and the testimonies and lifestyles of others are there as confirmation of the truth of what is claimed.

3. Renewal in Mainline Churches

The impact of FGBMFI particularly on non-Pentecostal traditions has been significant. Because of the non-sectarian nature of the fellowship and its insistence on responsible church membership, churches in Ghana are experiencing a renewal that may soon make it difficult to distinguish

---

[22] The term *post-first-generation Christian* is used with reference to people identifying themselves with the Christian faith on the basis of having been baptised into it by their parents or guardians.

between what constitutes a Pentecostal church in the Ghanaian context and what does not. A number of lay members of non-Pentecostal churches have experienced through these fellowships not only conversion but also baptism of the Holy Spirit with its attendant manifestation of charismata. Charismatic phenomena are finding active expression in many otherwise orthodox churches. Don Basham's admonition to his fellow neo-Pentecostals seems to be enacted by many of those of Pentecostal experience in Ghana:

> Let your experience of the Holy Spirit draw you into deeper and more loving participation in the life of your church, not only with some charismatic group you may join, but in the church's worship and service as well. Other members having heard your testimony will be waiting – and rightly so – to see the fruit of your experience in your actions, and they will be far more impressed with what you share if the experience leads you into a deeper love for the church and its people, than if they see you deserting the church to start off on some tangent of your own.[23]

The respectability and acceptability that Pentecostalism today enjoys in Ghana's historic mission churches has been due partly to the high social profile of many of the people manifesting charismatic gifts and retaining their membership in these churches. In Ghana, high-profile members of FGBMFI include university vice-chancellors, parliamentarians, ministers of state, military service commanders, heads of churches and many captains of industry.

Wherever the gospel has been preached, it has often been easier for the socially marginalised to respond than it has been for the well-to-do. Through the New Testament we discover that whenever socially prominent persons received the gospel, it was news: Nicodemus, Zacchaeus, Paul and Cornelius all made news when they responded to the gospel. The experiences of prominent people in Ghana, which compare favourably with the conversion experiences of these biblical characters, defy the theory that in Africa Pentecostal Christianity touches only the lower classes and the socially marginalised.

4. A Leadership Resource for Churches

The membership of FGBMFI and Women's Aglow provides a steady supply of people willing to serve as leaders of churches. Many have also entered the ministry of historic mission churches. Godfried Bamfo, the first president of the Accra airport chapter of the fellowship, is now serving as a Presbyterian minister; the immediate past president of the Accra premier chapter, Maxwell Aryee, a medical doctor, is a Methodist minister, and

[23] Cited in Richard Quebedeaux, *The New Charismatics II* (San Francisco: Harper & Row, 1983), 145.

Winfred H. Y. Ametefe, a former principal of the renowned Methodist teacher training institution Wesley College, in Kumasi, and now a bishop, is an ardent member of the fellowship.

The increasing number of adherents and leaders of transdenominational charismatic fellowships seeking serious theological education in Ghana is noteworthy. Dr. E.K. Opuni, a scientist with a prosperous pest control agency in Accra who served as the president of the airport chapter of FGBMFI from 1992 to 1994, completed a two-year course leading to a diploma in theology at the Trinity Theological Seminary, Legon, Accra, in 1995. Evangelist Hannah Arthur, a former national vice-president of Aglow, and Christina Darko, the founder of the Kumasi chapter, are both products of the Christian Service College.[24] Although they have taken theological courses from historic mission church institutions, these Pentecostals have not sought to enter the ordained ministry.

Countless others serve either as lay leaders or as pastors of independent charismatic churches in Ghana. Unlike traditional African religion, where women serve prominently as priestesses and cultic functionaries, and the AICs in which a significant number of women serve as prophetesses, women's roles in the Christian church have been generally marginalised for a long time. Partly as a result of the ministry of the Women's Aglow fellowship, many women have been catapulted into prominence as leaders in churches, where they manifest charismatic gifts and play significant roles in various Christian ministries.

The reception of avowed Pentecostals into the leadership of non-Pentecostal churches is significant because, until about a decade ago, persons of Pentecostal persuasion entered such positions with difficulty due to misgivings about their theological competence. This suspicion of persons manifesting spiritual gifts accounts in part for the many people who, after their experience of the Holy Spirit, seceded from the church to start an independent church.

5. Models of Ecumenical Fellowship

By virtue of their non-sectarian nature and emphasis on responsible church membership, FGBMFI and Women's Aglow effectively demolish denominational inhibitions. Those who experience Holy Spirit baptism claim the experience is so dynamic that it produces an all-embracing religious enthusiasm and renders denominational and theological divisions

[24] Trinity Theological Seminary and Christian Service College (now a University) are the two leading Protestant theological colleges in Ghana that combine pastoral training with university-level academic studies in theology. Trinity College is jointly owned by the Protestant mainline churches in Ghana, and Christian Service College is privately owned and also ecumenical.

irrelevant, for they are inhibitors to Christian fellowship.[25] David du Plessis calls FGBMFI truly ecumenical in that it has been bridging the gap between Pentecostals and 'mainliners', a claim equally true of Aglow.[26]

In the FGBMFI and Women's Aglow fellowships, we encounter a modern version of the kind of relationship that characterised the early beneficiaries of the outpouring of the Holy Spirit: 'They devoted themselves to the apostles' teaching and to the fellowship, to the breaking of bread and to prayer ... Every day they continued to meet together ... praising God and enjoying the favour of the people. And the Lord added to their number daily those who were being saved' (Acts 4:42-47).

In the application of this biblical model, the FGBMFI and Women's Aglow fellowships have not sought to achieve renewal at the expense of church affiliation. On the contrary, they have enriched the overall spiritual life of the church and in that sense have even become a source of unity rather than fragmentation. At the global level, this ecumenical spirit was championed by David du Plessis who, Charles Nienkirchen has recorded, 'though defrocked by the Assemblies of God in 1962 because of his ecumenical activities, especially his involvement with the World Council of Churches and Roman Catholics, nonetheless persisted in disseminating his vision of a charismatically renewed Church within all Christian traditions'.[27] Later, du Plessis was reinstated to the ministerial ranks of the Assemblies of God, USA.

It has become the tradition at the meetings of the FGBMFI and Women's Aglow fellowships to welcome people by denomination, and it is impressive to see groups of people stand up to applaud the mention of their respective denominations: Methodists, Presbyterians, Seventh-Day Adventists and different shades of Pentecostals. Many of these people cannot appear at the communion table together in their churches because of ecclesiastical barriers, but at FGBMFI and Aglow meetings they eat and drink and above all 'speak in tongues together'. In effect, 'names and sects and parties fall' as these believers participate in the common experience of the Holy Spirit.

6. Instruments of Christian Growth and Expansion

One of the key features of Pentecostal Christianity has been the deep sense of commitment that adherents show in sharing their faith with others. Glossolalia may mark out the Pentecostals from traditional Christians, but

[25] Quebedeaux, *New Charismatics*, 9.

[26] Quebedeaux, *New Charismatics*, 120.

[27] Charles Nienkirchen, 'Conflicting Visions of the Past: The Prophetic Use of History in the Early American Pentecostal-Charismatic Movements', in Karla Poewe (ed.), *Charismatic Christianity as a Global Culture* (Columbia: University of South Carolina Press, 1994), 129-30.

evangelism is the heartbeat of the movement. The gifts of the Holy Spirit are given as equipment for evangelism and not as ends in themselves: Jesus promised the disciples: 'But you will receive power when the Holy Spirit comes on you; and you will be my witnesses' (Acts 1:8). In the preface to Fire from Heaven, Harvey Cox pays tribute to the Pentecostal spirit to evangelise at the least opportunity:

> First, I rarely had any trouble getting Pentecostals to tell me about their faith. They talk about it at the slightest provocation. If there was a problem sometimes it was how I could delicately end the conversation. Also I never once felt any snubbing or suspicion. Wherever I went Pentecostal people welcomed me to their churches and invariably invited me to come back. Part of what made my work so easy and enjoyable was that Pentecostals tend to be very happy about their faith and they want you to share their happiness.[28]

For the FGBMFI and Women's Aglow fellowships, evangelism is their reason for existence. The breakfast meetings are occasions for inviting friends, fellow church members, neighbours and business associates to listen to the testimonies of others in the hope that the testimonies will lead the guests to a positive response to the gospel. More often than not, people will pay for breakfast for their guests, so that there is no chance of cost being used as an excuse for not attending. In Ghana, there have been cases of individual members sponsoring whole breakfast meetings, especially of newly established chapters.

A number of chapters in some regions in Ghana started through the initiative of early members who had business interests outside Accra. In the 1980s, for instance, Nana Kwesi Amoakohene II owned supermarkets in many towns in Ghana. As he indicates, 'anywhere my business took me I established a core group with whom I shared the vision and with time they took off'. Other members testify that Amoakohene personally invested a fortune in the activities of the fellowship, and he confirmed this in my personal interview with him, saying, 'If I would become poor for God's kingdom to increase, I will still find fulfilment.'

The proprietor of a very popular discotheque, Stereo Spot at Teshie-Nungua in Accra, had gone bankrupt because, having turned to Christ through the ministry of FGBMFI, he had quit that business and had not been able to find an alternative use for the building. The property was going to be sold to defray the mortgage. According to Amoakohene, 'I could not stand the idea that a place that had ruined the lives of so many young people and almost did mine (because I used to drink there), may be turned into a discotheque again. I raised the money, we paid off the mortgage, and stopped the action.' Stereo Spot, renamed 'Victory Centre',

[28] Harvey Cox, *Fire from Heaven: The Rise of Pentecostal Spirituality and the Reshaping of Religion in the Twenty-First Century* (Reading, MA: Addison-Wesley, 1995), xvii.

has become the worship centre for a branch of one of Ghana's burgeoning independent neo-Pentecostal churches, Victory Bible Church, and the regular meeting place of the Teshie-Nungua chapter of FGBMFI.[29]

Each chapter has an elaborate outreach programme for localities or towns and villages within easy reach. Within a ten-year period, the Accra airport chapter of FGBMFI, itself an outgrowth of the premier chapter, established chapters at Suhum in the Eastern region and at Anloga in the Volta region, and also one chapter at the University of Ghana at Legon in Accra and chapters in Madina, Adabraka, Tesano, Achimota, Teshie-Nungua – all suburbs of Accra – as well as gateway and city chapters, both in Tema.[30]

The outreach zeal of FGBMFI in Ghana has led it to establish branches in the neighbouring countries of Ivory Coast, Burkina Faso and Sierra Leone, where a member of the fellowship bore the entire expense of the outreach team, including the inaugural breakfast meeting. In addition, branches have been started for Ghanaian immigrants in London, Italy and Israel, and Joseph Kwaw opened a branch for immigrants in New York City in July 1996.[31] The impetus for the Ghanaian versions in these countries was provided by former members of the fellowship in Ghana who wanted to serve as 'missionaries to their own people' elsewhere. The Ghanaian international influence has been so remarkable that, as of August 1996, the presidents of the FGBMFI organisations in Gambia, Guinea, Israel, Italy and Senegal were all Ghanaians.[32]

The Women's Aglow fellowship runs similar outreach programmes to neighbouring towns and villages where, in addition to the spread of the gospel, they also provide relief for needy persons. The Accra premier chapter of Women's Aglow adopted a female ward at the Accra psychiatric hospital in 1986; in addition, it had an ongoing ministry to the female inmates of a number of Ghana's prisons and reached out to the Liberian refugee camp located at Buduburam, about thirty kilometres from Accra.[33]

As non-denominational lay charismatic fellowships, FGBMFI and Women's Aglow have been instrumental in populating Ghana's churches. Their policy of responsible church membership ensures that those who come to faith through their ministry not only worship, but also put both their human and material resources at God's disposal through their respective churches. Pastors regularly testify that members of these renewal

[29] Nana Kwesi Amoakohene II, interviewed by author.

[30] FGBMFI Ghana Airport Chapter, *Recapturing the Vision*, 10th Anniversary Handbook, 28 August-2 September 1995.

[31] Joseph Kwaw, personal communication.

[32] FGBMFI Ghana, *Watch and Pray*, 10th National Convention Handbook.

[33] Women's Aglow Ghana, *Mighty Women*, 185.

fellowships are not only the most practical in their Christianity, but also the biggest givers in their churches.

It must be admitted that in some cases the profession of commitment, in particular to historic mission churches, has not been carried out in practice. After going through the Pentecostal experience, some members adopt such a hypercritical attitude towards their original mainline churches that they withdraw their membership into Pentecostal ones. This attitude raises suspicions about the movement from mainline church leadership and to some extent denies the role that mainline churches have to play in the evangelisation of the nation.

Nevertheless, the praxis in the Christian living of fellowships like FGBMFI and Women's Aglow is evident in the seriousness with which members pray, study the Bible, support spiritual piety with ethical rigor and perform Christian duties like giving to others in expectation of divine multiplier effects. This praxis is often evident in the testimonies of success stories at fellowship meetings since people 'came to Christ'. This success orientation needs to be balanced to account for the setbacks in life that the Bible talks so much about, in order to avoid creating the impression that all difficulties abate once people become believers.

7. Impact on Social Life

FGBMFI, in particular, and Women's Aglow, to a more limited extent, have been criticised as being elitist in membership. To be sure, these fellowships started with the intent to evangelise a particular social class, that is, the middle and upper-middle socio-economic levels of society, but in Ghana at least, it is to the credit of the fellowships that, in spite of their defined targets, their doors are open to members of all classes of society. Be that as it may, the people whom the fellowships target are less likely to be in church than most individuals, and, if they do attend, for many of them it is for social respectability rather than as a genuine response to the call for a new relationship with God. If these people, whose circumstances in life make them managers of public institutions and finances, are able to bring their Christian principles to bear upon what they do, Ghana may be spared the large-scale corruption that has ruined many developing nations.

Friends and workmates testify to the impact of many of these fellowships. There are examples of doctors and nurses who pray with patients before the day begins, and early morning devotions in workplaces are now common occurrences. These activities by themselves may not be indicative of anything socially transformative, but once people begin to demonstrate their Christian beliefs in this way, they tend to become more conscious of the expectations of those workers closest to them as they go about official duties. There are also reports of wives pleading with members of FGBMFI to recruit their husbands because they had observed how a neighbour's husband had become more responsible after joining the fellowship.[34] Examples equally abound of the influence on their husbands of Pentecostal women who have become betters wives and mothers as a result of their conversion experiences.

Conclusion

The influence of FGBMFI, Women's Aglow and other charismatic renewal groups within Pentecostal and non-Pentecostal churches on Christianity in Ghana is significant. The great increase in the membership of Pentecostal fellowships, reflected in the growing number of chapters across the country, can be interpreted as a confirmation of what Arnold Bittlinger identifies as a threefold longing on the part of many Christians: the longing for a truly spiritual life, in reaction to an over-cerebral Christianity; the longing for fellowship in which the gifts of the individual are taken seriously, in reaction to a Christianity that reduced church members to minor functionaries; the longing for strength, in reaction to a Christianity that denied or explained away the miracles of the New Testament.[35]

Renewal seems to be sweeping across many non-Pentecostal churches in Ghana, partly because of the presence of individuals of Pentecostal persuasion in those churches. Worship has become more spontaneous and informal. There are constant advertisements for revival, healing and deliverance services, often led by lay members of these churches affiliated to the neo-Pentecostal fellowships. Even the Pentecostal churches have been affected to the extent that, in the Ghanaian context, the distinction between classical Pentecostals and the neo-Pentecostal churches is becoming virtually irrelevant.

The pressure on ordained ministers to respond is great. In the African context, religion is action-oriented, and people will seek help from whomever can produce results. It is not surprising that some ministers have been antagonistic towards individuals and groups of Pentecostals within their churches. Their parishioners are seeking 'pastoral' assistance from laypeople who are manifesting spiritual gifts and proving their worth as counsellors. In order to cope with the challenge of Pentecostalism, a number of churches have tried to introduce elements of the movement into their worship. This 'renovation' approach misses the point. The success of neo-Pentecostal fellowships like FGBMFI and Women's Aglow does not lie simply in spontaneity of worship or speaking in tongues. Fundamental to each movement's success is the emphasis placed on the personal experiences of conversion and of the empowerment of the Holy Spirit. Through these experiences, people without robes or theological education

---

[34] Nana Kwesi Amoakohene II, personal communication.

[35] Arnold Bittlinger (ed.), *The Church is Charismatic: The World Council of Churches and the Charismatic Renewal* (Geneva: World Council of Churches, 1981), 9.

become empowered to live the Christian life with conviction and to serve as missionaries to others.

As Douglas Petersen notes, Pentecostals 'are best defined as individuals who have strong convictions about participating in the subjective Christian experiences that are universally acceptable to, but often de-emphasised within, other Christian communions'.[36] In the Pentecostal movement, the individual is made part of a 'comprehensive redemptive programme' to which his or her own empowerment is expected to make a contribution.[37] One is not admitted to membership simply through the sacraments; rather, for Pentecostals, a personal and conscious decision enables an individual to share in the experience, which only the Father can bestow.

The empowerment of individuals for mission through the experience of the Holy Spirit demystifies the vocational pastoral ministry, particularly that found within mainline church missions. With the institutionalisation of Christianity, the awe and respect normally accorded to traditional priests and priestesses as mouthpieces of deities was extended to the clergy of the Christian church as representatives of God. This deferential regard for clergy no longer comes as a matter of course. Ministers must now be seen to be 'performing' the works of the ministry, because many churches have an abundance of Spirit-filled laypersons who can function effectively in ministry. In other words, pastors or ministers are no longer regarded as having exclusive access to 'deity'.

This situation explains in part the gradual eclipse of the once popular and vibrant African Independent Churches. For those churches, prophet-healers have always been the custodians of the spiritual power, and the church members, as clients, seek the Spirit's intervention in their difficulties through the prophet-healers. With the increasing number of laypersons manifesting similar charisma, those who operate such services are either losing 'customers' or are being viewed with suspicion and gradually marginalised.

In the Ghanaian context, the use of testimony underscores the point that mission is not theoretical. Instead, people are encouraged and enabled to experience the power of the Holy Spirit as deliverance from sin, illnesses, demons, principalities and powers, so that they too, like the Samaritan woman, may be able to tell others about God who revealed their past in order to save them. They, like the man delivered from demons, will go home to family and friends 'and tell them how much the Lord has done for you, and how he has had mercy on you'.

---

[36] Douglas Petersen, *Not by Might Nor by Power: A Pentecostal Theology of Social Concern in Latin America* (Oxford: Regnum Books International, 1996), 6.
[37] Petersen, *Not by Might*, 7.

Chapter 9
Holiness Unto the Lord: Ghana's Church of Pentecost

Most of the recent writing and research on Christianity in Africa, especially within the last decade, has focused on contemporary Pentecostalism or the new Charismatic Ministries. But the relevance and influence of Pentecostalism as a contemporary religious form in Africa goes beyond the newcomers. There are quite a number of indigenous classical Pentecostal denominations in Africa that are also doing extremely well. Historically, most of these, such as the Church of Pentecost (CoP), headquartered in Ghana, have their roots in the Apostolic Church tradition. The Christ Apostolic Church in Ghana and Nigeria and the Church of Pentecost are only two of the most important indigenous classical Pentecostal denominations in sub-Saharan Africa. The significance of Pentecostalism in Africa today cannot be properly appreciated without a discussion of the growth and influence of these older and more firmly established churches.

We have noted that Pentecostalism has become the fastest growing stream of Christianity in the world today. In line with this development, Harvey Cox writes that the growth of Pentecostalism worldwide 'holds within it a host of significant clues to the meaning of the general global spiritual resurgence we are now witnessing'.[1] I interpret the expression 'significant clues' in terms of those internal factors accounting for the growth and popularity of the global Pentecostal movement. In Africa, these factors tend to be of a religious nature. This chapter attempts to isolate and discuss some of the salient religious factors accounting for Pentecostal growth as manifested in the ministry of the Church of Pentecost. My aim is to illustrate the importance of religious experience to the growth of Pentecostalism as a distinctive stream of Christianity.

Spirit in Pentecostalism

The essential core of Pentecostal/charismatic revivals is the experience of the Holy Spirit in salvific transformation, radical discipleship and

---

[1] Harvey Cox, 'Foreword', in Allan H. Anderson and Walter J. Hollenweger (eds.), *Pentecostals after a Century: Global Perspectives on a Movement in Transition* (Sheffield: Sheffield Academic Press, 1999), 8.

manifestations of acts of power that demonstrate the presence of God among his people. In this book, I have consistently contended that revitalisation movements have to be credited for reminding historic mission denominations that the non-rational dimensions of religion, in this case the experience of the Spirit, are important to a relevant and dynamic church life. It needs to be emphasised that the experience of the Spirit as the source of life or renewal, it, remains a non-negotiable element of Christian mission. This truth about Pentecostalism, according to J.D.G. Dunn, 'is ignored to our common peril and impoverishment'.[2]

Religious History

Emmanuel Kingsley Larbi's Pentecostalism: The Eddies of Ghanaian Christianity has documented the history of the Church of Pentecost from its origins in a local faith-healing movement led by Ghanaian Pentecostalist Peter Anim (1890–1984).[3] The CoP is one of three apostolic churches to emerge from the initiative of Anim and his subsequent collaboration with the British Apostolic missionaries James and Sophia McKeown in the early 1930s. James McKeown and Anim initially worked together, but subsequently split up into separate apostolic churches, mainly over McKeown's reluctance to observe a strict faith-healing stance adopted by the African movement headed by Anim. In August 1962, after a series of intractable conflicts and court cases, a faction led by the McKeowns finally adopted the name the Church of Pentecost.

The CoP is listed as the single largest Protestant denomination in Ghana in terms of church attendance, next in size only to the Roman Catholic Church.[4] In 1998, the CoP claimed a membership of 496,000 adults, with 415 new assemblies formed between 1989 and 1998.[5] The 1999 Annual Report of the CoP General Council claimed a membership of 863,401 people located within 7,049 assemblies in Ghana alone. This report also claimed that the CoP existed in 43 countries spanning all the continents. At the end of 2001, there were CoP congregations in most major western European cities and in about twenty of the fifty states that make up the

[2] James D.G. Dunn, 'A Protestant Response' (to Juan Sepúlveda, 'Born Again: Baptism and the Spirit'), in Jürgen Moltmann and Karl-Josef Kuschel (eds.), *Pentecostal Movements as an Ecumenical Challenge, Concilium*, 3 (1996), 110.

[3] E. Kingsley Larbi, *Pentecostalism: The Eddies of Ghanaian Christianity* (Accra: Centre for Pentecostal and Charismatic Studies, 2001).

[4] Ghana National Evangelism Committee, *Facing the Unfinished Task of the Church in Ghana: National Survey Update 1993* (Accra: Ghana Evangelism Committee, 1993).

[5] Church of Pentecost, 'Reports for the 7th Session of the Extraordinary Council Meetings' (Koforidua, Ghana, 22-26 April 1999); Other figures from 2001, 2011 documents.

United States.[6] In 2011 the CoP claimed a total adult membership of 1,223,959 in Ghana spread over 12,238 assemblies and a worldwide membership of 1,431,364 spread over 15,805 assemblies. Internally generated religious statistics can be notoriously deceptive, so they have to be taken cautiously. However, popular opinion in Ghana supports the general opinion that even without the benefit of statistical data, it is clear from physical evidence that the CoP has grown as a classical Pentecostal denomination based in Ghana. Although it identifies with the classical Pentecostal tradition worldwide, the CoP – wherever in the world it is established – has acquired a unique indigenous character that marks it out as different in outlook from, say, the Assemblies of God, whose American imprint after almost a century of existence in Ghana is still quite visible.

Conversion Growth

Pentecostal spirituality emphasises the need for the Born-again experience through personal acceptance of Jesus Christ as Lord and Saviour. The constitution of the Church of Pentecost is unambiguous about what it means to be a member. First, you must have come to 'personal salvation through a conscious decision to give your life to Christ'. Personal witnessing in which members share their faith with others is a common feature of the life of the CoP. Those who accept Christ are integrated into the Church through baptism by immersion. Salvation, it is taught, must be a personal decision and therefore the CoP does not practise infant baptism. For Pentecostals generally, the teaching that Jesus Christ is Saviour is the entry point into the movement, and so preaching often requires people to take this step in response to Altar Calls at which the 'Sinner's Prayer of Repentance' is repeated.

Commitment and participation can be engendered through knowledge of what it means to 'belong' to a specific religious movement. In A Giant in Ghana, a popular mission history on the formation and development of the CoP, Christine Leonard makes the following observation on the relationship between personal decision-making and the growth and success of the CoP: 'The main reason the Church has grown is that its people love Jesus – they have been set on fire for Him. It shows in their worship and in their lives. The Church has never allowed compromise – they treat sin and reversion to cultic religious practices as seriously as each one takes his responsibility to Jesus Christ and the Church.'[7] Richard Foli identifies

---

6 Michael Ntumy, 'An Assessment of the Growth and Development of the Church of Pentecost with Particular Reference to its Impact on the Religious Life of Ghana'. Unpublished MTh Thesis, Regents Theological College, UK, June 2000, 5.

7 Christine Leonard, *A Giant in Ghana: 3,000 Churches in 50 Years. The Story of James McKeown and the Church of Pentecost* (Chichester: New Wine Press, 1989).

'conversion growth', that is, church growth and discipleship through personal conversion, as the most sustainable kind of growth.[8] As far as the CoP is concerned, one of the most enduring legacies in its heritage has been the emphasis James McKeown placed on personal experience in the process of incorporation into the church. This heritage has enabled the CoP to maintain its missionary focus in spite of its chequered history.

Its focus on the fundamentals of mission has helped the CoP to avoid the over-clericalism and nominalism associated with the Christianity of the older mission denominations, whose main missionary instruments were their socio-economic services to society. 'In much of Africa', Maia Green observes of the Christianity of the older churches, 'the widespread adoption of Christian religious affiliation was a direct consequence of mission over-schooling ... Often, Christian religious affiliation as an aspect of a person's identity is explicitly concerned with the presentation of an exterior state, not an internal one.'[9] So, among the Pogoro people of Southern Tanzania, Green notes, conversion to Christianity was not the result of the aggregate choices of individuals attracted by the 'message' of Christianity, but a direct consequence of colonial education policy.[10]

Baptism was the first stage of becoming 'officially' Christian for Pogoro Catholics, and similarly, many have been baptised in Ghanaian churches without knowing what it actually means to be a Christian. Parents scarcely know the significance of baptism and are therefore not in a position to give their children any education in accordance with it. Confirmation has all but lost its value as a means of personally affirming a faith that was affirmed on one's behalf as an infant in baptism. For many candidates the confirmation rite simply replaced the puberty rite, frowned upon as backward by city dwellers and those with some education. Not only do those who feel that they can get on in life without passing through the portals of the church stay away, but many of those who affiliated with the church became only nominal Christians.

Pentecostals are thus right to recognise that salvation is fundamentally about coming into an existential relationship with God in and through his Son Jesus Christ. There are two recognisable features of Pentecostal spirituality, as identified in the writings of Juan Sepúlveda: first, the rejection of a religiosity centred on the 'objectivity of dogma' (in which faith consists of formal, conscious and rational acceptance of determined beliefs or doctrines), in preference for a religiosity that gives primacy to the subjective experience of God (in which faith is a response to a kind of

---

[8] Richard Foli, *Church Growth in Ghana* (Accra: Methodist Book Depot, 2001), 11.

[9] Maia Green, 'Why Christianity is the "Religion of Business": Perceptions of the Church among Pogoro Catholics in Southern Tanzania', *Journal of Religion in Africa*, 25, no. 1 (1995), 26.

[10] Green, '"Religion of Business"', 29.

possession of one's being by the divine) Second, direct access to God available to poor, simple people, with a relationship that can be communicated in the language of feeling and the indigenous culture.[11]

Baptism of the Holy Spirit

Classical Pentecostalism contains a sense of urgency to warn the church and witness to the nations about the Second Coming of Christ. The church as the Bride must be prepared for the Bridegroom, and lost souls are to be brought into the Kingdom through the gospel. Thus the emphasis on judgement, that seems to have fallen off the theological agenda of the contemporary Pentecostals, remains a central aspect of the ministry of classical Pentecostal denominations such as the CoP. Members are expected to identify with the CoP 'doctrine of subsequence' by seeking the baptism of the Holy Spirit with the initial evidence of speaking in tongues.[12] Those who have experienced this gift of glossolalia testify proudly to the profound sense of transformation that it brings and the subsequent intense and deep relationship that it helps one to have with the Lord Jesus Christ. Those with the gift of tongues testify to a new sense of empowerment to pray, and to a confidence to intercede for others. In keeping with its classical Pentecostal orientation, the CoP holds that:

> All believers in Jesus Christ are entitled to receive, and should earnestly seek the Baptism of the Holy Ghost and fire according to the command of our Lord. This is the normal experience of the early church. With this experience comes power to preach and bestowment of the gifts of the Spirit. The believer is filled with the Holy Spirit and there is a physical sign of 'speaking in other tongues as the Spirit of God gives utterance'. This is accompanied by a burning desire and supernatural power to witness to others about God's salvation and power.[13]

William and Robert Menzies, in their remarkable work Spirit and Power, list 'strong faith' as a central feature of Pentecostal spirituality: 'Overwhelmed by the sense of God's immediate presence among them, Pentecostals were quick to believe in the fact of divine intervention in the affairs of this life. They prayed for the sick, expecting God to deliver the afflicted from suffering.'[14] Christian mission means 'to recognize what the Creator-Redeemer is doing in his world and allowing him to engage you in

---

[11] Juan Sepúlveda, 'Reflections on the Pentecostal Contribution to the Mission of the Church in Latin America', *Journal of Pentecostal Theology*, 1 (1992), 95.

[12] Ntumy, 'Growth and Development', 31.

[13] Larbi, *Pentecostalism*, 278.

[14] William W. Menzies and Robert P. Menzies, *Spirit and Power: Foundations of Pentecostal Experience* (Grand Rapids, MI: Zondervan, 2000), 23.

the enterprise'.[15] Whether it is used with reference to the Church as the 'body of Christ' or to the individual Christian, mission begins with an experiential encounter with God. So, from its origins, Pentecostal Christianity understood its experience, particularly the experience of the baptism of the Holy Spirit, as an empowerment for mission.

Ministry and Transformation

The processes that are part of joining the ordained ministry of the traditional churches do nothing to help the high rate of nominalism associated with western mission-related Christianity. The standards, unlike those of the CoP, are mainly academic, and many of those who enter ministry may do so in pursuance of academic and professional careers, rather than vocations in which they serve in a ministry meant to proclaim salvation in Christ. For service in God's church, the CoP does not consider lack of formal education a hindrance, believing that where the Holy Spirit is at work, he is the Great Teacher who can instruct, and that he can use even illiterates once they have come to a personal knowledge of Christ and received the baptism of the Spirit.[16] In its ministry in Ghana and abroad, the CoP has not relied on theologically sophisticated clergy and lay leaders. Pastors are very often simple and ordinary Christians who have received a calling into ministry and are trained on the job. The CoP considers theological knowledge important, but over the years such learning has not been allowed to determine the choice of people for ministry.

In the missionary enterprise of the Lord Jesus Christ, those he used were at some point referred to as 'unschooled ordinary men' whose only credential for mission was the fact that 'they had been with Jesus' (Acts 4:13). The calling of the church is first and foremost towards this missionary end. McKeown cited 'waiting on God', and not education, as the means of growth for the CoP: 'if we follow education, we will get what education gives … We have to seek the Lord and wait on Him – this is the secret of the Church's success and expansion.'[17] Experience is not everything … but clericalism that sacrifices vital experience for ecclesiastical authority and theological propriety is one of the main impediments to mission and renewal in the body of Christ.

---

[15] This is a slight modification of a definition by John V. Taylor who writes that 'mission … means to recognise what the Creator-Redeemer is doing and try to do it with him'. See Taylor, *The Go-Between God: The Holy Spirit and the Christian Mission* (London: SCM, 1972), 37.

[16] Ntumy, 'Growth and Development', 33.

[17] Leonard, *Giant*, 45-46.

Commitment of Membership

My observation is that the CoP has been successful on account of the very high degree of commitment to the church demonstrated by ordinary members. Gerlach and Hine identify such commitment engendered by religious experience as a crucial factor accounting for the growth of Pentecostalism. Pentecostals themselves, as Gerlach and Hine point out, 'verbalize one of the rewards of the Baptism [of the Holy Spirit] experience as the power to witness effectively.' [18] So, in the CoP the most obvious reason for growth, according to Leonard, 'is that their top priority has always been evangelism. James McKeown saw to that. Members consider witnessing faith in Jesus Christ as a personal responsibility, and not just the responsibility of the leaders.'[19]

Personal conversion and Spirit baptism, according to the study by Gerlach and Hine, are 'bridge-burning' and 'power-generating' acts that constitute for Pentecostals 'a highly motivating religious experience' that generates or sustains religious commitment.[20] On the relationship between religious experience and participation, they conclude as follows: 'Effective participation in a movement involves just such an act that sets the believer apart in some way from the larger social context, cuts him off from past associations, identifies him with other participants in the movement, and provides high motivation for changed behavior.'[21]

Members of the CoP are discouraged from joining or associating with other religious organisations, even Christian associations. On the face of it, such pressure might seem typically sectarian, but it has helped the CoP to hold on to its own. The older mission churches have had problems with 'split allegiance': people may belong to the church and simultaneously register as patrons of fraternities such as lodges, pseudo-religious welfare associations and other problem-solving religious centres that are common in African religiosity. Such split allegiance is virtually non-existent within the CoP, which is thus able to command the total allegiance of its members. Because of the emphasis on the sufficiency of the fellowship provided by the Church, members are able to detach themselves not only from past patterns of behaviour, but also from other associations and welfare groups.

From such total allegiance, the Church gains commitment to its principal mission through church attendance and effective participation in evangelistic conventions and prayer meetings. The CoP also grows because

[18] Luther P. Gerlach and Virginia H. Hine, 'Five Factors Crucial to the Growth and Spread of a Modern Religious Movement', *Journal for the Scientific Study of Religion*, 7, no. 1 (1968), 32.

[19] Leonard, *Giant*, 7.

[20] Gerlach and Hine, 'Five Factors', 32.

[21] Gerlach and Hine, 'Five Factors', 32.

its members are committed to giving.[22] Finances set aside for religious purposes are not split with rival religious organisations. The CoP is also a praying church, and prayer makes things happen. It is a very common sight at CoP Assemblies to find scores of members gathered for mass praying. In this praying culture, the CoP stands in continuity with the early Pentecostals, who 'believed ardently in intercessory prayer. They taught the principle of "praying through", of continuing a vigil before the Lord until they had the impression that the prayer was being answered.'[23]

Testimonies as Witness

The testimonies of life-changing encounters with God that participants are prepared to share account in large measure for the success of Pentecostalism in Christian mission. Cox recounts his experience with Pentecostals even as a researcher: 'I rarely had any trouble getting Pentecostals to tell me about their faith. They talk about it at the slightest provocation ... Part of what made my work so easy and enjoyable is that Pentecostals tend to be very happy about their faith and they want you to share that happiness.'[24]

On the importance of the global Pentecostal resurgence for mission, Taylor observes,

> Anyone who has a concern for the mission of the church to the six continents must come to terms with the fact that the vast majority of mankind is not going to find God through such a cerebral religion as the Christianity it has so far encountered. That is what the revival movements, the Zionist sects, the whole Pentecostal third section of the world-wide church, are saying to us.[25]

The need for an active Christian witness and mission led the CoP to set up a very strong and dynamic Witness Movement very early in its work. This movement, as the name suggests, is the department of the church dedicated to evangelical outreach. One of the weaknesses of independent church Christianity in Africa is that church activity and programmes tend to centre too closely on the charismatic personality of the founders. In the older independent church movements in particular, the ability of the prophet to pray for healing, to prophesy or to provide some ritual means for solving problems of barrenness, sterility, failing businesses and the like, tended to be what attracted people to those churches. The AICs thus had

---

22 Leonard, *Giant*, 8.

23 Menzies, *Spirit and Power*, 23.

24 Harvey Cox, *Fire From Heaven: The Rise of Pentecostal Spirituality and the Reshaping of Religion in the Twenty-First Century* (Reading, MA: Addison-Wesley Publishing Company, 1995), xvii.

25 Taylor, *Go-Between God*, 221.

large numbers of floating adult members, mainly women, who moved from prophet to prophet looking for God's intervention in their lives. Children and youth ministries from which sustained membership could be drawn were largely absent from these churches. The Charismatic Ministries also tend to be urban-centred. Their emphasis on prosperity and success and on a person's enhanced physical appearance and dress as signs of God's blessing, has made it difficult for them to operate in rural areas. The poverty, economic stagnation and low literacy levels in those areas simply cannot accommodate a charismatic Christianity that requires a large budget to sustain the flamboyant and expensive lifestyles of pastors and their churches.

Inter-Generational Ministries

The CoP, by contrast, has very rigorous evangelistic programmes in both urban and rural Ghana. The CoP Witness Movement, the Pentecost Students' Association (PENSA) and the Women's Fellowship are all evangelistic groups that target specific constituencies for mission. The 'Bombing Group' emerged from the Witness Movement. The name was taken from bombing raids carried out by allied forces in World War II to signify that their own prayer 'bombed' the devil and his agents. So spiritual warfare, a ministry that is very much cherished in African Christianity because of the precarious world in which people live, is part of the missionary methods of the CoP.

Andrew Walls argues that the church as a movement of the Kingdom calls people to repentance and to alertness to the presence of Christ within. But the presence of the church, the first test of Christian expansion, does not itself guarantee 'the continuing influence of Christ'. To guarantee this continuing influence through the church, Walls points out that 'the signs of the Kingdom' must also be present. These signs, as evidenced through the ministry of Jesus, include the triumph of God over principalities, powers and demonic influences.[26] That the power of Christ is effective in healing and delivering is one of the greatest lessons that Pentecostal Christianity teaches the church of Christ today, in its attempt at continuing his mission in the world.

Healing Camps

An important factor in the growth of the CoP is that, in keeping with its Pentecostal ethos, it takes seriously the manifestations of the Spirit. Pentecostals 'believe in the fact of divine intervention in the affairs of this

[26] Andrew F. Walls, *The Cross-Cultural Process in Christian History* (Maryknoll, NY: Orbis Books, 2002), 15.

life'.[27] In the African context, solutions to problems are often sought within the religious or theological realm. The normalisation of healing as an essential part of Christianity constitutes the single greatest attraction for the massive drift of people from the traditional western mission denominations into the independent churches. The popularity of healing led to the rise of a large number of charlatans, who swelled the ranks of African prophets and whose activities in time led to general scepticism about the authenticity of the older independent churches. The cry for salvation/liberation in Africa, it has been suggested, is primarily a cry for health and wholeness.[28]

The CoP gained an edge on the Sunsum sorè (Spiritual Churches), as the older independent churches are referred to in Ghana, and thus supplanted the activities of many prophets through the ministry of healing and deliverance. In order to avoid some of the excesses, suspicions and abuses surrounding the healing practices of 'prophetism in Ghana', the CoP has institutionalised, integrated and therefore brought under the Church's administrative control the activities of those of their number manifesting the gifts of healing and deliverance. In the process, some of these healers seceded to form their own independent churches,[29] but the healing camps set up and run by recognised CoP healers continue to function as the most popular and respected in the country.[30] The sick and afflicted from across denominations and many from foreign parts patronise these CoP residential healing facilities as alternatives to what the Sunsum sorè offer. The ministry of the CoP has therefore helped to demystify prophetism in Ghana by hastening the move of the Sunsum sorè from the centre to the periphery of Ghanaian Christianity.

The success of the CoP is a product not just of their offering the same 'services', but also because they do so from a more respectable position, with institutional structures to cater for abuses, which undoubtedly occur. The popularity of these healing camps is in part a product of their proven effectiveness as instruments of divine healing, and additionally, because

---

[27] See above, note 14.

[28] Mercy Amba Oduyoye, *Hearing and Knowing: Theological Reflections on Christianity in Africa* (Maryknoll, NY: Orbis Books, 1986), 44.

[29] In the mid 1950s, three members broke fellowship with the CoP to form their own independent churches: Brother Lawson of the Divine Healers' Church, Prophet C.S.T. Owuo of the Apostolic Reformed Church and Prophet John Mensah who founded the Church of Christ (Spiritual Movement).

[30] The most prominent of the healing camps operating under the auspices of the CoP include the Edumfa camp near Cape Coast, the Bantama and Sepe camps in Kumasi and the Okanta prayer and healing camp located near Suhum. They have not been without problems. In the mid-1990s Evangelist Owusu Tabiri, as a result of a misunderstanding with the CoP over the running of the Bethel Healing Camp at Sunyani, announced his independence from the Church. He reorganised the camp into a church and in 1995 returned from a trip overseas with the titles 'Rev. Dr' and 'Bishop'.

they operate within a recognised denomination, they have a high degree of credibility that the prophet-healer of an independent church may lack. The issue here is the authenticity of the experiences and ministries of those who mediate the power of God in healing. As with its indigenous religions, healing and prophecy often go together in the practices of the new religions of Africa.

Pentecostals believe prophecy to be the utterance under the influence of the Holy Spirit of a word of God addressed to a particular contemporary situation.[31] In the context of healing, prophecy helps in diagnosis, and for the ailing African who is familiar with the methods of the traditional diviner, prophecy is important in establishing the cause of one's condition. Many a vulnerable patient has fallen prey to the devices of prophets and pastors who make declarations in the name of God, supposedly under the influence of the Spirit, when God has not spoken. In the CoP healing camp, where the prophet is accountable to an establishment, there exists an authority to whom victims of deception could appeal.

Community Church-Planting Method

One of the hallmarks of the life of the early church, as chronicled in the Acts of Apostles and the Epistles of Paul, was the strong sense of community binding the members and resulting from their common experience of the Spirit. In many places, Paul speaks of the various Christian communities in terms of a single family. So the Thessalonians, for example, are addressed as 'brothers beloved by God' and mention is made of the 'joy of the Holy Spirit' associated with their conversion (1 Thes. 1:4, 6). In an insightful study on the formation of the ekklesia, Wayne Meeks shows how the spirit of hospitality, including care for the poor and needy, was also among the virtues that characterised the lives of the early churches, as stressed in the traditional admonitions of Paul in some of his letters (cf. Rom. 12:13).[32]

One of the reasons for the massive presence of the CoP across the length and breadth of Ghana and beyond is its community-based church-planting method. The Church encourages people to fellowship within their communities, a far cry from the situation where certain historic mission church congregations have acquired an elitist character because they provide a forum for the learned theologian to serve as pastor to the rich, powerful and famous. In the city of Takoradi in the Western Region of Ghana, for example, the Methodist Church was established in the late

[31] Simon Tugwell et al., *New Heaven? New Earth?: An Encounter with Pentecostalism* (Springfield, IL: Templegate Publishers, 1976), 24.

[32] Wayne A. Meeks, *The First Urban Christians: The Social World of the Apostle Paul* (New Haven, CT, and London: Yale University Press, 1983), ch. 3.

1920s. Until about ten years ago, everybody had to worship at that same location in a city that is now about ten times larger than when the Methodists arrived. The CoP established their first Assembly in the city more than two decades after the Methodists, and they have responded quickly to the geographic and demographic changes in Takoradi by establishing Assemblies in all the suburbs. At the last count, the Methodists had fewer than ten societies in Takoradi and its immediate environs. The CoP had about eighteen assemblies within the same geographical area, not only making their congregations accessible, but also fostering stronger communal bonds as members were likely to be living closer to one other. Community-oriented congregations engender meaningful fellowship and prompt pastoral care. Such communal bonds have been recognised as a highly stabilising factor in African traditional societies, as Dickson states:

> It is a commonplace that the sense of community is strong in Africa. A society is in equilibrium when its customs are maintained, its goals attained and the spirit powers given regular and adequate recognition. Members of society are expected to live and act in such a way as to promote society's well-being; to do otherwise is to court disaster, not only for the actor but also for society as a whole.[33]

The injunction laid upon members to avoid things that are inimical to the well-being of their communities, or sanctions from the gods, recalls the experience of the early church in which Ananias and Sapphira paid dearly for an attempt to lie to the Holy Spirit through their covetousness and greed (Acts 5:1-11). It is well known that, in the life of the CoP, members in good standing who find themselves in crises are ably supported in both prayerful and material terms.

Welfare

The CoP welfare system of support for members is key to that Church's ability to attract and hold members in a context where poverty and deprivation bring untold misery in times of sickness and bereavement. The welfare system is not unrelated to the overall experience of the worshipping community, because the support is an outflow of the common experience of the Spirit that motivates believers to care for each other. In the Acts of the Apostles, the massive growth in the fellowship of believers is closely tied to the integrated nature of their fellowship, which included teaching, prayer and sharing with 'sincere hearts'. As a result, 'the Lord added to their number daily those who were being saved' (Acts 2:42-47).

---

[33] Kwesi A. Dickson, *Theology in Africa* (London: Darton, Longman and Todd; Maryknoll, NY: Orbis Books, 1984), 62.

The Greek word for the 'fellowship' or 'communion' characterising the life of the early church was koinonia. This fellowship, which came into being at Pentecost, was more than the deepening of human intercourse: it was the expression of vertical-horizontal relationships that combined sharing with others what one shared with Christ. In other words, the new fellowship gave practical expression to the belief that to experience Christ is to belong to him, and to belong to Christ is to share his love in communion with others. This sense of renewal that affects human relationships is one of the reasons for the missionary impact of the CoP.

Liturgical Vernacularisation

The CoP has a very simple outlook, as can be seen in its ordered, but very informal, liturgy and its vernacularisation policy, which create the space and atmosphere for the Spirit to operate during worship. Corporate worship provides the highpoint for the experience of the Spirit through his manifestations in tongues, prophecies, visions and ecstasies. Informality creates the atmosphere for this experience to happen. The move away from written and stereotyped liturgical formulae ensures that Pentecostal worship is characterised by spontaneity and expectancy, because, during worship, God through his Spirit is expected to come and 'inhabit the praises of his people'. Pentecostals are thus able to make room for participatory worship in which people can worship God in languages that come naturally to them. Writing about worship among early Pentecostals, William and Robert Menzies have noted, 'The gatherings of Pentecostals, although generally following a simple form, nonetheless were punctuated by manifestations of the Spirit ... Church services were not boring repetitions of prearranged liturgy; rather, each service had the potential for being the occasion of a special outpouring of the Spirit.'[34]

A typical CoP worship service begins with a time of participatory and spontaneous prayer, which is followed by a time of intense and expressive praise involving drumming, singing and dancing. Wherever the CoP operates, the various tribes are allowed the use of their mother tongue and their indigenous song and dance. Worship services also make room for recounting God's interventions in people's affairs through salvation from precarious situations, healing and deliverances.

Spontaneous prophecy as communication from God is allowed and is not seen as an interruption to a 'beautiful' service. Those who do not have direct testimonies to share may sing a song, read an appropriate portion of Scripture or give an exhortation to encourage others. The last segment of worship is dedicated to the sermon, the offerings and then an Altar Call.

[34] William W. Menzies and Robert P. Menzies, *Spirit and Power: Foundations of Pentecostal Experience (Grand Rapids, MI: Zondervan, 2000)*, 23.

The use of the vernacular for prayer, singing, preaching and reading of the Scriptures helps CoP assemblies to function in congregations with low levels of literacy.

In Translating the Message Sanneh draws attention to a primary affinity between the vernacular and the gospel and the way in which, by carrying the gospel in its vernacular form into their communities, Africans have helped the church to grow.[35] Walls has also spoken about the critical role that ordinary lay Christians, rather than ordained clergy, play in the spread of the gospel in Africa.[36] From the outset, the CoP relied extensively on the evangelistic passion of its local members. Informants testify that James McKeown consistently paid glorious tribute to the passion and commitment of the indigenous personnel he worked with, and he attributed the growth and expansion of the CoP to the hard work of the African agents of the Church. In his words, 'this has been our aim in allowing the work in Africa to retain its native characteristics and it has resulted in producing some of the finest Christians I have met.'[37]

Vernacularisation in the CoP, which is given expression in locally composed choruses and songs, personal testimonies, public Scripture reading and the preaching of sermons, helps to give the CoP a certain appealing simplicity not found in other classical Pentecostal churches, for example in the Assemblies of God, or in the traditional mission churches. Much of this vernacularisation may not itself be new, considering that worship services in the older independent churches were also in the vernacular. Its importance as a source of attraction into the CoP is best understood against the backdrop of the CoP's wider demographic and geographic appeal, and in the context of the dwindling public image of these older independent churches.

Holiness Ethic

The CoP is noted for its uncompromising holiness ethic and high moral standards. There is a definite relationship between personal experiences of the Spirit and commitment to the cause of Christ and his mission through the church. Such commitment arises out of a sense of belonging that develops within the individual as a result of that intense encounter with the Holy Spirit. Heribert Mühlen compares the relationship that emerges between the Christian and God after an experience of the Spirit to the love between married people. In bodily intercourse, married people offer to one

---

[35] Lamin O. Sanneh, *Translating the Message: The Missionary Impact on Culture* (Maryknoll, NY: Orbis Books, 1989), 188-89.

[36] Andrew F. Walls, *The Missionary Movement in Christian History: Studies in the Transmission of Faith* (Maryknoll, NY: Orbis Books, 1996), 87.

[37] Leonard, *Giant*, 64.

another not only something like a physical gift 'but themselves, their whole persons'.[38] This act of self-giving was initiated by Christ because he loved the church and gave himself for her (Eph. 5:29-33).

The metaphorical comparison of the relationship between the Christian and the Spirit to self-giving, as in marital intercourse, would be very familiar in the African context. Among the Yoruba, for example, spirit possession uses the idiom of sexual intercourse.[39] Here the traditional priest is quintessentially the 'wife' of the deity possessing him or her. The Akan expression sunsum afa no, used to describe spirit possession, means a spirit has taken over the executive faculties of the candidate for priesthood. The critical word here is fa, 'to take'. The same expression is used for sexual intercourse, particularly when performed without the woman's consent.

When the Spirit of God takes hold of a person, it amounts to one's privacy being 'invaded'. The candidate, as with the making of prophets in the Christian context, is domesticated for service in a way that involves an intense emotional commitment demanding that a person's whole being be yielded to God. Among the demands that such a commitment makes on Christians is that they lead lives befitting their new status: as 'married' to God and his service. In Ephesians, we read that becoming a Spirit-filled Christian involves change from 'a former way of life'; the text records that it is time 'to put off' the old self, 'which is being corrupted by its deceitful desires', and 'to be made new in the attitude of your minds; and to put on the new self, created to be like God in true righteousness and holiness' (Eph. 4:22-24).

Thus the ultimate testimony of the Pentecostal is a testimony of personal transformation from life in the world to a new life in Christ, involving a renewal of the whole person for a life of holiness. In this sense, writes Mühlen, 'renewal of the Spirit is the renewal of our human spirit effected in us by the Holy Spirit: the renewal of our feeling, willing, thinking, of our whole person'.[40] In the minds of the generality of Ghanaians, the mainline churches are permissive in their ethical standards, but the Church of Pentecost is not. According to the constitution of the CoP, the following deviations attract sanctions: going to questionable places (such as visiting shrines, as some Christians do to supplement their faith) and falling into such sins as adultery, fornication and alcoholism. Divorce, embracing false doctrines, or not keeping the Lord's Day holy may all attract sanctions from church authority. The disciplinary sanctions include suspension from full membership for ordinary members, demotion (with or without suspension)

---

[38] Heribert Mühlen, *A Charismatic Theology: Initiation in the Spirit* (London: Burns and Oates, 1978), 119.

[39] J.D.Y. Peel, 'The Pastor and the *Babalawo*: The Interaction of Religions in Nineteenth-Century Yorubaland', *Africa*, 60, no. 3 (1990), 344.

[40] Mühlen, *Charismatic Theology*, 133.

for those in leadership, and outright dismissal for pastors. A member on suspension may attend church services but is not allowed to preach or give testimony in church. He or she is also not allowed to join the congregation in 'open-floor' dancing and when in church must sit at the back. Suspended members do not receive Holy Communion.

The seriousness of CoP evokes a very high level of membership commitment, which is evident in the intensity of participation in church life. Rodney Stark states that, in order to grow, religious movements must offer a religious culture that sets them apart from the general secular culture. This means, he says, that movements must be distinctive and impose strict moral standards.[41] Stark uses 'strictness' in reference to the degree to which a religious group maintains 'a separate and distinctive life style or morality in personal and family life, in such areas as dress, diet, drinking, entertainment, uses of time, sex, child rearing and the like'.[42] In Christian terms drinking and other such indulgences may be interpreted as being worldly, in light of Paul's counsel to Christians to avoid conformity 'to the pattern of this world' (Rom. 12:2). According to Stark, such strictness makes religious groups strong by screening out those he refers to as 'free-riders', i.e., those who may want to share in the benefits of the movement without 'contributing' to the collective enterprise. When free-riders are excluded, the average level of commitment increases, which in turn greatly increases the credibility of the religious culture and also mobilises resources very effectively.[43]

The Ghanaian public image of the CoP is that of a church that is making up for some of the failures and weaknesses – particularly in the area of morality – that have come to be associated with the Sunsum sorè and even the traditional mission churches. In keeping with its ethos as a Pentecostal denomination, CoP is serious about religious experience and things of the Spirit, and as a religious organisation it pursues a strict and uncompromising stance on what the church perceives as biblical ethical and moral standards. The CoP maintains a very conservative outlook that sets the church apart as an organisation that refuses to be drawn into worldliness. On the relation of such strictness to church life and growth, Leonard observes that the CoP is particularly strict in dealing with matters of marital infidelity and even stricter when such marital infidelity occurs among church elders or pastors.[44]

In traditional African religiosity, the maintenance of high moral standards in response to prescriptions by the gods is well known. Religion

---

[41] Rodney Stark, 'Why New Religious Movements Succeed or Fail: A Revised General Model', *Journal of Contemporary Religion*, 11, no. 2 (1996), 137.
[42] Stark, 'New Religious Movements', 137.
[43] Stark, 'New Religious Movements', 137.
[44] Cf. Leonard , *Giant*, 110.

functions as a means of social control.[45] After nearly two centuries of existence in Ghana, and with the benefit of the translated Scriptures, traditional communities are by no means oblivious to the standards required by the God of the Bible. If their own deities, which are discounted by the Christian church as powerless and inferior, expect such high moral standards, then converts have good reason to expect the Christian God to demand even higher standards, issuing in a more venerable and passionate commitment on the part of worshippers. Against this background, and as compared to what has come to be generally regarded as the dubious ways of African prophets and the compromised and moribund Christianity of traditional mission churches, the CoP's serious and strict approach to the gospel helps to endear it to potential members and admirers. The official greeting of the CoP women, 'ye kronkron ma Ewurade', 'be holy unto the Lord', underlines the church's strong holiness ethic.

Encapsulation Conversion Methods

Rambo uses 'encapsulation' with reference to a conversion strategy in which the converted are discouraged from contact with the 'outside world' by creating 'self-contained worlds' through which the process of conversion may be strengthened.[46] Encapsulation may be physical, with the practical isolation of members, as in the case of the early missionary communities for local Christians called 'Salems' in Ghana. It may also be social, with converts encouraged to adopt lifestyles that limit significant contact with 'outsiders'.[47] In relation to the Sunsum sorè, the CoP practises what Rambo refers to as 'ideological encapsulation', in which members are inoculated against alternative or competing systems of belief.[48]

Ideological encapsulation in the CoP takes the form of vicious attacks on the Sunsum sorè as occultic and spiritist churches who manipulate their followers and drive them along the paths of evil spiritual bondage. Those joining the CoP or Charismatic Ministries from a Sunsum sorè are thus required, as part of the conversion process, to undergo a symbolic severance from their former religious associations through the ministry of deliverance. The ideological encapsulation is part of the demonisation of African religious culture and its strong denunciation in Ghanaian Pentecostal hermeneutics as a 'demonic doorway'. In view of the fact that the Spiritual churches assimilate certain traditional religious practices, rituals and taboos associated with African culture into their worship, the

45 See Edmund Ilogu, *Christianity and Ibo Culture* (Leiden: E.J. Brill, 1974), 63-64, 201.

46 Lewis R. Rambo, *Understanding Religious Conversion* (New Haven, CT: Yale University Press, 1993), 103-8.

47 Rambo, *Understanding Religious Conversion*, 106.

48 Rambo, *Understanding Religious Conversion*, 106.

Pentecostal movement generally vilifies these Sunsum sorè as unchristian and belonging to the occult, thus adding to their unpopularity.

Tithing

From the example of the early church, 'giving', in terms of material contributions in support of the work of the believing community and of poor and deprived members, constitutes an important outflow of the Pentecostal experience. In the Acts of the Apostles, Luke suggests a correlation between the dynamism of the new community of believers and the material support that they wholeheartedly provided in order that those in need could be catered for. So members sold their possessions and goods and 'gave to anyone as he had need' (Acts 2:45). Luke mentions elsewhere that, as a result of this act of giving, 'there were no needy persons among them', as those who had anything to dispose of did so willingly and laid the proceeds 'at the apostles' feet' for distribution (Acts 4:32-37).

Indeed, so important was the act of giving among the believers that when Ananias and Sapphira conspired to cheat on the community, the Spirit terminated their lives: an incident that brought great fear on the whole church and presumably enhanced reverence for God among the believers (Acts 5:1-11). In praising the churches in Macedonia for their exceptional commitment to giving, Paul also suggests a correlation between the experience of the Spirit and the act of supporting God's work. The spirit of giving found in Macedonia was explicable in terms of 'the grace that God has given the Macedonian churches'. That was why they could give out 'overflowing joy' in spite of their unfortunate circumstances. In fact, the churches in Macedonia saw giving as a 'privilege of sharing in [God's] service' to the saints, a view of giving that was possible because of their Christian experience: 'they gave themselves first to the Lord and to us in keeping with God's will' (2 Cor. 8:1-7).

It is theologically revealing that Paul refers to the spirit of giving as an 'act of grace'. In giving towards the needs of the saints, Christian workers and the church, the believer was only appreciating God's ultimate sacrifice in Christ on behalf of all who believe and accept him as Lord and Saviour: 'For you know the grace of our Lord Jesus Christ, that though he was rich, yet for your sakes he became poor, so that you through his poverty might become rich' (2 Cor 8:9; also Phil. 2:6-7). In Ghana the spirit of giving in the CoP has become a point of reference for the traditional mission churches, particularly in encouraging their members to give. 'Giving' as an 'act of grace' has been translated into tithing in the CoP, a church that has been financially self-supporting since its emergence. Ntumy has proposed that McKeown's intention from the inception of the church was 'to build an indigenous church with Ghanaian culture, Ghanaian ministers and finances generated from within the church'.[49]

The members of CoP tithe with zeal and understanding. Tithing has become part of the spirituality of the church and a way of giving that the older churches – after more than a century of existence in Ghana – are still struggling to emulate. Funding the programmes of a church through local resources is a major strength because it enables the church to plan and execute its own work without foreign interference. In a deprived economy like Ghana's, where institutions, including the government, continue to rely heavily on foreign donor assistance, it is to the credit of the CoP that it integrates the experience of being Christian and making one's financial resources available for supporting the mission of the church.

The Role of Women

In the African context, as Mercy Oduyoye notes, 'women are religion's chief clients'.[50] The survival of the church in Africa has been made possible to a very large extent by the active role that women have played in her life and work. The older independent churches of Africa broke the male hegemony in Christian ministry because a large number of the founders were prophetesses. The role of women as founders and patrons of independent churches in Africa is one area where missionary tutelage was overthrown with dramatic effect. I share Lamin Sanneh's view that this timely intervention of women as recipients of spiritual gifts and as possessors of charismatic power saved Christianity from terminal decline in much of Africa.[51]

The CoP is a patriarchal church that does not ordain women. Men and women do not even sit or dance together in church. Wives are supposed to refer to and address their husbands as me wura, 'my Lord', as a sign of submission and respect. This patriarchal outlook, regrettable as it may be, does not, however, deny women full participation in the life of the church. One of the major strengths of the CoP is its strong women's movement, and women's participation dates back to the origins of the church. Sophia McKeown provided leadership for the local women who were at the frontlines of mission. In the words of James McKeown himself, in sharp contrast to his experience in the Apostolic Church of the United Kingdom, in Ghana, 'it was women who came and were baptised in the Holy Spirit;

---

[49] Ntumy, 'Growth and Development', 24.

[50] Mercy Amba Oduyoye, *Daughters of Anowa: African Women and Patriarchy* (Maryknoll, NY: Orbis Books, 1995), ch. 5.

[51] Lamin Sanneh, 'The Horizontal and Vertical in Mission: An African Perspective', *International Bulletin of Missionary Research*, 7, no. 4 (1983), 165-171.

women who gave money and committed their time and women who prayed'.[52]

One woman, Mrs Obo, has been described as 'a real rock in the foundation of the Church'. In times of real financial need, she was said to have sold her personal jewellery and other valuable items to support James McKeown, for whom she also served as an interpreter. Mrs Obo organised the women at Saltpond in the Central Region for Bible study, prayer and evangelism. She was a leader in the women's movement of the CoP from its inception, in 1938, until 1974.[53] Women are found in the various assemblies as prophetesses and interpreters of preachers when the latter cannot communicate in the mother tongue of the area. In other words, the spiritual gifts of women are recognised in the local congregations.

In his work on the growth and development of the Church of Pentecost, Ntumy points out that in the CoP the operation of the gifts is not limited to any one group of people. As regards healing, and miracles in general, it is noteworthy that those whose ministries are singled out as unique in the history and development of the CoP are all women. Among these figures, Ntumy mentions Maame Dede, a deaconess who was said to have been active in the 1960s in the areas of healing, word of knowledge, prophecy and discernment of spirits. Ntumy also mentions Grace Mensah, who is the founder and leader of the popular Edumfa Revival Centre, which operates under the auspices of the CoP.[54]

Pentecost International Worship Centre

As a classical Pentecostal church, the CoP maintained a very strict holiness ethic and discouraged her members from using anything or participating in any events that are considered worldly. Until fairly recently, women were supposed to cover their hair in church, a policy that alienated many young women and professionals from the denomination. As noted, in CoP assemblies, men and women neither sit nor dance together in church. The denomination frowned upon the wearing of expensive jewellery and the extensive use of makeup by women. All that was to change a little over a decade ago, when the CoP started what is now called the Pentecost International Worship Centre (PIWC). The first of these centres was started in Kumasi and has been replicated throughout the country and beyond. The PIWCs are English-speaking assemblies in which the conservative rules of the traditional assemblies have been completely relaxed.

Unlike in the classical assemblies, the mode of communication in PIWCs is English. Women are no longer required to cover their heads in

---

[52] Leonard, *Giant*, 54.

[53] Leonard, *Giant*, 43.

[54] See note 28.

church, and there are no requirements in terms of seating. The CoP has in the last few years engaged quite a number of university graduates and professionals as pastors, with some specifically earmarked for these modern or contemporary assemblies. The new arrangements have helped the CoP attract young people into the PIWCs and have stemmed the tide of people drifting into charismatic churches because of the conservative rules. A typical PIWC assembly looks like any contemporary Pentecostal or charismatic church; the willingness of the CoP to adapt has paid off in terms of dynamism, exuberance and the attraction of young people and students into these new paradigm assemblies.

Church of Pentecost Grassroots Theology

Afua Kuma is a useful example of the contributions that women have made to the dynamic presence of the CoP in African Christianity. Afua Kuma, whose prayers have been the subject of theological analysis by Kwame Bediako and his student Philip Laryea, was a member of the Church of Pentecost. Her church background, which to my mind is crucial to her theological thinking, is not sufficiently prominent in the writings of the two scholars. Although she was illiterate, it is highly significant that, in the work of both Bediako and Laryea, Afua Kuma is referred to as a 'grassroots theologian' who has played an important role 'in the development of Christian thought' and whose theology 'is foundational for Christian theology in the twenty-first century'.[55]

In Afua Kuma's prayers, prayers that I submit are born out of her Pentecostal experience, Jesus is imaged as Obaatanpa (Capable Mother), Kronkron (Holy One), Otumfo Nyankopon (Almighty God), Ohene (King) and Nyansabuakwa (Custodian of Wisdom). These titles, some of which have been borrowed from traditional appellations for Ghanaian chiefs, were analysed by Laryea in his work. For our purposes I single out Afua Kuma's application of the Akan expression Obaatanpa for God. As Laryea rightly points out, the image is derived from the natural and biological roles of women as mothers with exceptional qualities of emotional attachment and care for children. The expression is, however, not restricted to the female gender. It is also used for males and for any human institutions that perform the functions of caring and emotional support. The theological import of Jesus as Obaatanpa lies in the fact that 'although the Jesus of history comes to us as a male, our conception of him as Jesus of faith transcends gender … To invest the Jesus of faith with the Obaatanpa image is to attest to the fact that in him both genders cohere.'[56] The deep theological thinking

[55] Philip T. Laryea, 'Mother Tongue Theology: Reflections on Images of Jesus in the Poetry of Afua Kuma', *Journal of African Christian Thought*, 3, no. 1 (2000), 50-60.
[56] Laryea, 'Mother Tongue Theology', 50.

behind the prayers of Afua Kuma also comes to the fore in the following prayer, in which Jesus is presented in his supremacy as having no equal in the universe, not even among the chiefs of Ghana with their sacral personalities as representatives of the ancestors:

> Mere chiefs and kings are not his equals,
> Though filled with glory and power,
> Wealth and blessings, and royalty
> in the greatest abundance
> But of them all, he is the leader,
> And the chiefs with all their glory follow after him.[57]

What comes to mind as one reads this prayer is Paul's reference to Jesus as one 'for whom all things were created … whether thrones or powers or rulers or authorities; all things were created by him and for him ... so that in everything he might have the supremacy' (Col. 1:16-19). In the African imagination, one who is greater than the chiefs who sit on the stool of the ancestors as custodians of power, authority and tradition must be supreme indeed. This status has serious implications for the experience of Christian conversion in Africa. If Jesus is the 'leader' of all the authorities, and if the chiefs with all their glory follow after him, then it is in order that conversion in Pentecostal experience means the dethronement of all rival authorities in the traditional religio-cultural sphere. Such dethronement of rival authorities covers worship of ancestors in whose stead the chief rules.

As a grassroots theologian, Afua Kuma gained prominence during CoP conventions in which she was invited to mount the crusade platform and, through her oral theological skills in the Akan language, narrate the nature of God in her prayer. Her ministry was not unlike that of the women in the traditional churches who use ebibindwom (African lyrics) to recount the mighty deeds of God as outlined in the Scriptures and experienced in the daily life of the African Christian. Shenk outlines the relationship between the experience of the Spirit and the novel ministries of Pentecostal women like Afua Kuma:

> The sense of the immediacy of the Holy Spirit in the life of the faith community has fostered an ethos in which women are free to acknowledge and exercise their gifts, including leadership roles in the churches. Pentecostal/charismatic churches have long recognized the leadership of women. Indeed, numerous prophetesses have founded churches. Now a shift is under way as women in these churches are

[57] Afua Kuma, *Jesus of the Deep Forest*, Fr Jon Kirby SVD et al (eds & trans.) (Accra: Asempa Press, 1980), 20.

> being encouraged, in the freedom of the Spirit, to forge their own style of ministry rather than fitting into the conventional patterns of ministry of the past.[58]

It is very significant that Kwame Bediako reveals Afua Kuma's prayers as paradigmatic of 'grassroots' or oral theology in action. Prayer, as an oral theological form and the medium of communication with the object of worship, provides access to the belief and theology of worshippers. In Bediako's assessment, the prayers of this Pentecostal woman are 'an illustration of that spirituality which gives a clue to the vibrant Christian presence … which forms the true basis of African theology'. In these prayers, as Bediako further reflects, Jesus is presented not only as Lord, but also as a living reality, Protector, Provider and Enabler, who has conquered the ubiquitous forces and mysterious powers whose activities would have made it difficult for the Christian to come to a full appreciation of abundant life in Christ.[59]

In the experience of Pentecost, the message that is proclaimed is that of the availability of power in the name of Jesus Christ. The reception of power is very ardently and consciously sought, so that, in witnessing, the world is made to realise that Christians are more than conquerors amidst the uncertainties of life. Paul reminded the Corinthian church that the belief that the Kingdom of God came with power was central to mission: 'My message and my preaching were not with wise and persuasive words, but with a demonstration of the Spirit's power, so that your faith might not rest on men's wisdom, but on God's power' (1 Cor. 2:4-5). By implication, then, the church of today has also been brought into being by God so that in the name of the risen Lord and through the power of the Holy Spirit, she could serve as a conduit for God's transforming grace to the world.

Conclusion

In this chapter I have discussed spiritual experience as a non-negotiable element of Christian mission, using Ghana's Church of Pentecost as an example. African churches are now at the forefront of mission and most of these churches are Pentecostal in nature. Mission in African hands has ceased to be defined in terms of the overseas activity of western mission agencies; mission frontiers, if lessons in modern African Christianity have anything to teach us, have also ceased to be geographical. Pentecostal churches are thriving in Africa and among African communities in the west

58 Wilbert R. Shenk, 'Recasting Theology of Mission: Impulses from the Non-Western World', *International Bulletin of Missionary Research*, 25, no. 3 (2001), 102.

59 Kwame Bediako, *Jesus in Africa: The Christian Gospel in African History and Experience* (Akropong-Akuapem, Ghana: Regnum Africa, 2000), 9.

primarily because of their emphases on belief, experience, conviction and commitment to what the Spirit of God is doing in the world.

The CoP, as an example of this new development in mission, possesses a strong prophetic and healing ministry, an uncompromising holiness ethic, a wider demographic appeal with an equally extensive geographic spread, a community-oriented approach to church planting, a diversified ministry including provision for children and youth, and a strong women's movement. These factors have made the CoP one of the most popular churches in the West Africa sub-region. Among African churches being established in western Europe and North America at the present time, the CoP has the best organised network. With the features characterising its spirituality, the CoP stands for what is widely perceived in Ghana to be a more accessible and 'more respectable option' in indigenous Pentecostalism.

In Pentecostalism, religion is expected to be a matter of personal choice rather than of institutional presence.[60] Pentecostalism is an experiential religion par excellence. The CoP is serious about the Bible, prayer, evangelism and, above all, things of the Spirit. Although the early Pentecostals revelled in the glory of spiritual experience, most of them readily organised their lives around the principle of reaching out to a lost world and touching lives for God.[61]

Those who will work for God in mission must first come to an experiential knowledge of him. That is why Pentecostals take serious exception to the routine manner in which people become Christian in the mainline churches, through the processes of infant baptism and confirmation. These routine processes of incorporation into the church have in the immediate past not been helped by an approach that has seen Christian mission conducted through the provision of educational facilities and social services, important as these may be. Although the older mission churches have made major contributions to the life of the Christian church in Africa, through the Pentecostal movement God is teaching his church a vital lesson about the need to return to the fundamentals of Scripture through experience.

---

[60] Bryan R. Wilson, 'The Functions of Religion: A Reappraisal', *Religion*, 18 (1988), 199.
[61] Menzies, *Spirit and Power*, 22.

Chapter 10
Moving Against the Gates of Hell: Exorcism in Evangelism

Pentecostalism, in all its forms, is popular in Africa because, as we have noted in the chapter on the prophetic, it restored to the heart of Christianity something that resonated with African religious sensibilities. Pentecostalism's relationship with primal piety is identified in a number of the chapters in this volume as critical to its popularity among African Christians. What is of primary importance to Pentecostal religion, though, is not necessarily to be ethnically contextual. Pentecostalism is a religion that seeks first and foremost to be biblical and to stay true to what was evident in the ministry of Jesus Christ and in the ministries of the apostles, including Paul. Thus the words of Jesus to his disciples that the gates of hell cannot move against his church, are understood to mean that the might of the church in the power of the Spirit stands against opposing demonic forces. Demonisation and exorcism are therefore significant features of Christianity, especially Pentecostal Christianity, in Africa. Evangelism in most Pentecostal contexts involves preaching the word and casting out demons of affliction.

In healing, exorcism and deliverance, Pentecostalism has distinguished itself as a religion of the Bible that relives the ministry of Jesus Christ in the power of the Holy Spirit for our time. Exorcism has to do with the casting out of demons; deliverance includes exorcism and the reversal of the effects of negative physical and spiritual forces that may be working against peoples' destinies. The following quotation from Amos Yong's Pentecostalism and Political Theology captures all that can be placed under the heading of deliverance, which in principle encapsulates healing and exorcism and everything else that goes into them:

> From the beginning ... Pentecostals have experienced Jesus as saving them not only from their sins, but also from their sicknesses and diseases. In the world Pentecostal context, especially in the global south, this salvation includes a redemption from the powers of the devil and his demons since these are, ultimately, the causes of sickness (both physical and psychosomatic), poverty, and other material and socio-economic ills that keep human beings from experiencing the abundant life promised by God. Especially in the global south, it is not unusual to find Pentecostals blaming the demonic for the prostitution industry, the

AIDS virus, medically inexplicable conditions, unemployment, political corruption, and other real life challenges. Given these assumptions, Jesus as savior is understood not only as healer but also as deliverer, and, in some cases, as exorcist, and Pentecostal evangelistic services thus include moments in the liturgy devoted to prayer for the sick as well as rituals of deliverance and exorcism.[1]

This chapter examines the ministries of healing and exorcism in African Pentecostal evangelism. Evangelism in this context refers to the conscious attempt to proclaim 'Christ as Saviour' and trusting the Holy Spirit to convict of sin and evoke responses that will lead those so convicted to accept Christ as their Lord. In other words, the simple definition of evangelism from a Pentecostal perspective is to get people to be Born-again. This process explains why 'personal testimonies' of conversion are important in Pentecostal evangelism. Evangelism that takes place during mass crusades often includes praying for the sick and casting out demons in order to affirm the power and viability of the message. Opoku Onyinah has pointed to the fact that dealing with evil is so important in African Christianity that the Pentecostal practice of exorcism or deliverance has now been incorporated into all streams of Ghanaian Christianity. Failure to take on healing and deliverance ministries by certain historic mission denominations in particular has contributed to the loss of members to other churches.[2] Based mainly on his experiences with the Church of Pentecost, Onyinah reports that from the early years of the life of the denomination, confronting and countering the attraction of local people to traditional medicine shrines in the name and power of Christ led to many conversions to Christianity.[3]

African Pentecostal and charismatic Christians still believe in mass evangelisation methods in which people are invited through the Altar Call to give their lives to Christ.

In line with the media explosion on the continent, some of these events are broadcast as part of sponsored television programmes, with dramatic effects on audiences.

These ministries of supernatural intervention are usually justified on the basis of Scripture. Two passages come to mind, both of them from the Acts of the Apostles. First:

Those who had been scattered preached the word wherever they went. Philip went down to a city in Samaria and proclaimed the Christ there. When the crowds heard Philip and saw the miraculous signs he did, they all paid close attention to

[1] Amos Yong, *In the Days of Caesar: Pentecostalism and Political Theology* (Grand Rapids, MI: William B. Eerdmans, 2010), 123.

[2] Opoku Onyinah, *Pentecostal Exorcism: Witchcraft and Demonology in Ghana* (Dorset: Deo Publishing, 2012), 2.

[3] Onyinah, *Pentecostal Exorcism,* 141-142.

> what he said. With shrieks, evil spirits came out of many, and many paralytics and cripples were healed. So there was great joy in that city. (Acts 8:4-8)

And second:

> God did extraordinary miracles through Paul, so that even handkerchiefs and aprons that had touched him were taken to the sick, and their illnesses were cured and evil spirits left them. (Acts 19:11-12)

Themes of overcoming, conquering, dominating or defeating evil powers and breaking through debilitating afflictions, as seen in the ministry of the apostles in Acts, are familiar in Pentecostal and charismatic discourses. Pentecostalism, as I have stressed, is about the experience of the power of the Holy Spirit. It is the Spirit who enables healing and the casting out of evil spirits to take place in the context of evangelism. That is the key to understanding the two passages cited above. The restoration of people to health, exorcising them of the demonic and bringing deliverance to them, was a central, not a marginal part of the ministry of Jesus Christ and the Apostles. Thus Pentecostal Christians in Africa have found the categories of power, dominion and alleviation of suffering by the power of the Spirit relevant in the general struggle with fears and insecurities within a universe in which supernatural evil is considered hyperactive.[4]

In John 10:10, Jesus is reported as saying, 'The thief comes to steal, kill and destroy but I come that you might have life and have it abundantly.' In Pentecostal hermeneutics, 'the thief' here is the devil and any entity that acts as his agent and spiritually or physically 'terrorises' people. Obstacles, including sin, spiritual and physical afflictions and other such negative influences that prevent people from realising the abundance of life in Christ, are cast as 'strongholds' that must be pulled down by the authority of the risen Christ and the power of the Holy Spirit. Pentecostals preach, speak, teach, sing about and practise these 'interventionist theologies', as I call them, in ways and to degrees that one cannot find in other streams of Christianity. 'I/We believe in the Holy Spirit' is an aspect of the Christian creed that every Christian and church may be willing to affirm. For Pentecostal and charismatic Christians, however, 'belief' and 'experience' are always expected to move in tandem if the power of God is to be seen in evangelism.

The Akan [African] universe, Ghanaian philosopher Kwame Gyekye argues, 'is a spiritual universe, one in which supernatural beings play

---

[4] André Corten and Ruth Marshall-Fratani (eds.), *Between Babel and Pentecost: Transnational Pentecostalism in Africa and Latin America* (Bloomington and Indianapolis: Indiana University Press, 2001), 5.

significant roles in the thought and action of the people'.[5] Christian Baëta articulates that view thus: 'In a worldview which assumes the effective presence of numberless spirits, and regards all life as one; with no clear distinctions between the material and the non-material, the natural and supernatural let alone the secular and the religious, or even between man and other created beings, this could hardly be otherwise.'[6]

Classical Pentecostal spirituality, including its contemporary neo-Pentecostal and charismatic forms, is popular in Africa because its interpretations and responses to evil have continuity with the traditional religious ideas described above. In Translating the Devil, based on ethnographic data on the Peki-Ewe of Ghana, Birgit Meyer notes how the inability of historic mission churches to take the experience of the Holy Spirit seriously, to 'ward off or cast out evil spirits' and to offer people 'protection and healing' in his power, is a cause of drifts into Pentecostal churches and movements.[7]

These reflections proceed from an African perspective where the Eurocentric distinctions among evangelical, charismatic and Pentecostal streams of Christianity may often appear blurred. Many non-Pentecostal churches take a very evangelical or charismatic approach to the gospel in which the 'proclamation of the gospel' is accompanied by 'signs and wonders'. African traditions generally hold a strong belief in spirit possession. Spirits of deities possess people in order to make them priests, but evil spirits can also hijack a person's faculties to torment that person. The Akan of Ghana, for example, make a distinction between akom, possession leading to the priesthood, and adambo, possession leading to insanity.

I see the ministries of healing and exorcism as important hallmarks of Pentecostal/charismatic evangelistic activity in Africa because, as I argue, that theology fits into African interpretation of mystical causality. The impact of Pentecostalism on African religious life has been so profound that there is currently an ongoing 'pentecostalisation' of African Christianity in which historic mission churches consciously incorporate pneumatic phenomena, including healing and exorcism in particular, into their worship and spirituality.

---

[5] Kwame Gyekye, *African Philosophical Thought: The Akan Conceptual Scheme*, rev. ed. (Philadelphia: Temple University Press, 1995), 69.

[6] Christian G. Baëta, 'Christianity and Healing', *Orita: Journal of Religious Studies, University of Ibadan*, 1 (1967), 19.

[7] Birgit Meyer, *Translating the Devil: Religion and Modernity among the Ewe in Ghana* (Edinburgh: Edinburgh University Press, 1999), xviii.

Spiritual Warfare in African Pentecostal Hermeneutics

Bishop Charles Agyinasare is the founder and leader of the Word Miracle Church International in Accra. He has emerged as Ghana's equivalent of Oral Roberts, Benny Hinn or Morris Cerullo, with a powerful ministry of healing, exorcism and deliverance at his international open-air crusades. He has written a number of books cataloguing his experiences in this endeavour, and here I quote from one of them as he describes the 'power demonstration' that has accompanied his ministry:

> I realized that my commission was just a re-echoing of Scripture by the Spirit to me ... It meant that God expected me to go round the cities and towns like the disciples did when they followed Jesus to see how he healed the sick and cast out devils. I therefore began to read and study the gospels of Jesus avidly and there I learnt some of the principles.
>
> I visited Konongo next and during the meetings many healings took place. A man who had passed off or was considered dead was brought back to life when I called back his spirit into his body. In 1985, at Asamankese, [the wife of] a watchman of the Presbyterian Church [who] had been paralyzed for five years jumped and started walking and running. The husband [ran] throughout the town and told people what the Lord had done for his wife. This caused my meeting to grow from 400 to 3,000 people in one day, and we continued this crusade for 21 days.
>
> In October 1990, I went to preach in Somanya for two days. I was praying the second day when I heard that a lady from Accra was looking for me. She had a mental problem and always heard voices that had told her to swallow gravels, and coins. She said she had gone to Tamale and heard I had gone to Accra. She came to Accra and heard I was in Somanya; and she chased me up there. Since 1983 in over 51 nations of the world including North America, India, Israel, Pakistan, Japan, Europe, most of Africa I have seen God save and perform incredible miracles of the Holy Spirit.[8]

Such healing, exorcism and deliverance occurs within the context of what Pentecostals describe as 'spiritual warfare', that is, the deployment of the power of the Holy Spirit in the fight against destructive powers in peoples' lives. Sometimes exorcism is even carried out on physical spaces, such as haunted homes perceived to be occupied by the 'forces of the devil'. The reinvention of spiritual warfare in the ministry of contemporary Pentecostalism is based on Paul's submission: 'for our struggle is not against flesh and blood, but against the rulers, the authorities, against the powers of this dark world and against the spiritual forces of evil in the heavenly realms' (Eph. 6:12). Commenting on this passage, Agyinasare explains:

---

[8] Charles Agyin-Asare, *Power Demonstration: Understanding the Holy Spirit and His Gifts* (Accra: Agyin-Asare, 2008), 177-78.

> Prayer is being engaged in spiritual warfare. In any war, weapons are used. In natural wars, carnal weapons are used but in spiritual warfare weapons used are more dangerous than inter-continental ballistic missiles; these weapons are in prayer. To succeed in any war, you need to learn to fight and use your weapons or artillery! ... If you do not know how to fight, you will become a spiritual casualty of war. May God teach your spiritual hands and fingers to fight … This wrestling is fiercer and more dangerous than the World Wrestling Federation Matches in America because here you are dealing with unseen beings, more powerful than human beings. One demon in a lunatic could break chains and fetters and could not be tamed by anyone (Mk. 5:2-5). One demon in a man could beat the seven sons of Sceva (Acts 19:14-17). Beloved it is not everything that is happening around you that is physical. The devil wants you to believe the problem is caused by those around you but the root cause can always be dealt with in prayer. Someone said 'when you stop wrestling principalities and powers, you will wrestle flesh and blood,' so pray, pray, pray.[9]

For a typical contemporary African Pentecostal under-standing of the phenomenon of evil powers and how to deal with them, consider the following example: Steve Mensah is the founder of the Charismatic Evangelistic Ministry, one of the new Pentecostal/charismatic churches based in Ghana. He is widely acknowledged as a leading exponent and practitioner of the 'healing and deliverance' ministry. In a Sunday sermon, Mensah told his members: 'when you are "born again" you must be prepared for "spiritual warfare"'. God's command to humankind to subdue the earth meant that from the beginning 'we were given power and authority'. Just as 'in the name of the state' a uniformed police officer would be deemed to have the authority to stop traffic, Mensah explained to the congregation, 'each of you has the authority to raise your hand and stop the activities of demons'. The Christian who is plagued by evils has therefore no need to panic: 'when in trouble, simply take authority in the Name of Jesus' over the problem.

Making reference to Philippians 2:10, 'in the name of Jesus every knee shall bow', Mensah stated that 'sickness knees', 'marital problems knees', 'financial difficulties knees', 'business problems knees' and 'demons knees' should all bow to the mightier power and authority located in the name of Jesus. The message concluded with an assurance to the congregation that, as believers, they each had power to resist the devil and chase him out of their affairs, which he listed as marriages, homes, finances, business endeavours, and the lives of their families and children. Obviously inspired by the message, the congregation spontaneously burst into the following chorus as they waved white handkerchiefs, the symbols of victory:

---

[9] Charles Agyin-Asare, *Power in Prayer: Taking Your Blessings by Force* (Hoornaar, Netherlands: His Printing, 2001), 16.

We conquer Satan
We conquer demons
We conquer principalities
We conquer powers

Refrain: Shout Hallelujah

'Satan', 'Demons', 'Principalities' and 'Powers' have one thing in common – they are considered the principal sources of evil.

Mensah's reference to the name of Jesus during the message is thus very instructive. The icons and images of the Christ event – his name, his authority, his blood and his cross – are constantly invoked in pronouncements of curses on traditional religions, evil and other enemies including the devil, witches, demons or the principalities and powers that cause difficulties in life. The name and blood of Jesus in particular feature very frequently in indigenous Christian prayers and gospel music as powerful instruments for the conquest of evil and change of destiny. In the words of some Ghanaian Pentecostal/charismatic local choruses: dzin no mbonsam suro (devils/demons fear that name [Jesus]) and bogya no tumi ne ayaresa wo mu (there is power and healing in the blood). According to the first chorus, the name also 'performs wonders', 'it heals diseases', 'cures lepers and cripples' and 'destroys the powers of witches'.

Pentecostalism and the African Worldview

In the African context, the spirits of the ancestors and traditional deities have all survived in the Christian imagination as demons that must be resisted, pure and simple. My preliminary conclusions from a study based on Ghana shows that Christians from diverse confessional backgrounds visit Pentecostal/charismatic healing camps and centres, as well as Prayer Mountain sites, in search of ayaresa, 'healing', ogyee, 'deliverance', and tumi, 'power' to overcome evil. People visit these prayer sites to engage in spiritual warfare: the prodigious struggle to break through in all the conditions that prevent the Christian from realising a positive destiny. With such a strong belief in the power of spirits and the desire to seek deliverance within a religious context, it is not surprising that healing and exorcism are two of the most important phenomena that draw people into Pentecostal churches.

The point has been made that this 'power approach' to evangelism, which takes demon possession seriously, coheres with African philosophical thought. This worldview differs from that of the typical historic mission church, in which the Christian faith, as Kwame Bediako points out, reflects that which has been transmitted through the intellectual history of the west:

> Coinciding as it did with significant advances in scientific discoveries, the Enlightenment acted to direct intellectual attention away from the realm of transcendence to the empirical world that could be seen and felt – away, that is, from the intangible to the tangible. By and large, Christian theology in the West made its peace with the Enlightenment. It responded by drawing a line between the secular world and the sacred sphere, as it were, and so established a frontier between the spiritual world on the one hand, and the material world on the other, creating in effect, a dichotomy between them. Many earnest Christians have been attempting by various means since then to bridge the two worlds.[10]

It is here, as Bediako further notes, that Africa has followed a different path culturally and intellectually from the Enlightenment heritage.[11] Among the Akan of Ghana, 'evil' is mbusu, and most of the time it is supernaturally caused. When used in connection with life generally, mbusu is that which prevents people from living a holistic lifestyle. In the Christology of one Ghanaian chorus, Jesus is presented as 'the changer of evil destinies'.

In that sense, in both traditional and indigenous Christian worldviews evil is anything that destroys lives. Thus the performance of traditional ritual, described by Meyer as 'the pivot of Ewe religious life', is aimed at achieving 'health, fertility, protection, and success in life'.[12] In the process of conversion, the Ewe Christians, we are told, 'measured the success of Christianity by its capacity to counteract evil at least as successfully as Ewe traditional religion'.[13] Pentecostalism thus provides the ritual context within which the consequences of evil and spirit possession may be dealt with. Thus in Ghana, the Pentecostal/charismatic phenomenon of 'ayaresa ne ogyee', 'healing and deliverance', is now not restricted to that tradition.

The need to struggle, fight and conquer supernatural evil is, without exception, a central sociological and theological issue for contemporary Pentecostal/charis-matic Christianity in Africa. Earlier in this volume, we encountered the Church of Pentecost (CoP), the largest single Protestant denomination in Ghana. The CoP has a very well defined healing and deliverance ministry and agenda for evangelism that are carried out by the Witness Movement of the church. Annual reports of the Church of Pentecost to the highest decision-making body of the Church, the General Council, give much space to accounts of healings and exorcisms that have taken place in its various assemblies during the year. The success of the CoP as a Pentecostal denomination can be attributed in part to its healing

---

[10] Kwame Bediako, 'Worship as Vital Participation: Some Personal Reflections on Ministry in the African Church', *Journal of African Christian Thought*, 8, no. 2 (December 2005), 3.

[11] Bediako, 'Vital Participation', 3.

[12] Meyer, *Translating the Devil*, 61, 68.

[13] Meyer, *Translating the Devil*, 138.

centres, spread throughout the country, where the sick and afflicted go for prayerful interventions in their problems.

The Pentecostals' creation of Christian ritual contexts and spaces for resistance to evil is not historically and theologically discontinuous with the activity of the older independent churches. The internalisation of the gospel in vernacular form, and the inability of historic mission Christianity to respond to the African spiritual quest for 'deliverance from evil' and survival, we have noted, accounted for the rise of the AICs at the turn of the twentieth century. The pastoral strategy of these older indigenous and newer Pentecostal and charismatic churches has been to produce integrated syncretistic rites as effective African Christian alternatives to traditional rituals of coping, protection and prevention of evil. Contemporary Pentecostal churches in Africa have not departed significantly from the religious culture of fighting evil through religious ritual, rather, new rites have been reinvented to deal with the perceived prevalence of evil in spiritual warfare.

Shifting Paradigms in Evangelism

I studied at the Trinity Theological Seminary, Legon, Ghana, which was established in 1942 on the western European pattern of theological education. In the last twenty years, I have been amazed to see how the lives of students and professors have changed in many ways, including in relation to the teaching curriculum. Over the years courses have broadened to include African Theology, Evangelism and Church Growth, Pentecostal and Charismatic Theologies and African and Biblical Charismaticism, which is offered at the graduate level. A former professor at Trinity, Rev. Prof. Emmanuel Martey, who returned to Ghana in the early 1990s after training under James Cone at Union Theological Seminary in New York, USA, has, for instance, made a dramatic shift from his liberation/inculturation theologies to embrace and advocate a ministry of spiritual warfare that demonises the most mundane of problems. Like most of the lecturers at Trinity, Martey is an alumnus of the seminary, with its deep roots in western Protestant theology, yet he is now a leading exponent of healing and deliverance in Ghana.

It has been suggested that Martey's election as Moderator of the Presbyterian Church of Ghana in 2010 was partly a result of his leanings towards the renewal movement in his Church. That possibility underscores the fact that we have seen not just one influential theologian embrace charismatic renewal phenomena as a practitioner, but also the Presbyterian Church as a whole move towards pneumatic Christianity and away from its roots in the Reformed tradition of the west. The story of Martey's transformation from what his classmates at Trinity in the 1970s saw as a growing liberal Presbyterian pastor, into an avowed advocate and practitioner of exorcism, is best told in his own words:

> On my return from Union Theological Seminary, I was posted to the Presbyterian Church of Ghana congregation at Kaneshie in Accra. The Church had a Bible Study and Prayer Group which was made up of lay members who met to pray, read the Bible, heal the sick and cast out spirits. Some of the elders lodged a complaint with me about the activities of the group, which they considered 'un-Presbyterian'. I asked them to give me time to study things for myself and make a decision. I visited the group and discovered that they spent long hours in prayer. When the leaders laid hands on those needing prayer some of them were 'slain in the Spirit' and fell down. I did not understand what was going on, but was sure of one thing: the activities were genuine and those who fell down during prayer were not faking their fall. I felt drawn towards the activities of the group and today I am in it big time.[14]

At the end of every academic year, Trinity Theological Seminary holds a 'family week' for final year students. Students bring their spouses to campus for a week during which seminars are organised to help prepare for life as a pastor and as a pastor's spouse. Martey was for a time in charge of this programme and during this period every evening of the family week was dedicated to teaching the students how to exorcise spirits. Such an exercise in exorcism on the campus of Trinity, a seminary set up and run for a number of years by white western Protestant theologians, would have been unthinkable prior to the engagement of Martey as a lecturer in the early 1990s.

As one who takes a charismatic orientation to my Methodist faith, I have been interested in how seminary professors in Africa, who embrace charismatic or pneumatic phenomena in their personal lives, are helping to reshape historic mission Christianity in their countries. In the early years of the neo-Pentecostal movement in Ghana, almost three decades ago, leaders of the movement openly chastised Trinity Theological Seminary for its critical approach to the Bible. One leader, who has since apologised for his vituperations, described Trinity as no more than a 'cemetery' from where only 'dry bones' could emerge. Three decades after these attacks, Pentecostal and charismatic pastors now apply in their numbers to study at Trinity. Not only have they come to appreciate the need for rigorous and critical academic training, but Trinity itself has responded positively to changing paradigms in Christianity by creating space for the ministries of healing, exorcism and deliverance in the curriculum.

My familiarity with charismatic Christianity started in high school and some of my personal encounters with exorcism occurred when I was

---

14 Emmanuel Martey, speaking at a World Council of Churches Forum on Healing in Accra, Ghana, May 2003.

serving as a circuit minister. One example will suffice: I started my pastoral ministry in a small town in the Central Region of Ghana. The Jesus of Nazareth Healing Church in the town held church services and prayer meetings at which God's intervention was sought on behalf of sick and troubled persons – with great results. There were facilities for quarantining those whose conditions needed time to be dealt with. One day, a quarantined patient grew violent and strayed to my house. 'I have had a vision', she said, continuing, 'I saw angels who told me to come to your house and you can help me.' I tried talking to the patient, but for long periods of time she would become dissociated, speaking with a small shrill voice that in my interpretation indicated another 'personality' at work in the woman. Occasionally during our encounter, I would call the woman's name, and whatever 'spirit' was at work in her would repeatedly call the name, telling her, 'pastor wants to speak to you'. I would then speak to the woman until the spirit told me, 'you are wasting my time' and took over the woman's mental faculty, leading her into all kinds of disturbing gestures including contortions of her face.

With the help of fellow Methodist ministers and members of the Methodist charismatic renewal fellowship, we did pray for her and exorcise the spirit. The woman was able to return to her home and business. When my students, many of whom come from evangelical, charismatic and Pentecostal backgrounds, hear these personal stories, they are encouraged that this sort of ministry is equally important. Whatever reservations people may have about Pentecostalism, it has definitely restored something that is genuinely biblical and of which the evangelism ministry of the church stands in need.

Conclusion: Healing, Exorcism and Evangelism

Healing, exorcism and deliverance are important for us because they were critical to the ministry of Jesus Christ. He so integrated these ministries into his work that it is difficult to separate them from evangelism that is done in the way Jesus wished. Mark, for example, begins his record of the sending out of the Twelve Disciples by referring specifically to its healing and exorcism component: 'Calling the Twelve to him, he sent them out two by two and gave them authority over evil spirits.' Subsequently, 'They drove out many demons and anointed many sick people with oil and healed them' (Mk. 6:7, 11).

In my writings, I often make a distinction between 'demonic possession' and 'demonic oppression'. In demonic oppression, as used in African Pentecostal discourse, evil powers simply make life miserable through all kinds of failure, without necessarily inhabiting the person. In demonic possession, an alien spirit actually takes control of a person's faculties, as we find in Mark 5. The story of the Gerasene demoniac recorded in that chapter is a classic example of the relationship between exorcism and evangelism. We are told that the man had come under the influence of evil spirits, sending him into a very pitiful state: 'No one was strong enough to subdue him,' we read. 'Night and day among the tombs and in the hills he would cry out and cut himself with stones' (v. 4-5).

Following the man's encounter with Jesus, there was a total transformation that made a strong impression on those who saw the change: 'When they came to Jesus, they saw the man who had been possessed by the legion of demons, sitting there, dressed and in his right mind; and they were afraid.' Subsequently, 'the man went away and began to tell in the Decapolis how much Jesus had done for him' (v. 15, 20). The evidence of transformation was there for all to see, and I believe it was sufficient to make the man's testimony, and the message and person of Jesus credible. Such ministries of supernatural intervention are critical to the evangelisation efforts of African independent indigenous Pentecostal churches just as they were for the Apostles before and after Pentecost.

In contemporary African Christianity, exorcism can be extended to include dealing with 'territorial spirits' that trouble communities and spaces such as haunted homes. These ministries are so important that not only do many African churches consciously place the expression 'healing' in their names, but the fact that healing from sickness and deliverance from the demonic encumbrances of life are available is advertised. In my understanding and experience, three things make the theology of divine intervention through exorcism an important part of Christian evangelism in Africa.

First, the biblical worldview of mystical causality within which exorcism operates resonates very strongly with African worldviews on the causes of evil, including the belief in spirit possession. The traditional African lives in an intentional world in which things do not happen by chance. Even when problems are naturally caused, evil spirits are able to quickly get in and exploit the situation to the disadvantage of the victim. The general belief is that 'events have causes', and so when Paul speaks about wrestling with 'principalities and powers' or an 'agent of Satan' in his body, he speaks in categories and idioms that are not alien to African cosmological ideas.

Second, the primary motivation of African Pentecostals as far as the ministry of healing and exorcism is concerned is to be biblical. Pentecostals speak of a different kind of 'apostolic succession' that puts the emphasis not only on ecclesiastical authority and inheritance but also on the power of God that was evident then and now. Translations of the gospel into the vernacular enabled another level of apprehension of the ways of the God and father of our Lord Jesus Christ as a God of power and deliverance. If he took the Israelites through the Red Sea and brought down the walls of Jericho, then it makes sense to establish 'Jericho Hour' so that the walls of hostility and strongholds in the lives of his people can be pulled down even today. Similarly, if those who believe in Jesus Christ must do 'greater works', then it stands to reason that those who are possessed by the spirits of the traditional world – ancestors, deities, demons and other malevolent forces – must be cast out in order that 'the captives' can be set free.

Third, any Christian or church that takes the ministries of healing and exorcism seriously also knows how to pray and 'wait upon the Lord'. It is a very challenging ministry that calls for transparency, commitment, prayer and fasting, because dealing with evil spirits can be a dangerous venture for those who take it lightly. The story of the 'sons of Sceva' in Acts 19 is there as an example of the fact that God's grace in evangelism should not be taken for granted.

In contradistinction to what pertains in indigenous Christian ministries, Christoffer Grundmann concedes that 'the theologies that missionaries were exposed to while receiving their training did not equip them to take up the challenge of pneumatological reflection properly'.[15] The processes of healing and exorcism invite us to rethink traditional methods of evangelism and pneumatology. The ministry of exorcism in particular constitutes within the context of evangelism a response to the reality of evil, a non-negotiable element in the religious consciousness of all Christians who are alive to the world of the Bible. In this way Africa, through the ingenuity of the Pentecostals, has emerged as a new centre of theological creativity, 'a laboratory' as Bediako calls it, where 'Christian answers to African questions are hammered out'.[16]

---

[15] Christoffer H. Grundmann, 'Inviting the Spirit to Fight the Spirits? Pneumatological Challenges for Missions in Healing and Exorcism', *International Review of Mission*, 94, no. 372 (January 2005), 53.

[16] Kwame Bediako, interviewed by Kim A. Lawton, 'Faith without Borders: How the Developing World Is Changing the Face of Christianity', *Christianity Today* (May 19, 1997), 44.

Chapter 11
Health and Wealth:
A Theological Response to the Prosperity Gospel

I have addressed the gospel of prosperity and its challenges in other places.[1] In this chapter I provide a brief theological response because of the increasing concern that the gospel of prosperity has generated within evangelical Christianity in particular. The gospel of health and wealth, as it is also called, simply teaches that God rewards faithful Christianity with material abundance, well-being and perfect health. It is not uncommon for those who preach that gospel to cite their personal material acquisitions as examples of faithful Christianity, with some claiming that because of their faith they never fall sick. Several principles are presented as undergirding prosperity, including confessing positives and the faithful fulfilment of tithing obligations.

The biblical texts used to support the principle of giving in particular, also known as 'sowing and reaping', are Malachi 3:10 and Luke 3:38. In Malachi the prophet makes a direct connection between the failure of agricultural fortunes and the failure of Israel to fulfil her religious duty in the payment of tithes. The passage in Luke reads as follows: 'Give, and it will be given to you. A good measure, pressed down, shaken together and running over, will be poured into your lap. For with the measure you use, it will be measured to you.' Jesus made this statement within the context of the Sermon on the Mount, where he taught about reciprocal benevolent behaviour.

The prosperity gospel, which was originally associated with North American televangelism, has become synonymous with contemporary Pentecostalism in Africa. Until the late 1970s, being a Christian religious functionary in Africa was associated with a lifestyle of modesty, sacrifice and service, a model of Christian ministry introduced by western European missionaries from the early years of the nineteenth century. Those in the ministerial employment of the church were provided with housing and paid a modest stipend. In most cases ministers, evangelists and catechists of the church supplemented their incomes with gifts of food from church members or income from the work of their spouses. The model of Christian

[1] Notably, J. Kwabena Asamoah-Gyadu, *Contemporary Pentecostal Christianity: Interpretations from an African Context* (Oxford: Regnum International, 2013).

ministry that existed in Africa for many years became associated with economic deprivation, to the extent that in Ghana jokes about extreme rationing of resources in the 'mission house', as the minister's residence is still called, are well known.

In these older churches, the faithfulness of God was recounted in testimonies of his ability to see 'children of the manse' through their education into top positions in public life in spite of the difficult economic conditions in which they were raised. There can be no justification for the virtual penury into which some churches – both the historic mission and classical Pentecostal denominations – consigned their pastors and ministers through a particular understanding of ministry as 'sacrificial'. Material wealth was seen as evil and as an obstacle to faithful Christianity and entry into the Kingdom of God. Thus, both Christian ministry and Christian discipleship meant turning away from the world of materialism and extravagance. Suffering had to be embraced in the hope of the restoration of fortunes in the other world. This was not necessarily only an African interpretation of spirituality; James Shelton has written of western evangelicals and classical Pentecostals:

> Another assumption was that God allowed suffering to teach lessons and refine souls. This is truly a biblical teaching, but it was not tempered with the healing power of God, which, it was asserted, only happened long ago or was only rarely granted in the present [as, for example, during evangelistic crusades]. In regard to material things, poverty was considered a spiritual state of blessedness (Luke 6:20).[2]

It was not unusual for Christian ministry to become the preserve of retired schoolteachers, who, having served the local church as caretakers and catechists, regularised their 'calling' by opting for the ordained ministry. Until fairly recently, very few highly educated people entered the ministries of the classical Pentecostal denominations in Africa because on the whole they attracted people from the margins. In the Ghanaian city of Sekondi-Takoradi, where I grew up, a popular Pentecostal pastor who did his pastoral rounds on a Honda motorbike was blessed with a small Nissan saloon car in the early to mid-1970s. That this Assemblies of God pastor now drove his own private car became news in the whole metropolis, raising his profile significantly in the eyes of both his members and the general public.

---

[2] James B. Shelton, 'A Pendulum Swing between Prosperity and Suffering: What is the Role of Faith?', in Vinson Synan (ed.), *Spirit-Empowered Christianity in the 21st Century* (Lake Mary, FL: Charisma House, 2011), 358.

Shifting Paradigms

Things have changed considerably since then. With its modern outlook, attraction to an upwardly mobile youth, educated, professional and media-savvy charismatic leadership, fashion consciousness, messages of empowerment, endorsement of the 'material' as divine right, and modern styles of worship, contemporary Pentecostalism has changed the ministry-equals-material-sacrifice mindset. The new message is that God is good and powerful to save and prosper his children. It is one of the legacies of contemporary Pentecostalism that it has helped to create a certain awareness that pastors need to be taken care of properly and Christians must feel free to enjoy the material things of life as blessings from a good God. The older churches have not fully embraced the prosperity gospel. However there is evidence that they have been challenged to improve the general material conditions of their agents and be a little more open to modern fashion, for example. In other words, much of the awareness about those who work for God being entitled to a certain level of wellbeing is due in part to prosperity preaching. Christians are now taught to feel and look good because the preacher embodies the message of prosperity and this message is expected to filter down into the lives of those who believe.

Thus, in responding to the older form of spirituality and the redirection provided by the Pentecostals, there are questions to ask. This is because excessive, materialism is a vice and it is good to hold lightly to the things of the world. One is tempted to ask in the midst of the preaching on materialism in the gospel of prosperity: where is the 'blessedness' of starving children, rampant disease, oppression, and exposure to the elements? At some point, the old Gnostic beliefs that St John had attacked seemed to be creeping back into the churches, specifically the false and accursed view that material things are inherently evil and the flesh is not good (Jn. 1:14; 1 Jn. 4:2, 3). This disparagement of God's good creation led to an emphasis on spiritual salvation and a lack of concern for works of charity and social justice (1 Jn. 3:16-18).[3] The Pentecostal movement, through its message of empowerment, provides a healthy redirection by preaching that God is good and is still in the business of healing and blessings. Christian theology needs this healthy rebalancing of the issues.

The problem with the prosperity gospel is that, in many cases, contemporary Pentecostals take things far beyond merely making pastors comfortable or making Christians feel at home in the use of material things. Pastors preach in support of their extravagant and materialistic lifestyles, sometimes in subtle competition with their church's affluent members. In discussing prosperity gospel, there is no need to throw the baby out with the bath water by attacking those who, through hard work, acquire certain

---

[3] Shelton, 'Pendulum Swing', 358.

material luxuries in life. Good and comfortable living is not evil. There is nothing wrong with having material things, because everybody needs them to live and people must be free to enjoy the fruits of their labour. The good things of this world are there to be enjoyed, but, as far as the Christian evangel is concerned, there is everything wrong with promoting materialistic and extravagant lifestyles, especially when they are presented as the prime indicators of faithful Christianity.

In my judgement, the biggest problem caused by the prosperity message is its selective use of the Scriptures to promote materialism as a non-negotiable indicator of faithful Christianity. Consider, for instance, the passage from Luke quoted in the first paragraph of this chapter. This context is the Sermon on the Mount, parts of which teach that we should not 'judge' or 'condemn' others because the standards we use for others would be used against us. It is with that understanding that Jesus also taught that forgiveness was reciprocal: 'Forgive, and you will be forgiven.' We give not just money but also forgiveness. A useful example comes from the Parable of the Unforgiving Servant, in which the servant refused to forgive even though he had been forgiven his greater debt. Unfortunately, whenever this passage is preached, the focus is on giving money, which does not do justice to the context within which Jesus taught. In using Scripture selectively, regardless of context, contemporary Pentecostal theology shoots itself in the foot by marginalising the poor and vulnerable and finding itself short of answers in the midst of poverty, pain and misfortune.

Elsewhere, I have noted that the kind of materialistic prosperity that is preached in the name of 'biblical prosperity' accounts in part for the inability of large numbers of those who preach them to establish rural ministries.[4] The three idols identified by evangelical theologian Christopher Wright as characterising aspects of contemporary Christianity come into play here: first, the idols of power and pride; second, the idols of popularity and success; and third, the idols of wealth and greed.[5] Idolising power leads to pride and a craving for popularity and success for their own sake. It is difficult to see how the idolisation of wealth would not lead to greed. What has happened then is that ministry has taken on an executive tone that distances it from ordinary people who are not considered symbols of material prosperity. Thus many prosperity preachers are unable to establish churches in poor communities because African rural economies and levels of deprivation are unable to sustain name-it-and-claim-it models of Christian spirituality. They are therefore unable to support the materialistic

---

[4] Asamoah-Gyadu, *African Charismatics*, ch. 7.

[5] Chris Wright, 'Calling the Church Back to Humility, Integrity, Simplicity', in Julia E.M. Cameron (ed.), *Christ our Reconciler: Gospel, Church, World* (Downers Grove, IL: Intervarsity Press, 2012), 149-58.

lifestyles of those who preach materialistic models of prosperity as the right of every Christian. From the lips of a contemporary African Pentecostal pastor one might hear claims that he or she has been called only to the educated middle class, and that those who do not benefit from the messages he or she preaches would have their biblical needs satisfied elsewhere. The truth is that the model of spirituality presented by this preacher of material prosperity can fit the lifestyles only of those who are already rich or on their way up.

Prosperity Gospel and Contemporary Christianity

Contemporary Pentecostal pastors in Africa today claim a divine right to travel first class on airplanes, drive top-of-the-range cars, wear designer clothing, live in five-star-hotel-like accommodation, and have access to other such material acquisitions that are supposed to be indicators of God's favour on his servants. The issue is not with the material things as such, but with the theological interpretations that are given to their acquisition. In other words, materialistic lifestyles are being justified on the basis that the Bible endorses them. David Oyedepo, the Nigerian bishop of the Living Church Worldwide ('Winners' Chapel') owns more than one jet, and in Ghana one pastor opened his home and wardrobe to a local TV station to film his luxurious estate and expensive cars. Pastors constantly illustrate their sermons with their international travels, the money they receive from influential members and the fact that their children were either born in the United States or are in school there. This attitude has created a new religious sub-culture within contemporary Christianity in which, contrary to the teaching of Jesus, a person's worth is assessed on the basis of his material wealth. A man's life, Jesus taught, does not consist in the abundance of his possessions (Luke 12:15).

Additionally, contemporary Pentecostal prosperity preach-ing has introduced an executive model of leadership into Christianity in which the pastor must be 'waited upon' because s/he is a man or woman of God.[6] In Ghana's New Christianity, Paul Gifford has rightly noted that the emphasis on success in these churches is found everywhere. It is found in the names of the churches; it is found in the claims made on their car-bumper stickers, and it is found in the names of their evangelistic crusades. Suffice it at this point to cite Gifford's list of crusade themes from this new type of Pentecostalism:

---

[6] See J. Kwabena Asamoah-Gyadu, 'Touch Not the Lord's Anointed: Leadership in Ghana's New Charismatic Communities', in Akintunde Akinade (ed.), *A New Day: Essays on World Christianity in Honor of Lamin Sanneh* (New York: Peter Lang, 2010), ch. 9.

> 'Taking your Possessions'; 'Winning Ways'; 'Experiencing Open Heavens for Divine Blessings'; 'Stepping into Greatness'; 'The Force of Divine Progress'; 'Be a Winner in Jesus Christ'; 'Come and Possess your Promised Land'; 'From Captivity to Restoration'; 'The Best is Yet to Come'; 'Highway to Success'; 'Dawning of a New Day'; 'Taking New Territories'; 'I Will Restore unto You'; 'Breaking your Barriers'; 'Breaking the Yoke'; 'Abundance is my Portion'; 'Going up to Higher Places'.[7]

Within Africa, although the message of prosperity is usually identified with the new Pentecostals, versions of it are now also heard among some preachers serving with classical Pentecostal denominations and ministers of the historic mission churches. Even among those who preach the prosperity gospel, the emphasis differs from preacher to preacher. What is preached may also be defined by the occasion and the audience. Thus in talking about prosperity gospel, I gather the evidence not just from its selective hermeneutics but also from what is promoted through lifestyle choices in the name of renewal and empowered Christianity. I am responding, therefore, to the bottom line of a message with different variations and not just the thoughts of a particular preacher or church, whether Pentecostal or otherwise.

Foundations of Prosperity Gospel

In the minds of the general public, prosperity gospel is an interpretation of the Scriptures with an emphasis on personal and material wellbeing. In the new churches, there is a disproportionate emphasis on money, cars, houses, international travel, jewellery, clothes and other such visible manifestations of personal and material wellbeing as signs of God's favour. These blessings from God also include good health and family life with children as returns for good Christianity. The inability of many people to enjoy such 'glorious living', invariably symbolised by the pastor's own success, results in prayer meetings, conventions and summits, at which their shortfalls of prosperity are addressed. Here, at these prayer sessions, the 'fire of God' is invoked in imprecations upon family members, witches and demons that are supposed to be hindering the breakthroughs being sought.

There is a bridge between what is preached as far as the prosperity gospel is concerned, and what is heard in church and through the media. David Oyedepo of the Living Church Worldwide, for example, includes in his personal testimony the claim that God called him specifically to make people rich. The popular name of his Church, Winners' Chapel, is a reflection of this mindset. While the conservative evangelical movement preached modesty in life, the dangers of wealth, and caution in the pursuit

---

7 Paul Gifford, *Ghana's New Christianity: Pentecostalism in a Globalizing African Economy* (London: Hurst and Co., 2004), 45.

of material things because they could be obstacles to the kingdom, among the new Pentecostals wealth is flaunted as an indicator of God's blessing and faithful Christianity. To some extent, the gospel of prosperity is a direct response to conservative evangelical values that in some cases, whether advertently or not, saw deprivation as a sign of deep spirituality. That sort of preaching also hurt people, as they were inflicted with guilt for enjoying God's material graces to them. The more thoughtful conservative evangelicals and classical Pentecostals did not condemn wealth as such, but sustained the teachings of Jesus Christ on its dangers. The dangers of materialism were emphasised against the backdrop of the eschatological orientation of those older streams of Christianity.

As I have come to understand it, therefore, prosperity gospel is the teaching that, when a person comes to Christ, God makes available to that Christian certain spiritual and material blessings that lead to well-being. There are variations of the prosperity gospel, including some that teach that poverty is a sign of unfaithfulness, sinfulness or failure in the fulfilment of tithing obligations towards God. Some have even taught that a pastor must be as wealthy as the wealthiest member of his congregation. The teachings of the prosperity gospel are justified by its advocates on three main grounds: first, that the Bible teaches it. Among the many passages that are used to support the gospel of prosperity is Galatians 3:13-14, which reads, 'Christ redeemed us from the curse of the law by becoming a curse for us … He redeemed us in order that the blessing given to Abraham might come to the Gentiles through Christ Jesus, that by faith we might receive the promise of the Spirit.' The expression 'blessing given to Abraham' is understood by prosperity preachers – regardless of the context and the general tenor of Paul's message in Galatians – to refer to the modern-day equivalents of the material blessings that God made available to Abraham.

Second, that Jesus lived it. To make the gospel of prosperity Christian, there are attempts to make it Christological. Thus some argue that the donkey on which Jesus rode to Jerusalem was the best means of transport of his day and that his seamless robe was designer-made and that was why the soldiers at the cross fought to have custody of it. His statement in John 10:10 that he came that we might have life and, in particular, have in abundance, is often interpreted to mean abundance in the material things of life.

Third, that faith makes it possible because God has willed it. Those who can appropriate the promises of the prosperity gospel are expected to exercise faith in Jesus Christ through faithful payments of tithes and offerings. This giving is not simply to the church, but also to the 'anointed of God', which, in the understanding of those who preach prosperity, means the pastor who exercises 'spiritual authority' over the individual. The biblical passages used to justify this transactional means of coming into prosperity include the episode involving the prophet Elijah and the widow of Zarephath. The story as recorded in 1 Kings 17:8-16 reads:

> Then the word of the Lord came to him: 'Go at once to Zarephath of Sidon and stay there. I have commanded a widow in that place to supply you with food.' So he went to Zarephath. When he came to the town gate, a widow was there gathering sticks. He called to her and asked, 'Would you bring to me a little water in a jar so I may have a drink?' As she was going to get it, he called, 'And bring me, please, a piece of bread.'
>
> 'As surely as the Lord your God lives', she replied, 'I don't have any bread – only a handful of flour in a jar and a little oil in a jug. I am gathering a few sticks to take home and make a meal for myself and my son, that we may eat it – and die.'
>
> Elijah said to her, 'Don't be afraid. Go home and do as you have said. But first make a small cake of bread for me from what you have and bring it to me, and then make something for yourself and your son. For this is what the Lord, the God of Israel, says: "The jar of flour will not be used up and the jug of oil will not run dry until the day the Lord gives rain on the land."'
>
> She went away and did as Elijah had told her. So there was food for every day for Elijah and for the woman and her family. For the jar of flour was not used up and the jug of oil did not run dry, in keeping with the word of the Lord spoken by Elijah.

For a number of reasons those who preach the prosperity gospel prefer such passages. First, we find a vulnerable woman in need. That she was a poor widow with a son to feed and that they were at their wits end in terms of their material circumstances is important. Second, the way out of a dire situation of poverty occasioned by widowhood, that passage seems to suggest, was to give something to 'the man of God'. From this idea comes the principle of 'sowing and reaping', which is a cardinal preaching of the prosperity message. In this particular case, the little the woman owned had to be 'sowed' as an offering in the life and ministry of Elijah, and our modern-day Elijahs claim the same privileges. Third, the sowing was done at God's command, and therefore sowing in tithes and offerings and giving to the men and women of God are not optional when it comes to the principles of prosperity. As a result, it is those who can afford to give who normally come to the attention of the pastor in terms of the provision of care.

Fourth, in any day, it takes a great amount of 'faith' for a widow in that condition to serve the prophet first, before herself and her son. The prosperity gospel is based on the exercise of faith because sometimes – and this is particularly so in Africa – external circumstances may dictate otherwise, but a faithful Christian must learn to give, even if to do so means emptying bank accounts. Some even teach that the payment of tithes is such a sacred duty in terms of one's blessing that the obligation must be fulfilled even by borrowing money. I heard one pastor teaching that anyone who does not pay tithes is worse than an armed robber because 'the armed robber robs mortals but those who do not pay tithes rob God'. Fifth, and finally, the faith of the widow of Zarephath paid off, as she and her son, if prosperity preachers are to believed, lived in great abundance. This woman is an icon in prosperity preaching because her story provides the principles for it; as I heard one preacher say, 'even in your poverty God needs something from you to bless you'.

In the rest of the story as recorded in 1 Kings 17:17-24, even when the widow's only son died, as a result of ill health, God restored him to his mother through the prophet Elijah. Thus, not only do we have in this story the restoration of wealth and abundance, but we also have a classic case of the restoration of health to a dead son. Thus, what I discuss in this chapter has to do with expositions and interpretations of the Bible that suggest that material things in particular, including health and wealth, are non-negotiable indicators or rewards for faithful Christianity. Conversely, it is preached in prosperity messages that those who do not enjoy these material benefits of life may be under curses either for not being faithful in their Christian walk or for being unfaithful in the payment of tithes and offerings. The critical text is always Malachi 3:7-10:

> Ever since the time of your forefathers you have turned away from my decrees and have not kept them. Return to me, and I will return to you, says the Lord Almighty.
>
> But you ask, 'How are we to return?' Will a man rob God? Yet you rob me. But you ask, 'How do we rob you?' In tithes and offerings. You are under a curse – the whole nation of you – because you are robbing me. Bring the whole tithe into my store house that there may be food in my house. Test me in this, says the Lord Almighty, and see if I will not throw open the floodgates of heaven and pour out so much blessing that you will not have room enough for it.

This challenge, the challenge to 'test me and see', has been taken on squarely by Pentecostals. If the widow of Zarephath gave to the prophet as 'a man of God' and received her breakthrough, those who withhold from God have curses unleashed on their activities. This understanding of misfortune and calamity is also preached from a scriptural basis, for God has promised that, if tithing obligations are fulfilled, curses will be reversed in the affairs of his people: '"I will prevent pests from devouring your crops, and the vines in your fields will not cast their fruit", says the Lord Almighty. "Then all the nations will call you blessed for yours will be a delightful land", says the Lord Almighty' (Mal. 3:11-12).

In using this text to support the relationship between tithes and prosperity, contemporary Pentecostals have developed what I have referred to as a 'transactional' approach to giving. In other words faithfulness in tithes and offerings virtually guarantees security and protection for one's endeavours. There have been cases in which people seeking pastoral care during crises have been told bluntly that 'pests are devouring your crops' and the 'vines in your fields are casting their fruits' because you have 'stolen' from the Lord in tithes and offerings. Businessmen in particular have become vulnerable in the face of this teaching, with some even developing specific transactional relationships with pastors, because to bring the tithes into the 'storehouse' of the Lord has also been interpreted in many cases to mean 'give it to your pastor'.

Understanding the Practice and Theology of Prosperity

Faithful payments of tithes and offerings have enabled African Pentecostal churches in particular to raise enormous amounts of money for running their churches and projects. In this particular area, they have proven more innovative and theologically relevant than almost all the historic mission denominations. Many of the older churches have still not been able to wean themselves off subventions from mission partners in the west. In contrast, let us consider what Mensa Otabil, leader of the International Central Gospel Church in Ghana, has to say about his calling, as far as resources are concerned:

> When the Lord called me to pioneer a church, He impressed on me strongly to found a church that would not be tied to the apron-strings of a foreign mission board. The Lord called me to teach my congregation to stop looking to Europe or America as their source of supply but to cultivate a new spirit and ethic of national development. I fully believe that wherever God puts you He has enough resources in place to take care of your needs. As a result of that conviction, our church has pursued a vigorous policy of indigenous financing and government.[8]

The faithful payments of tithes and offerings have helped the new churches to 'prosper' materially, including enabling these churches to support their extremely expensive media programmes, which make the general message of the gospel available to a wider public.

On the relationship between the principles and signs of prosperity, it is important to note that a 'redemptive uplift' is possible following the conversion experience. There are testimonies of transformation, empowerment and deliverance among the people of God that underscore a strong connection between 'being in Christ' and 'prosperity in life'. Material prosperity is good because it affirms the dignity of the human person as created in the image of God. There is no dignity in poverty and

---

[8] Mensa Otabil, *Beyond the Rivers of Ethiopia: A Biblical Revelation on God's Purpose for the Black Race* (Accra: Altar Media, 2004), 8, 64.

deprivation. The Bible therefore does not encourage believers in God to embrace poverty. What it does is enjoin those who believe to take care of the material needs of the poor. Tithes and offerings, one would think, should properly be used by the churches in part for poverty alleviation programmes for their members, many of whom do not give – simply because they do not have the means to do so. In this way, human beings take care of creation and responsibly appropriate God-given resources for the benefit of the created and to the glory of the Creator God.

Material blessings and spiritual well-being are not alien to Scripture. In the promises and examples of the Bible we encounter people who prospered, and also promises that those who are obedient to God and love him will do well in life. Abraham, is one such model, and Paul in Philippians writes that God will supply our needs according to his riches in glory as found in Christ Jesus (Philippians 4:19). A testimony delivered at the twenty-fifth anniversary of the International Central Gospel Church, in 2009, narrated how three months' savings of what would have been spent on alcohol enabled the testifier, a middle-aged man, to buy a new car and redirect resources previously 'wasted on drinks for friends and womanising' into supporting family life. We have in that testimony, and in many others I have heard, clear cases of God's redemption in Christ and the empowerment of the Holy Spirit that have led to spiritual and material prosperity. Prosperity is not alien to the experiences of Christians today as long as the right choices in life are made.

Giving is a biblical mandate, and it must be done as part of our total response to God in worship. We worship God with our verbalisations of his majesty and goodness. Nowhere is this done more powerfully than in Pentecostal/charismatic churches in Africa, where, because of the oral nature of their theology, worshippers can rise in church, even interrupt a sermon, to sing and bless the name of the Lord. We also worship God with our gestures, i.e. raising arms, kneeling, prostrating ourselves and, if the examples I find in Pentecostal settings are anything to go by, even running around the auditorium. God must also be worshipped with our substance. All three – words, gestures, and substance – come together so beautifully in the words of Psalm 116:12-15, 17-19.

> How can I repay the Lord for all his goodness to me? I will lift up the cup of salvation and call on the name of the Lord. I will fulfil my vows to the Lord in the presence of all his people. ... I will sacrifice a thank offering to you and call on the name of the Lord. I will fulfil my vows to the Lord in the presence of all his people, in the courts of the house of the Lord – in your midst O Jerusalem. Praise the Lord.

Christian giving must always be done as part of worship, because it is our response to what God has done for us in Christ. Jesus Christ is our ultimate example in giving. Thus, in Philippians 2:5-11, Paul talks about cultivating the same attitude as we find in Christ who, though he was God, 'emptied himself' and took on the form of a servant. Christians give as part of our own 'self-emptying', indicating that what we have belongs to God and we return it to him. Payment of tithes and offerings is good, but the intention must never be to use them in transactional ways, as if God's grace is for the highest bidder.

Why Has Prosperity Theology Become a Contentious Issue?

Tithes and their relationship to prosperity have become contentious issues for other reasons also. The first is its Old Testament emphasis. The evidence in support of any Christian doctrine is usually marshalled from both the Old and New Testaments, but, when it comes to the issue of tithes, the evidence is obtained almost exclusively from the Old Testament. Second, the relationship between tithes and offerings makes theology 'formulaic'. Life is not formulaic, so, for instance, although Jeremiah the prophet assures God's people that 'there is hope for the future' and that God's plans for his people are 'for good and not for ill' (Jer. 29:11), it is also true that life does not always move in one direction.

Third, those who live in Africa know that poverty does not discriminate between believers and unbelievers. There are Christians who are poor, materially speaking, and non-Christians who are wealthy. The Christian life, Jesus promised, would be full of challenges that required only the grace of God to endure. For some, these challenges will continue until either they are called home or Christ returns in glory, whichever comes first. Fourth, Jesus was not materialistic and the Church must follow his example, yet the prosperity gospel tends to be materialistic in orientation. Materialism should not be confused with godly prosperity. Materialism pursues material things as ends in themselves and over-projects them as the sole indicators of God's favour. When that happens, pastors tend to preach about cars, furniture, houses, international travel, etc.

Fifth, the gospel of Jesus Christ must have something to say to both 'the rich and the poor'; 'the winner and the loser'; 'the champion and the defeated'; 'the successful and the struggling'; 'those celebrating and those mourning'. Jesus had a message for Nicodemus but also had something for the woman who was haemorrhaging. Two families might appear in church on Sunday morning to worship, one to thank God for the gift of a new child and the other to attend a memorial service for the loss of a child of the same age; the Christian message must have something to say to both.

Sixth, the prosperity gospel has a hermeneutical problem: prosperity thinking usually relies too much on proof-texts and so tends to interpret the Scriptures in a selective manner, without due attention to context. Its message tends to be one-sided. It privileges the rich and marginalises the poor, weak and underprivileged. This imbalance may not always be conscious, but in a religious context where the emphasis is always on health and wealth, the weak and helpless do not find the space to function and the comfort they need.

Conclusion: Is There Biblical Prosperity?

Yes, in my thinking, there is biblical prosperity, but biblical prosperity is never materialistic in orientation. There is a difference between being prosperous in Christ and being materialistic. Time and again, Jesus denounced those who pursued material things to the neglect of spirituality at the deeper levels. The matter becomes even more theologically confusing when preachers uphold their personal mat-erialistic lifestyles and those of the affluent members of their congregations as indicators of God's favour. That emphasis leaves the poor without any testimony. Thus Femi Adeleye serves us well with his submission that the problem with the materialistic orientation of the prosperity gospel is that: first, it distorts the mission of Jesus Christ as primarily to save from sin; second, it fails to see that all forms of giving to God are primarily acts of worship; third, it distorts the person of Christ by portraying Jesus as one who was materially rich; fourth, it feeds on greed; fifth, the prosperity gospel lacks an explanation for the sufferings of believers in particular.[9]

In Mary's Magnificat, we have a useful example of what it means to prosper from God's perspective: 'From now all generations will call me blessed, for the Mighty One has done great things for me – holy is his name. His mercy extends to those who fear him, from generation to generation … He has filled the hungry with good things but has sent the rich empty away' (Lk. 1:48ff.). The 'rich' in this context are like the Pharisee who went into the temple to pray and decided to present his 'curriculum vitae' to God. He was sent empty away (Lk. 18:9-14).

Another example is Zechariah's prophetic song on Israel's salvation:

> Praise be to the Lord, the God of Israel, because he has come and has redeemed his people. He has raised up a horn of salvation for us … salvation from our enemies and from the hand of all who hate us … to rescue us from the hand of our enemies, and enable us to serve him without fear in holiness and righteousness before him all our days (Lk. 1:67ff.).

Israel is delivered in order to enable the nation to 'serve God without fear in holiness and righteousness'. Sometimes in the desire to raise funds in tithing, the moral dimensions of the gospel tend to disappear completely

---

[9] Femi Adeleye, 'The Prosperity Gospel', in Julia E.M. Cameron (ed.), *Christ our Reconciler: Gospel, Church, World* (Downers Grove, IL: Intervarsity Press, 2012), 161.

from the theological radar of the churches. One influential Nigerian charismatic preacher even used to say that tithing works whether the person is a believer or not, because it is God's formula for success. Biblical prosperity encapsulates God's physical and spiritual deliverance and personal and communal well-being. All the people who had been blessed materially were expected to extend hands of support to those who did not have, and also to serve God in holiness and righteousness. Prosperity in the Scriptures was never conceived entirely in material terms, and those who do not have material things should not feel left out of God's grace.

In response to the materialistic prosperity mindset, the call of the church is to preach a holistic gospel that prepares the materially rich to acknowledge God and the materially poor not to feel 'cursed' or neglected by God. This would be a holistic gospel in which the existential and eschatological dimensions of the faith are seen as continuous with each other. Jesus warned against the accumulation of material wealth and dependence upon it; in preaching, therefore, we need to practice 'Christological hermeneutics' in which Jesus Christ becomes the standard and our focus is on the Cross.

Chapter 12

Sighs and Signs of the Spirit: Pentecostalism and the Future of Christianity in Africa

The main thesis of this volume is that Pentecostalism and the various charismatic movements that are its historically younger and theologically more versatile progenies have been inspired by the Spirit of God. The Christian communities in Africa that I describe as Pentecostal include older independent churches with a clear Christian orientation, classical Pentecostal denominations of both foreign and local provenance, and the various contemporary Pentecostal renewal movements, churches and transnational fellowships, such as the Full Gospel Businessmen's Fellowship International. Within the last century these streams of pneumatic Christianity have together transformed the face of Christianity in Africa. There is every indication that the future of Christianity in Africa will be determined by how seriously the churches remain open to the work of the Holy Spirit. This conclusion is based on the following observations.

First, religion in Africa generally tends to value experience more than creeds. Pentecostalism, with its emphasis on the experiential dimension of spirituality, offers a stream of Christianity that appeals more to African religious sensibilities than do the traditional forms found in the historic mission churches.

Second, the presence and force of charismatic renewal movements within existing historic mission denominations has helped to stem the tide of members drifting into Pentecostal and charismatic churches. The haemorrhage has not stopped completely, but there is every indication that, if the historic mission churches continue along the path of toleration for renewal, they may not have the numbers on their side, but they will survive.

Third, demographically speaking, the advantage, in terms of the growth and influence of Christianity, belongs to the contemporary Pentecostal churches. We have learnt that not only do they have a strong appeal for the upwardly mobile youth but they also make innovative uses of modern media technologies. Their brand of Christianity, with its diversified religious menu, means that in the future most African Christian professionals and people of influence are likely to belong to these new religious communities.

Four, Pentecostal spirituality, as we saw in the case of the prophetic and healing and deliverance ministries, resonates very strongly with African traditional religious piety; healing, exorcism, Spirit-inspired worship, the power of words, and the prophetic ministries are familiar ideas. This is why Harvey Cox referred to Pentecostalism as a movement that recovers for our time 'primal speech' (ecstatic utterance), 'primal piety' (mystical experience, trance and healing) and 'primal hope' (the unshakable expectation of a better future). In Cox's words: 'However they may define it theologically, there can be little doubt that Pentecostals have rediscovered a powerful and primal form of religious expression.'[1]

Fifth, on the part of the new Pentecostals in particular, there are very conscious attempts to 'take territories and raise champions', seen, for example, in the recent establishment of institutions of higher learning, including private universities. In addition to the recognition and space given for people to use their spiritual gifts, a number of the new Pentecostals, unlike, say, the older AICs, have also developed ministry at the inter-generational level. Thus the average charismatic ministry in Ghana has strong children's, men's, women's and youth ministries. The more institutionalised a religious organisation becomes, the more likely it is that it will endure and influence its environment. I see this as one of the major strengths of Pentecostalism.

Encountering the Spirit as the Spirit of Christ

The Pentecostal movement deserves credit for drawing the attention of the Church to the centrality and importance of the Holy Spirit in Christian life and theology. The way the presence of the Spirit is expressed in Christian life today, however, has tended to create the impression that the Spirit is only a supernatural power from God, a power that responds to human invitations to 'possess' people, to enable the speaking of tongues, to effect healing, exorcism and deliverance; a power that helps to effect curses on enemies and activate blessings and that inspires worship, including the manifestations of prophecy, visions and revelations. All this may be true. Nevertheless, this view of the Spirit has not been helped by the tendency to speak of him in dispensational terms, by beginning with Pentecost.

It was to correct such impressions that Jesus said, 'before Abraham was I am'. If Jesus existed prior to the Incarnation, in what form did he exist? In his own response to the woman of Samaria, Jesus explained that God is Spirit and those who worshipped him were supposed to do so in 'spirit and in truth' (Jn. 4:21-24). The Spirit appears in the understanding of Jesus

---

[1] Harvey Cox, *Fire from Heaven: The Rise of Pentecostal Spirituality and the Reshaping of Religion in the Twenty-First Century* (Reading, MA: Addison-Wesley, 1995), 88.

Christ, as the 'Spirit of truth', and that is how he is expected to be encountered.

The inability to understand that the Holy Spirit of God is also the Spirit of Christ, has led to situations in which the works of the Spirit in contemporary Pentecostalism have often been interpreted without reference to the standard that Christ lays down for those who believe in him. In recent times, a number of powerful Pentecostal pastors in Ghana and Nigeria have come under the public spotlight for lack of accountability in the use of church resources. The use of the media for prophetic activities has caused confusion and will require extensive research. I have referred to the development of an executive model of leadership among contemporary Pentecostal leaders, in contrast to the servant-leadership model recommended by Jesus Christ. There are cases of leaders demanding that tithes and offerings be paid directly into their own bank accounts. The following summary from Ruth Marshall reflects what I have observed in churches:

> With the arrival of the prosperity gospel, money has become incontestably the most significant object in the creation of a common language, seen both as the mode of organizing churches and as the means of entering into contact with God … During the request for 'seed offerings', the pastor called individuals to bring their 'gifts' up to the altar, rather than using the standard practice of placing their money in a discreet and concealed fashion into a basket passed around, or remitting sealed envelopes … We can see with the rise of these charismatic 'miracle' workers an attempt to impose pastoral control and develop an economy of power and prestige in which divine power and secular power become interchangeable and mutually supportive.[2]

Marshall continues by noting that, although the modern Pentecostal movement continues to preach on corruption and sin, the abuse of power in these movements means their preaching against vices has become 'increasingly fraught with contradictions'.[3] These and other such practices, although by no means part of all the churches, have led to very critical comments by members of the public.

The sighs of the Spirit denotes the attempt of the Spirit of God to express his presence and power through the human vessels and communities that confess the lordship of Jesus Christ. To avoid the pitfalls that could undermine the signs of the Spirit among his people, the pneumatology of the church must have a Christological focus. The Spirit that is at work in the church must be understood as the Spirit of Jesus Christ. One of the clearest statements on the personality of the Holy Spirit is found in John

---

[2] Ruth Marshall, *Political Spiritualities: The Pentecostal Revolution in Nigeria* (Chicago and London: University of Chicago Press, 2009), 183-84.

[3] Marshall, *Political Spiritualities,* 184.

14:18, where Jesus says, 'I will not leave you as orphans but I will come to you.' In other words, Jesus was telling his disciples, 'I will not leave you without support'. Jesus was speaking in the run-up to his Passion, which culminated in the withdrawal of his physical presence from the world. 'In a little while you will see me; and in a little while you will not see me,' was how he put it to the disciples. In effect, that phase of God's self-disclosure in which the 'word became flesh' in order that the disciples could physically touch, see, communicate and engage with Jesus Christ was virtually coming to an end with his death on the Cross. That withdrawal of physical presence was, however, according to Jesus, not going to mark an end to his presence in the world, which explains his statement, 'I will not leave you as orphans but I will come to you.' But how did he return to the disciples?

The Return of Christ as Spirit

Jesus Christ fulfilled the promise to 'return' to the disciples in the Presence of the Holy Spirit. In other words, a proper understanding of the Spirit must see him in terms of 'God's continuing Presence in the world'.[4] He remains among those who believe in him to continue the ministry of God as revealed in Jesus Christ in very specific ways. First, the Holy Spirit, according to Jesus Christ is to serve as Comforter or Counsellor to those who believe in him. He is also their teacher. Second, Jesus was recognised as one who taught with authority. If the Holy Spirit was going to continue the ministry of Jesus Christ, then it was logical to expect that he would take that which was of Christ and make it clearer to the people of Jesus. What the Holy Spirit makes clear is that which is true of Jesus Christ because he is 'the Spirit of truth'. In other words the Holy Spirit, when he is present, never contradicts anything that Jesus has said or represents. Jesus represents God, for as he noted: 'I am here not to do my own will but the will of him who sent me.' The Holy Spirit is therefore among us to exercise the will of God as revealed in Jesus Christ. Third, the Holy Spirit serves to remind believers of what Jesus has taught and represents. Anyone who needs a 'reminder' is a person with limitations. The fact the Spirit of God is supposed to remind his disciples of what Christ has taught is an indication that human beings have limitations.

How does the Holy Spirit continue the work of Jesus Christ among his people? The answer can be found in what we refer to as 'ministry'; Jesus called it 'greater works'. Greater works does not necessarily mean that what Christians will accomplish would be bigger than what Jesus did. We read from John that 'Jesus Christ laid down his life for us' (I John 3:16).

---

[4] Gordon D. Fee, *God's Empowering Presence: The Holy Spirit in the Letters of Paul* (Peabody, MA: Hendrickson, 1994).

Jesus was God who laid down his life for us, so what greater things can we do that Christ has not already done? Jesus worked as God in human form, but we work with all the accompanying limitations of the human person. Human beings, no matter how much they are filled with the Holy Spirit, do not become divine, but remain human. But, if they can be so filled with the Holy Spirit of God that by the enabling strength of the Spirit they can accomplish things that only God can accomplish in Christ, then that amounts to greater works. To perform greater works is to perform above human limitations – and that is possible only through the presence and power of the Holy Spirit, who is the continuing Presence of Jesus Christ among those he has called.

Pentecostalism and Greater Works

I am aware that there are many criticisms of Pentecostal/Charismatic Christianity, but on the whole I take a very positive view of the movement today. The impressive congregations that have been built, the attraction for our upwardly mobile youth, the media ministries developed and the religious menu constantly rolled out for the public suggest that the Pentecostal churches have indeed restored something to the heart of Christianity. As we have seen from some of the chapters in this volume, not everything that is happening in contemporary Pentecostalism can be attributed to the power of God. Nevertheless, there is every indication that the phenomenal growth of Christianity in Africa can be explained partly in terms of the rise of Pentecostalism, with its pneumatic or experiential Christianity.

When Jesus said that he was not going to leave us as orphans, he was not talking to any particular church or denomination. He was talking first to his disciples and then to all those who would come to believe in him. The Pentecostals have latched onto that promise, helping the movement to spread like wildfire across continents. A church that flows in the power of the Spirit can never be an orphan.

Bibliography

Books and Articles

Adeleye, Femi, 'The Prosperity Gospel,' in Julia E.M. Cameron (ed.). *Christ our Reconciler* (Downers Grove, IL: Intervarsity Press, 2012): 159-166.

Agyin-Asare, Charles, *Power in Prayer: Taking Your Blessings by Force* (Hoornaar, Netherlands: His Printing, 2001).

________. *Power Demonstration: Understanding the Holy Spirit and His Gifts* (Accra: Agyin-Asare, 2008).

Anaba, Eastwood, *Breaking Illegal Possession: Dislodge the Enemy and Possess the Land!* (Accra: Design Solutions, 1996).

________. *God's End-Time Militia: Winning the War Within and Without*, rev. ed. (Accra: Design Solutions, 1997).

________. *The Quest for Supremacy* (Bolgatanga, Ghana: Desert Leaf Publications, 2004).

________. *The Workability of Faith* (Bolgatanga, Ghana: Desert Leaf Publications, 2004).

________. *Speak the Word* (Bolgatanga, Ghana: Desert Leaf Publications, 2013).

Anderson, Allan, *To the Ends of the Earth: Pentecostalism and the Transformation of World Christianity* (Oxford: Oxford University Press, 2013).

Anderson, Allan, 'Varieties, Taxonomies, and Definitions', in Allan Anderson et al. (eds.), *Studying Global Pentecostalism: Theories and Methods* (Berkeley: University of California Press, 2010): 13-29.

Asamoah-Gyadu, Johnson, 'The Church in the African State Towards the Twenty-First Century: The Pentecostal/Charismatic Experience in Ghana.' *Journal of African Christian Thought.* Vol. 1, 2 (1998): 51-57.

Asamoah-Gyadu, J. Kwabena, 'Unction to Function: Reinventing the *Oil of Influence* in African Pentecostalism', *Journal of Pentecostal Theology*, 13, 2 (2005): 231-256.

________. *African Charismatics: Current Developments within Independent Indigenous Pentecostalism in Ghana* (Leiden: E.J. Brill, 2005).

________. 'Touch Not the Lord's Anointed: Leadership in Ghana's New Charismatic Communities', in Akintunde Akinade (ed.), *A New Day: Essays on World Christianity in Honor of Lamin Sanneh* (New York: Peter Lang, 2010): 142-157.

________. *Contemporary Pentecostal Christianity: Interpretations from an African Context* (Oxford: Regnum International; Akropong-Akuapem, Regnum Africa, 2013).

Ashimolowo, Matthew, *The Coming Wealth Transfer: Believing the Prophecy, Applying the Principles, Preparing to Be a Millionaire for God* (London: Mattyson Media, 2006).

Baëta, Christian G., *Prophetism in Ghana: A Study of Some Spiritual Churches* (London: SCM, 1962).

________. 'Christianity and Healing', *Orita: Journal of Religious Studies, University of*

Ibadan, 1 (1967): 51-61.

Beckford, James A. (ed.), *New Religious Movements and Rapid Social Change* (London: Sage, 1986).

Bediako, Kwame, *Christianity in Africa: The Renewal of a Non-Western Religion* (Edinburgh: Edinburgh University Press, 1995).

________. *Jesus in Africa: The Christian Gospel in African History and Experience* (Akropong-Akuapem, Ghana: Regnum Africa, 2000).

________. 'Worship as Vital Participation: Some Personal Reflections on Ministry in the African Church', *Journal of African Christian Thought*, 8, 2 (December 2005): 3-7.

Bittlinger, Arnold (ed.), *The Church is Charismatic: The World Council of Churches and the Charismatic Renewal* (Geneva: World Council of Churches, 1981).

Castells, Manuel, *Communication Power* (Oxford: Oxford University Press, 2009).

Cone, James, *God of the Oppressed* (Maryknoll, NY: Orbis Books, 1975).

Corten, André, and Marshall-Fratani, Ruth (eds), *Between Babel and Pentecost: Transnationalism in America and Latin America* (Bloomington and Indianapolis: Indiana University Press, 2001).

Cox, Harvey, *Fire From Heaven: The Rise of Pentecostal Spirituality and the Reshaping of Religion in the Twenty-First Century* (Reading, MA: Addison-Wesley Publishing Company, 1995).

________. 'Foreword', in Allan H. Anderson and Walter J. Hollenweger (eds), *Pentecostals after a Century: Global Perspectives on a Movement in Transition* (Sheffield: Sheffield Academic Press, 1999).

De Witte, Marleen, Altar Media's *Living Word:* Televised Charismatic Christianity in Ghana, *Journal of Religion in Africa*, 33, 2 (2003): 172-202.

Dickson, Kwesi A., *Theology in Africa* (Maryknoll, NY: Orbis, 1984).

Duncan-Williams, Nicholas, *Destined to Make an Impact* (Lanham, MD: Pneuma Life Publishing, 2004).

Dunn, James D.G., 'Ministry and the Ministry: The Charismatic Renewal's Challenge to Traditional Ecclesiology', in Cecil M. Robeck, Jr. (ed.), *Charismatic Experiences in Christian Worship* (Peabody, MA: Hendrickson, 1985): 81-101.

________. 'A Protestant Response' (to Juan Sepúlveda, 'Born Again: Baptism and the Spirit'), in Jürgen Moltmann and Karl-Josef Kuschel (eds), *Pentecostal Movements as an Ecumenical Challenge: Concilium*, 3 (1996): 109-115.

Ekem, John D.K., *Priesthood in Context: A Study of Priesthood in Some Christian and Primal Communities of Ghana and its Relevance for Mother-Tongue Biblical Interpretation*, rev. ed. (Accra: Sonlife, 2009).

Ephirim-Donkor, Anthony, 'Akom: The Ultimate Mediumship Experience among the Akan', *Journal of American Academy of Religion*, 76, 1 (March 2008).

Fee, Gordon D., *God's Empowering Presence: The Holy Spirit in the Letters of Paul* (Peabody, MA:Hendrickson, 1994).

________. *The Disease of the Health and Wealth Gospels* (Beverly, MA: Frontline Publishing, 1985).

Foli, Richard, *Church Growth in Ghana* (Accra: Methodist Book Depot, 2001).

Gerlach, Luther P., and Hine, Virginia H., 'Five Factors Crucial to the Growth and Spread of a Modern Religious Movement', *Journal for the Scientific Study of Religion*, 7, 1 (1968): 21-40.

Gifford, Paul, *Ghana's New Christianity: Pentecostalism in a Globalizing African Economy* (London: Hurst and Co., 2004).

________. (ed.), *The Christian Churches and the Democratization of Africa* (Leiden: E.J. Brill, 1995).

Green, Maia, 'Why Christianity is the "Religion of Business": Perceptions of the Church among Pogoro Catholics in Southern Tanzania', *Journal of Religion in Africa*, 25, 1 (1995): 25-47.

Grundmann, Christoffer H. 'Inviting the Spirit to Fight the Spirits? Pneumatological Challenges for Missions in Healing and Exorcism', *International Review of Mission*, 94, 372 (January 2005): 51-73.

Gyekye, Kwame, *African Philosophical Thought: The Akan Conceptual Scheme*, rev. ed. (Philadelphia: Temple University Press, 1995).

Hastings, Adrian, 'Christianity in Africa', in Ursula King (ed.). *Turning Points in Religious Studies: Essays in Honor of Geoffrey Parrinder* (Edinburgh: T&T Clarke, 1990): 201-210.

Heward-Mills, Dag, *Why Non-Tithing Christians Become Poor and How Tithing Christians Become Rich* (Wellington, South Africa: Lux Verbi, BM, 2009).

Hocken, Peter D., 'Charismatic Movement', in Stanley M. Burgess and Gary B. McGee (eds.), *Dictionary of Pentecostal and Charismatic Movements* (Grand Rapids, MI: Zondervan, 1989).

Hollenweger, Walter J., 'Charismatic Renewal in the Third World: Implications for Mission', *Occasional Bulletin of Missionary Research*, 4 (April 1980): 68-76.

________. 'After Twenty Years' Research on Pentecostalism', *International Review of Mission*, 75 (January 1986): 3-12.

Idowu, E. Bolaji, *Olódùmarè: God in Yoruba Belief* (New York: Frederick A. Praeger, 1963).

Ilogu, Edmund, *Christianity and Ibo Culture* (Leiden: E.J. Brill, 1974).

Jenkins, Philip, *The Next Christendom: The Coming of Global Christianity*, rev. ed. (Oxford: Oxford University Press, 2007).

Kalu, Ogbu, *African Pentecostalism: An Introduction* (Oxford: Oxford University Press, 2008).

________. 'The Third Response: Pentecostalism and the Reconstruction of Christian Experience in Africa. *Journal of African Christian Thought*, 1, 2 (1998): 3-16.

Kuma, Afua, *Jesus of the Deep Forest*, Fr Jon Kirby SVD et al (eds & trans.) (Accra: Asempa Press, 1980).

Larbi, E. Kingsley, *Pentecostalism: The Eddies of Ghanaian Christianity* (Accra: Centre for Pentecostal and Charismatic Studies, 2001).

Lartey, Emmanuel Y., 'Healing: Tradition and Pentecostalism in Africa Today', *International Review of Mission*, lxxv, 297 (January 1986): 75-81.

Laryea, Philip T., 'Mother Tongue Theology: Reflections on Images of Jesus in the Poetry of Afua Kuma', *Journal of African Christian Thought*, 3, 1 (2000): 50-60.

Lawton, Kim A., interview with Kwame Bediako, 'Faith without Borders: How the Developing World Is Changing the Face of Christianity', *Christianity Today* (May 19, 1997).

Leonard, Christine, *A Giant in Ghana: 3,000 Churches in 50 Years. The Story of James McKeown and the Church of Pentecost* (Chichester: New Wine Press, 1989).

Marshall, Ruth, *Political Spiritualities: The Pentecostal Revolution in Nigeria* (Chicago and London: University of Chicago Press, 2009).

Martin, David, *Tongues of Fire: The Explosion of Protestantism in Latin America* (Oxford: Basil Blackwell,1990).

Masamba ma Mpolo, 'Perspectives on African Pastoral Counseling', in Masamba ma Mpolo and Wilhelmina Kalu (eds), *The Risks of Growth: Counselling and Pastoral Theology in the African Context* (Geneva: WCC, 1985).

Meeks, Wayne A., *The First Urban Christians: The Social World of the Apostle Paul* (New Haven and London: Yale University Press, 1983).

Menzies, William W., and Menzies, Robert P., *Spirit and Power: Foundations of Pentecostal Experience* (Grand Rapids, MI: Zondervan, 2000).

Meyer, Birgit, *Translating the Devil: Religion and Modernity among the Ewe in Ghana* (Edinburgh: Edinburgh University Press, 1999).

________. *Religious Sensations: Why Media, Aesthetics and Power Matter in the Study of Contemporary Religion* (Amsterdam: Vrij Universiteit, 2006).

________. 'Pentecostalism and Globalization', in Allan Anderson et al. (ed), *Studying Global Pentecostalism: Theories and Methods* (Berkeley: University of California Press, 2010): 113-130.

Miller, Donald E, *Reinventing American Protestantism: Christianity in the New Millennium* (Berkeley:University of California Press, 1997).

Morgan, David, *Visual Piety: A History and Theory of Popular Religious Images* (Berkeley, Los Angeles and London: University of California Press, 1998).

________. *The Sacred Gaze: Religious Visual Culture in Theory and Practice* (Berkeley, Los Angeles and London: University of California Press, 2005).

Mühlen, Heribert, *A Charismatic Theology: Initiation in the Spirit* (London: Burns and Oates, 1978).

Nienkirchen, Charles, 'Conflicting Visions of the Past: The Prophetic Use of History in the Early American Pentecostal-Charismatic Movements', in Karla Poewe (ed.), *Charismatic Christianity as a Global Culture* (Columbia: University of South Carolina Press, 1994): 119-133.

Ntumy, Michael, 'An Assessment of the Growth and Development of the Church of Pentecost with Particular Reference to its Impact on the Religious Life of Ghana'. Unpublished MTh Thesis, Regents Theological College, UK (June 2000).

Nwankpa, Emeka, *Redeeming the Land* (Accra: ACP, 1994).

Oduyoye, Mercy Amba, *Hearing and Knowing: Theological Reflections on Christianity in Africa* (Maryknoll, NY: Orbis Books, 1986).

________. *Daughters of Anowa: African Women and Patriarchy* (Maryknoll, NY: Orbis Books, 1995).

Olukoya, Daniel K, *Prayer Rain* (Lagos: Mountain of Fire Ministries, 1999).

Omenyo, Cephas, 'The Charismatic Movement in Ghana', *PNEUMA: The Journal of the Society for Pentecostal Studies* 16 (Fall 1994): 169-189.

Onyinah, Opoku, *Pentecostal Exorcism: Witchcraft and Demonology in Ghana* (Dorset: DEO Publishing, 2012).

Osteen, Joel, *I Declare: 31 Promises to Speak Over Your Life* (New York: Faith Words, 2012).

Otabil, Mensa, *Four Laws of Productivity: God's Foundation for Living* (Tulsa, OK: Vicom Inc., 1991).

________. *Beyond the Rivers of Ethiopia: A Biblical Revelation on God's Purpose for the Black Race* (Accra: Altar Media, 2004).

________. *Buy the Future: Learning to Negotiate for a Better Future than your Present* (Accra: Altar International, 2002).

________. *Prophetic Declarations: 2005-2011* (Accra: ICGC, 2011).

________. *Pathways to Success: 21 Sure Tips on the Way to the Top* (Mansfield, TX: Blaze Publishing, 2008).

Oyedepo, David O., *Walking in Dominion* (Ota, Nigeria: Dominion Publishing House, 2006).

________. *Possessing Your Possessions* (Ota, Nigeria: Dominion Publishing House, 2007).

Peel, J.D.Y., 'The Pastor and the *Babalawo*: The Interaction of Religions in Nineteenth-Century Yorubaland', *Africa*, 60, 3 (1990): 338-369.

Petersen, Douglas, *Not by Might Nor by Power: A Pentecostal Theology of Social Concern in Latin America* (Oxford: Regnum Books International, 1996).

Prince, Derek, *Blessings and Curses* (Kent: Sovereign World, 1994).

Quayesi-Amakye, Joseph, 'Let the Prophet Speak: A Study of Trends in Pentecostal Prophetism with Particular Reference to the Church of Pentecost and some Neo-Pentecostal Churches', unpublished MPhil thesis (Accra: Central University College, 2009).

________. *Prophetism in Ghana Today: A Study on Trends in Ghanaian Pentecostal Prophetism* (Accra: Quayisi-Amakye, 2013).

Quebedeaux, Richard, *The New Charismatics II* (San Francisco: Harper & Row, 1983).

Rambo, Lewis R., *Understanding Religious Conversion* (New Haven: Yale University Press, 1993).

Ray, Benjamin C., 'Aladura Christianity: A Yoruba Religion', *Journal of Religion in Africa*, 23, 3 (1993): 266-291.

Sanneh, Lamin O., *West African Christianity: The Religious Impact* (Maryknoll, NY: Orbis Books, 1983).

________. 'The Horizontal and Vertical in Mission: An African Perspective', *International Bulletin of Missionary Research*, 7, 4 (1983): 165-171.

________. *Translating the Message: The Missionary Impact on Culture* (Maryknoll, NY: Orbis Books, 1989).

________. 'Translatability in Islam and Christianity in Africa: A Thematic Approach', in Thomas D. Blakely, Walter E.A. van Beek and Dennis L. Thomson (eds.), *Religion in Africa: Expression and Experience* (London: James Currey; Portsmouth, NH: Heinemann, 1994): 23-45.

Sepúlveda, Juan, 'Reflections on the Pentecostal Contribution to the Mission of the Church in Latin America', *Journal of Pentecostal Theology*, 1 (1992): 80-88.

Shakarian, Demos, *The Happiest People on Earth: The Long-Awaited Story of Demos Shakarian as Told to John and Elizabeth Sherrill* (Chappaqua, NY: Steward Press, 1975).

Shelton, James B., 'A Pendulum Swing Between Prosperity and Suffering: What is the Role of Faith?', in Vinson Synan (ed.), *Spirit-Empowered Christianity in the 21st Century* (Lake Mary, FL: Charisma House, 2011).

Sinitiere, Philip Luke, 'Preaching the Good News Glad: Joel Osteen's Tel-e-vangelism', in Pradip Thomas and Philip Lee (eds), *Global and Local Televangelism* (London: Palgrave Macmillan, 2012): 87-107.

Shenk, Wilbert R., 'Recasting Theology of Mission: Impulses from the Non-Western World', *International Bulletin of Missionary Research*, 25, 3 (2001).

Smith, Wilfred C., *What Is Scripture?* (London: SCM, 1993).

Stark, Rodney, 'Why New Religious Movements Succeed or Fail: A Revised General Model'. *Journal of Contemporary Religion*, 11, 2 (1996): 133-146.

Stark, Rodney, and Bainbridge, William Sims. *The Future of Religion: Secularization, Revival, and Cult Formation* (Berkeley, Los Angeles, London: University of California Press, 1985).

Stoll, David, *Is Latin America Turning Protestant? The Politics of Evangelical Growth* (Berkeley: University of California Press, 1990).

Taylor, John V., *The Primal Vision: Christian Presence amid African Religion* (London: SCM, 1963).

________. *The Go-Between God: The Holy Spirit and the Christian Mission* (London: SCM, 1972).

Tugwell, Simon, et al., *New Heaven? New Earth?: An Encounter with Pentecostalism* (Springfield, IL: Templegate Publishers, 1976).

Turner, Harold W., *Religious Innovation in Africa: Collected Essays on New Religious Movements* (Boston, MA: G.K. Hall, 1979).

Van der Leeuw, G., *Religion in Essence and Manifestation*, trans. J.E. Turner (Princeton, NJ: Princeton University Press, 1986 [1938]).

Van Dijk, Rijk A., 'From Camp to Encompassment: Discourses of Transsubjectivity in the Ghanaian Pentecostal Diaspora', *Journal of Religion in Africa*, 27, 2 (1997): 135-159.

Währisch-Oblau, Claudia, *The Missionary Self-Perception of Pentecostal-Charismatic Church Leaders from the Global South in Europe* (Leiden: E.J. Brill, 2009).

Waldo, César, 'From Babel to Pentecost: A Socio-Historical-Theological Study of the Growth of Pentecostalism' in André, and Marshall-Fratani, Ruth (eds), *Between Babel and Pentecost: Transnationalism in America and Latin America* (Bloomington and Indianapolis: Indiana University Press, 2001): 22-40.

Walls, Andrew F., *The Missionary Movement in Christian History: Studies in the Transmission of Faith* (Maryknoll, NY: Orbis Books, 1996).

________. *The Cross-Cultural Process in Christian History* (Maryknoll, NY: Orbis Books, 2002).

Wanner, Catherine, *Communities of the Converted: Ukrainians and Global Evangelism* (Ithaca, NY, and London: Cornell University Press, 2007).

Wilson, Bryan R., 'The Functions of Religion: A Reappraisal', *Religion*, 18 (1988).

Wright, Christopher J.H., *Knowing the Holy Spirit through the Old Testament* (Downers Grove, IL: Intervarsity Press, 2006).

_______. 'Calling the Church Back to Humility, Integrity, Simplicity,' in Julia E.M. Cameron (ed.), *Christ our Reconciler* (Downers Grove, IL: Intervarsity Press, 2012).

Yong, Amos, *In the Days of Caesar: Pentecostalism and Political Theology* (Grand Rapids, MI: William B. Eerdmans, 2010).

Other Documentary Sources

Church of Pentecost, 'Reports for the 7th Session of the Extraordinary Council Meetings' (Koforidua, Ghana, 22-26 April 1999), Appendix 1B.

FGBMFI, *Constitution and By-Laws and Articles of Incorporation*, revised version July 1985.

FGBMFI Ghana Airport Chapter, *Recapturing the Vision*, 10th Anniversary Handbook, 28 August-2 September 1995.

FGBMFI Ghana, *Watch and Pray*, 10th National Convention Handbook 1995.

Ghana National Evangelism Committee, *Facing the Unfinished Task of the Church in Ghana: National Survey Update 1993* (Accra: Ghana Evangelism Committee, 1993).

Women's Aglow Ghana, *Mighty Women of Valour of Our Generation*, 10th Anniversary Handbook, 25-27 November 1993.

Index

Regnum Studies in Mission

The Regnum Studies in Mission series is born out of the lived experience of Christians and Christian communities-in-mission, especially in the fast growing churches among the poor of the world. These churches have more to tell than just stories of growth. Their work is making a significant impact in shaping their cultures in the power and image of Christ. Through Regnum, these practitioners are expressing the reality of the Christian faith as it is manifested in their societies and making the work of God known, globally.

Titles in the Regnum Studies in Mission series are the fruit of rigorous research to the highest international standards. They demonstrate authentic Christian engagement that has led to the transformation of people and societies. These books are designed to impact the world, as the formation of Christian theology, missiology, and practice in the twenty-first century will depend to a great extent on the active participation of growing churches. Through Regnum, these ministries will be able to contribute biblically faithful and culturally appropriate expressions of Christian practice.

Volumes in this series are printed in paperback, unless otherwise stated.

Conflict Transformation: Churches in the Face of Structural Violence in Northern Nigeria

Ayuba Mavalla

2014 / 978-1-908355-60-7 / 278pp

Both Christian Missionaries and Indigenous Christians believed that their fundamental role is evangelism. However, the provision of education and health services are often done as an opening wedge for the Gospel. Rarely do the Christians perceive these development projects as means of transforming structural violence.

Stopping the Traffick: A Christian Response to Sexual Exploitation and Trafficking

Glenn Miles and Christa Foster Crawford (Eds)

2014 / 978-1-908355-51-5 / 318pp (eBook available)

How do we even begin addressing such an important – and yet overwhelming – task? If you are a practitioner striving to assist victims or a faith-based organization wondering how to get involved you may be wrestling with questions like: How should we go about working with exploited people? Where should we focus our response? How do we deal with the challenges?

Roots and Fruits:
Retrieving Scotland's Missionary Sory
Kenneth R Ross (Ed)
2014 / 978-1-908355-29-4 / 173pp

Scotland has played a major role in the worldwide movement of Christian mission. Equally, the missionary movement has played a big part in Scotland's story. The distinctive contribution of this book is its attempt to offer a comprehensive and synchronic assessment of the movement as a whole

---

Called Out for Witness : The Missionary Journey of Grace Korean Church
Daniel Taichoul Yang
2014 / 978-1-908355-49-2 / 170pp

This book investigates the theological motivation for GKC's missions: Reformed theology, Presbyterian theology, and mission theology. The book also shows the extent of the church's mission engagement by continents. Finally, the book turns its attention to the future with an evaluation of the church's missionary journey.

Mangoes or Bananas?: The Quest for an Authentic Asian Christian Theology (2nd Ed)
Hwa Yung
2014 / 978-1-908355-47-8 / 232pp (eBook available)

Over the past few decades there has been a growing awareness of the need for contextual theologies throughout Asia. Based on the premise that theology and mission are inseparable, the author applies four missiological criteria to representative examples of Protestant Asian writings to assess their adequacy or otherwise as contextual theologies.

Female Education and Mission
A Burkina Faso Experience
Philippe Ouedraogo
2014 / 978-1-908355-11-9 / 263pp

This volume is the result of six years research in 'Overcoming Obstacles to Female Education in Burkina Faso'. It narrates how Christians and religious groups can speed up female education and contribute to the socio-economic growth of Burkina Faso. The evidence from this research shows that Christianity is part of the solution to female education, a key factor of socio economic growth.